Toni McClintock

ALL ABROAD

3 Kids, 2 Years, 1 New Perspective

An American Family in Paris

To Dave, Julia, Matthew, and Katherine,
for being curious and courageous...

April 2007

A ripping pain shot up my leg as I slammed my foot down on the brakes. I barely avoided hitting a silver Aston Martin that had just sped in. The driver, a new mom I didn't recognize, stopped her car smack in the middle of the preschool parking lot, flung open the door, and pulled out a very posh, pint-sized version of herself. Dressed to kill for lunch at the club, she gave an, *Oh, I'll just be a minute, I'm running late* wave and left her fancy car blocking me and at least three other moms from leaving.

I refrained from yelling, "ARE YOU KIDDING ME? THERE IS NO VALET AT PRESCHOOL DROPOFF," maintaining my calm mommy demeanor instead. Breathe in. Breathe out. Stay in the slow lane, I reminded myself—a reference to a decision I made for freeway driving, which had metaphorically seeped into many other situations in my life. I glanced around the parking lot for some consolatory jaw dropping, but none of the other moms appeared bothered by the audacity of the situation. One mom gave me a winking "hang in there" look. Why was she so understanding? Another, talking intently on her cell phone, was oblivious. I sat there, fuming, waiting for her to return; the throbbing pain in my leg an unpleasant reminder of my latest war wound: a badly torn calf muscle ruptured in a sprint to the net for a drop shot in a recent doubles battle against the rival tennis club in Ojai.

It wasn't just the pain that bothered me, but the train of thought it triggered about my situation: Crutches for six weeks—the third time with this infuriating injury. It was pretty severe, the doctor said. No more tennis for a long time… maybe forever. Of course, things could be worse. I knew that. A ripped calf muscle was not a death sentence. But tennis had represented my precious social time with friends. It was my exercise and fun, all in one, and, as any mom with young kids knows, you have to carve out time for yourself or you won't get any.

I was deep in "dwelling mode" as Dave, my husband, has labeled my tendency to over-think things, and when I find myself in "dwelling mode," I like to write to clear my mind. That's why I've always kept a diary in my handbag. I pulled it out.

April 22

Now what am I going I do? Who am I? Okay, really? It's just tennis! Why the heck am I so worked up this morning? Tennis doesn't define me! There's obviously more going on here if I'm having an identity crisis in the preschool parking lot! Is this my mid-life crisis? Hmmm... I AM thirty-eight years old—the ripe age for it, I guess. I feel like my body is breaking down. Okay... wow... this injury is giving me way too much time to dwell.

Ms. Inconsiderate finally came out of the preschool gate. I stared at her from my minivan, a highly perturbed look that I hoped she could not misinterpret, not that she cared in the slightest that she had inconvenienced anyone. She just waved her perfectly manicured red nails, hopped in her sports car, and sped off, as if the Saks Half Yearly Sale doors were opening early. I flipped the music on. I was definitely over-caffeinated. That didn't help. Some curse-infested rap song was playing on the radio, which irritated me even more. I changed the station to classical and started feeling better. I reminded myself: slow lane... okay... breathe. I stared out at the sparkling blue ocean. I opened the windows and let the salty smell waft in. Taking the beach route home for an attitude adjustment was a great idea. It was working. I felt myself relax.

I arrived home to my barking dog, unlocked the door, and walked into my messy home office. I definitely felt better, but I felt the need to keep writing.

9:50 a.m.

Maybe I should start working again… but what would I do? Go back to the bank where I used to work before the kids were born? No, too boring! Start my own business? Hey, that might be fun. What kind of business? Oh, maybe a bar! I've always secretly wanted to be a bartender. No, I don't think Dave would like that very much! Hmmm… maybe I could open a small restaurant?

I looked around the room. Stacks of bills, school bulletins, and kids' artwork overflowed my desk. I started pawing through it until I came across a yellow piece of paper with a handwritten list and doodling around the edges. It wasn't one of my everyday errand lists. It was our Road Trip List—a kind of "bucket list" where Dave and I had brainstormed about our goals and ideas on one of our annual, fourteen-hour, family road trips to the mountains. I looked down the list and saw one entry that jumped out at me:

Work out

Cook interesting dinners

Date nights with Dave

Watch kids practice piano

SPEND A YEAR ABROAD

… Ah, yes. The great escape plan. My all-time favorite fantasy swooshed in, taking the foreground with its seductive images:

Dave and I are sitting at a delicate, wrought iron table for two with the vibrant orange, yellow, and purple rolling hills of Provence, France behind us, discussing the latest international news in Le Monde, a French newspaper. I'm savoring a bite of a buttery croissant with raspberry jam, and Dave is stirring a sugar cube around a small cup of espresso. Our three kids are running around in the grass, laughing their infectious, giddy laughs. Then, a bustling city at night flashes in: It's cold and snowy, and Dave and I are strolling in downtown Paris with the kids, all dressed up in warm coats and hats, admiring elaborate Christmas displays in the store windows.

The daydreams were a tease, transporting me out of my daily busy work into a tantalizing reverie—one that had taken me far away many times in the past—every time I came across that little Road Trip List.

Dave and I often contemplated spending a year abroad, but the blueprint of *when* and *how* always eluded us. Each time we abandoned the idea with an excuse like: it's not the right time, or it's too complicated, or, more importantly, how could we afford it? And we were in full, fervent, family mode—married thirteen years with three kids: Julia, eleven, Matthew, eight, and Katherine, five. We had just bought our first house next door to a park. We had a yellow Labrador named Barley, a goldfish named Goldie, and not one, but two minivans. My identity was defined as Julia's Mom, Matthew's Mom, or Katherine's Mom— a worthy identity, as far as I was concerned. I was a successful "domestic engineer." Running a household and facilitating my children's busy schedules was a full-time job. There were piano lessons, tennis lessons, water polo practices, roller hockey games, and soccer games. I took pride in all their accomplishments and felt lucky to be able to stay home with them.

10:00 a.m.

So, why do I feel like something is missing? I do feel blessed and lucky, but I guess I'm a little burned out. The kids are busy, busy, SO busy, and I spend all day driving around in circles. I need more challenges and more intellectual stimulation, I think tennis has kept me entertained until now, but my tennis days are over, I'm afraid, at least for a while. However, I don't think the answer is to get another job. I love being a stay-at-home mom. I don't want to give that up. But here I am… dwelling on the meaning of life.

4

Barley found his slimy tennis ball under the sofa and dropped it on my foot. *Ew!!* I picked it up with two fingers and saw him looking at me eagerly.

"Okay, Barley, I'll throw it for a few minutes."

10:32 a.m.

Weirdest thing just happened! I went out in the back yard and threw the ball up the hill, still holding the Road Trip List in my other hand. I glanced down at the list and noticed I had written "The Secret" on the edge of the paper, and I remembered it was a book I had just finished that claimed, "If you write it down, it will happen," and "Positive thinking creates life-changing results." [1] *I kept throwing the ball for Barley, but when I looked back at the Road Trip List again, "Spend a year abroad" was yelling out at me. I saw a light bulb flash on in my head, and I thought: Is this a sign? Is this the challenge I'm craving? And that was it. That was the moment I decided YES, it WAS a sign. It was the perfect time to spend a year abroad.*

When Dave walked in from work that night, I was waiting for him at the door.

"Let's move to Paris," I said with great enthusiasm. Dave looked right at me, didn't blink, and a slight smile formed on his face. That statement probably would surprise most husbands, or they'd ignore it, thinking it was a wistful but passing thought, but not Dave. He grabbed a beer, sat down, and listened calmly as I explained why I thought it was time for a cathartic and daring change in our lives. We had contemplated the idea a few times in the past, so it wasn't the first time he'd heard it, but I had never really taken it seriously before. Dave, I should mention, is open-minded but deliberate. He's good at helping me consider all sides

---

[1] *The Secret*, Rhonda Byrne, 2006

of a subject—things that aren't always obvious to me. He also loves a good controversial conversation. But this conversation didn't provoke him, not in the slightest. He agreed wholeheartedly that the time felt right.

April 23

> *I'm just thinking about living in Paris and not being able to speak a word of French. That will make things difficult, but it's also one of the main reasons "Spend a year abroad" is on our goal list. Dave and I both think that being bilingual is hugely beneficial in today's world. Unfortunately, our public school administration doesn't agree. I've even heard people say that English is necessary for everyone, but another language is just a bonus. We disagree, but try telling that to our state budget administrators who are recycling mobile homes into classrooms these days.*

Dave and I read a fascinating study about brain synapses and how they're linked to the ability to acquire language. The study said that "children acquire language by forming new neurons and neural connections, and at around twelve to thirteen years old, that window of native language acquisition starts to close. After that, we learn language by reprogramming existing neurons and neural connections, because no new neurons or neural connections are formed. That's why music and foreign languages are more difficult to learn as an adult." [2] We also knew that becoming fully bilingual would require immersion for an extended period of time. So, immersion was ideal, and we needed to make it happen soon, because Julia was already eleven. Her "window" was only open for another year or two.

---

[2] Huttenlocher and Dabholkar, Journal of Comparative Neurology, Vol. 387, Issue 2, October 1997

April 25

Just got back from picking up Julia and Matthew from school, where I mentioned the idea of spending a year abroad to Matthew's teacher. She got super excited. She told me that she did the SAME THING when her kids were young, but in Japan. She said, "It was, without a doubt, the most rewarding experience of their lives." And she told me, unequivocally, if this was an opportune time, we had to do it.

"Make it happen, Toni!" she told me.

I'm thinking about Julia's fifth grade class now, and how it's been academically mediocre (at best). Sixth grade is not looking like it's going to be much better. We've been contemplating private school—which is very expensive—and she'd have to change schools again for junior high. Hmmm... Sixth grade in Paris instead... it's kind of a crazy idea, but it seems like the timing works.

9 p.m.

Tonight, Dave and I sat down with two glasses of yummy French wine and shaped a pitch to his company. He'll ask if they'll consider letting him work from abroad for a year. In this day of the Internet and Skype, working from abroad is completely plausible. We assume they'll probably say no. Then we'll move to Plan B. What is Plan B? No idea yet, but we'll try Plan A first. What do we have to lose?

Dave didn't waste any time. When he arrived at work the next day, he went straight in to talk to George, his boss. He was anxious to see what he'd say. Dave thought it was a viable

7

proposal, but of course, he was prepared for some resistance. He did not think it would be as easy as it turned out to be. George loved the idea! He said that he too would like to do something like this some day, but his wife would never consider it. He said that if spending a year abroad was our dream, he would not stand in the way. In fact, he'd help Dave make it work. Dave called to tell me:

"Toni, guess what? George said yes."

I was startled… actually stunned was more like it.

"WHAT? Are you kidding? Holy %#*!!!" I felt the blood drain from my face, and a sudden sense of panic came over me.

April 26

I'm excited, but I cannot think clearly. I never predicted George would say yes. Honestly, I wasn't sure Dave would even ask. I never imagined he'd go for it today, and realistically, we were ready to start formulating Plan B. But Dave did it. And George said YES! I can't believe it. We're doing this. We're moving abroad for a year! I'm feeling a bit blindsided here, but there's no time to overthink things now. I need to focus. I have to get to work quickly. It's almost May! The next school year is only a few months away!

May 2007

May 2

We've been knocking on doors to see if they open, and they're all opening so far. It seems like it's meant to be. Imagine the vacations we can go on once we live in Paris... London, Venice, Barcelona, Biarritz, Monaco...

May 3

Okay, I'm dwelling, but should we consider other options besides Paris? I mean we could potentially move anywhere. What about Hawaii? That would be a complete 180-degree turn, but it would be so easy. Geez, all we'd need are flip-flops, sarongs, and bikinis. Yes, I should check out schools in Hawaii. But wait! Hawaii? The kids wouldn't learn a foreign language there, and that's one of our main reasons for doing this... and the kids would probably never want to come back! A vacation in Hawaii, maybe, but moving there does not sound like what we're looking for. Paris, on the other hand, is a different culture, a different language... a different everything! So many books are written about the magic of "The City of Light." I want to know why! I want in on the secret!

I remember the three romantic days we had in Paris on our whirlwind tour of France and Italy before kids. Yes, that's definitely where the love story with Paris began for me. I had too small a taste of its culture, art, food, and intrigue. Those three days really left me wanting more.

Dave and I had heard all the generalizations and misperceptions about the French—and Parisians in particular—but we knew we couldn't blame the French for being French, just like we couldn't blame Americans for being American. We knew the French culture was different from ours, but we were ready for different. I wanted different. That is not to say I wasn't anxious. I was anticipating the "Paris Intimidation Factor": Even the most confident woman can feel self-conscious in Paris, and the best non-French-person-speaking-French can feel insecure there. But even with all the intimidation factors and the challenges in store, I savored the idea of it.

Santa Barbara is gorgeous. The weather is almost always a perfect seventy degrees year round. The beach is down the street and the mountains ascend from the other direction. Sounds picture-perfect, doesn't it? But after twenty years of it, even that gets boring. I needed a change, and change is what we'd get if we moved to Paris. Nothing would be the same, and that sounded fine to me. Plus, our kids were taking their Santa Barbara lifestyle for granted. Attitudes of entitlement surrounded them. They needed to get out of their comfort zones and experience some challenges. French school certainly sounded like a great start!

It wasn't as scary as it sounds. Dave had spent a summer in Paris with family friends during junior high, and had lived and worked there for a year after college. He could speak French fluently and he knew the city well. I loved hearing him speak French. It sounded so romantic. The kids and I would get to learn this beautiful language, too.

As to our kids' over-scheduled lifestyle in Santa Barbara, we planned to clear the calendar completely for our year in Paris. They'd take a break from all their after-school activities, so we could enjoy our time together as a family. They were doing way too much anyway. Matthew was playing soccer, roller hockey, and tennis. Julia had evening water polo practices four times a week, which made family dinners problematic, if not impossible. With out-of-town tournaments every other weekend, our family unit was constantly being broken up. Katherine was only five, and she was already doing gymnastics and dance, and all three kids took piano lessons weekly. As family chauffeur, it's no wonder I was feeling burned out. We were on activity overdose. On top of all that, there was Barley, our high-maintenance yellow Lab, who monopolized any available spare time I had for myself because he needed his exercise, too. He'd look at me with his sad dog eyes, saying "WALK? WALK?" Truly, I felt like I had fallen into a very deep, over-scheduled rut that I couldn't climb out of... unless... we moved away.

I was filled with fantastic ideas for our adventurous year: We'd focus on learning the beautiful French language, making new friends, and having as much fun as possible. No piano lessons for a year, no more organized sports teams, and no more driving—just free time for new experiences or even to just do nothing.

May 6

I can't believe we're really moving to Paris. I can't wait to walk through the parks and along the banks of the Seine. I want to wander aimlessly around the city, introducing my kids to the beauty of everything French... like the sand colored buildings with decorative, wrought iron balconies and the statues in the parks. For myself, I can't wait to saunter into random stores I come across, and to explore the endless galleries and museums. I want to learn more about art. I want to learn all the different ways to tie a scarf. I want to walk and walk and walk for as long as I feel like walking, and I want to sit and relax in cafés without this hurried feeling all the time.

May 7

*Okay, I do plan to learn French, just not right away.
Sitting in a classroom for hours doesn't fit into the
"freedom from all binding time commitments plan"
I'm determined to enact. I hope this new lifestyle will
stimulate and inspire me. Maybe it'll encourage all of
us to try new things. Is this realistic? Will it be like I
imagine it—stimulating, challenging, and fun? Or will
it be really hard? No idea... but I intend to find out.*

Of course, we expected there would be difficult times,
but we wanted the kids to see that there was a bigger world out
there, a very different world than we were used to. We were
going on an adventure. We had no expectations really, besides
the kids learning French. The rest was unknown. And what we
didn't know couldn't worry or deter us. Beautiful Santa Barbara,
California would be here when we got back. Were the kids up
for it? All three of them gave an enthusiastic YES! Paris sounded
like fun to them. Paris sounded exciting! I was so thrilled that my
kids were curious and open-minded. No convincing or
persuading was necessary.

There were other factors we took into account regarding
our family situation, and on all counts, everything seemed to be a
go: We were all in good health. Both Dave's and my parents
were doing okay, health-wise. Dave had a job that he could do
from afar for a year, and we owned an easily rentable house that
we could come back to. It really seemed like the time was right.

May 8

*So where do we start? Schools. I guess I could home-
school... that would be easier than finding a school in
Paris. Ugh! I'm so NOT the home-schooling type. Just
trying to do homework with the kids is challenging for
me. We don't speak the same language, and we're all
speaking English! That's not the experience we're
looking for any way. We want the kids to rise to the*

12

challenges of French school and new friends. Plus, I
want my freedom during the day. We could potentially
do the local, French, neighborhood school, but that
sounds scary—too many variables. We don't even
know which will be our neighborhood school, and I
can't find any information online. I don't like that.

We started looking for schools on the Internet. I found the International School of Paris and the American School of Paris, but they were very expensive, more than we could afford. There were a few Montessori Schools, but they were just for the younger grades. Then we found some bilingual (French/English) schools. They were partly public, partly private, which made the price a lot less. The French government paid for the public, French speaking portion, and the tuition covered the non-French part. These schools looked like the best option, but there were a bunch to choose from. All we had to use in our decision process were the websites, and some websites—even though they were for bilingual schools—were all in French.

10:30 p.m.

What if we pick wrong and the school is terrible?
What effect could that have on our kids, our family,
our experience in Paris? Ahh, stop dwelling! Three
kids can go to a bilingual school in Paris, France for
the price of one kid going to a private school in Santa
Barbara. It's surprising these schools are so affordable.
They're actually feasible. We have to go for it!

Unfortunately, we soon found out that the application deadlines had already passed, so Dave started calling the schools directly. First, he called the bilingual school that was just outside of Paris. They only had one place open. I started to worry. Was it going to be too late for all the schools? He moved on to the next one. It was in Paris, and it had the most information on its website in English. Dave also liked the location. He spoke in French to the woman in the admissions office, and I listened

13

excitedly, while nervously pacing back and forth in an adjoining room. I couldn't understand a word he was saying, but he sounded upbeat. When he hung up, I ran into the room. She said there was a place available in the sixth grade for Julia and a place in the fourth grade for Matthew, but most likely there was no room for Katherine. The classes for Julia and Matthew were special Adaptation classes for non-French, first-year students. It sounded ideal for Julia and Matt, but what about Katherine? The woman in the admissions office recommended that we apply for admission for Katherine too, just in case a spot opened up.

May 9

What should we do? We can work on another plan for Katherine. It's only kindergarten anyway. Some kids don't even go to kindergarten. We'll find another school for her—maybe Montessori?

We decided to apply. But before we could start the process, the *Directrice* of the school wanted to meet our kids for an interview in Paris. Clearly, that wasn't possible! We didn't even have passports for the kids yet. Thankfully, she agreed to a phone interview with Dave instead, and again, I listened nervously. Dave sounded extremely charming to me, but he was speaking in French, so I had no idea what he was saying. Apparently, he charmed the French toast right off her plate because she said we could apply.

I dove in full-force at that point. The rigorous application process was my first indication of how difficult everything is in Paris: long applications, interviews, copies of all the kids' transcripts, test scores, multiple letters of recommendation. I even had to take Katherine to a psychologist for an IQ test, which the schools required. I did everything that was requested, and sent the paperwork off, Air Mail to Paris. Then, we waited. Every day, I went out to the mailbox anxiously, hoping to get some news. A week and a half passed. It was Monday again… no letter; then Tuesday… no letter.

14

May 24

*What will we do if they don't get in? Maybe we should
apply somewhere else? Can they go to the neighborhood
school? Is it allowed for non-residents? Should I try to
home-school the kids? No! I just want them to get in
to that school! I guess this was pretty dumb, putting all
our eggs in one basket.*

I focused on my list of other things that needed doing. I
researched schools for Katherine, but I wanted to wait and see
if, by chance, she got into the bilingual school first. We needed
to get passports for the kids, which were on backlog. We were
cutting it close, and expediting them would cost a lot more, so
we needed to get that done soon. We had to find an apartment
in Paris—probably the biggest undertaking—and there was also
the not-so-small hurdle of preparing and renting out our house
in Santa Barbara.

I knew I could handle the details of finding renters for
our Santa Barbara house, and Dave could handle the search for
an apartment in Paris in the evenings and on weekends. Because
I was curious, I made an attempt at the Paris apartment search,
but quickly realized that I couldn't do it. I knew nothing about
locations in Paris, and the websites were almost all in French.

May 28

*Okay, wow, it's time to buy our airline tickets. I've
been watching the prices every day, and today they've
dropped. Non-changeable, non-refundable tickets are
half the price, but buying them is like sending out
wedding invitations! We'll be committed—but we're
doing this, right?*

May 29

*I have to deal with the pets. I could flush the goldfish,
but I don't think the kids will go for it. No, they'd be*

15

very bummed. It shouldn't be that hard to find someone to take care of her. It really does seem like a lot of effort to find a babysitter for a goldfish, but she isn't just ANY goldfish. She's at least ten years old. I doubt she'll really live too much longer. I wonder how old the oldest goldfish is???

Julia got Goldie at her first dentist appointment when she was two years old, and Goldie was still living nine years later. Goldie was part of our family. And then there was Barley, our hyperactive yellow Lab. Grandma would most likely agree to taking care of Goldie, but not Barley. It was not an understatement to describe Barley as "high-maintenance." Like *Hans and Franz,* the buff Austrian muscle men from the old Saturday Night Live skits, who always wanted to "pump you up," Barley was the *Hans and Franz* of the Labrador world. He was a super-muscular, never-to-tire-out, barking, ball-obsessed nightmare of a dog. A walk did nothing for Barley. He needed a five-mile run or a swim out to the buoys in the ocean, fifty times—no exaggeration—to wear him out, and that only lasted an hour or so. Then, he was barking at that little, green tennis ball once again. The dog trainer told us that Labs usually calm down by three years old, some not until seven, but Barley was one of those "special" Labs that probably would never calm down. Even after he was "fixed," he still had wanderlust. He'd regularly dig himself out, under the fence in our yard, whenever he was left alone. Animal Control picked him up more times than I want to remember. He loved to dig. He'd dig up anything he could. I'm sure he thought he was "helping" the gardeners when he dug up the whole irrigation system at our house. Was it a ball or a bone under there, he wondered? (Neither!) And, for some reason he also loved the taste of Ugg boots—Yes, ugh is right! Needless to say, finding a home for Barley was a big undertaking, not to mention that the kids all loved him and would find it hard to leave him. One friend said she'd try him out. How bad could he be? When I took him over for a trial weekend, he tried to eat her Koi fish. They cost about $1000 each! That obviously didn't work out. Another brave friend said she'd try him, and guess what? She changed her mind too; said they realized they weren't cut out for having a family dog. *Ha!* Finally, a nice family we knew who lived on a ranch in the Santa Ynez Valley said they'd take him, no trial needed. They had a large property and lots of animals, so he'd fit in, no problem (or so they thought). I could've kissed them.

Next on the list was deciding on an apartment in Paris. Dave was determined to find something in the 7th arrondissement, where he had lived before. He loved the 7th and knew it the best, but the 7th is very expensive and we needed room for five. We couldn't take a trip to Paris to look at places. It wasn't in our budget, and we didn't have the time. We had to rent the apartment "sight unseen." After Dave came home from work, he perused the websites, trying to find something we could afford. Everything in the 7th was too expensive or too small. I was getting frustrated and impatient.

May 30

Dave thinks he's found a couple apartments with potential. One is really big with four bedrooms, and it even comes with a little French car for our use, but it's far away from the 7th arrondissement. It's pretty cheap and BIG by Paris standards, but the decorating is tacky. I'm trying, but I cannot imagine living there. It's not the image of Paris I had in mind. And I don't even want a car! I don't want to drive. I want to walk and take the Métro. But all the apartments that are big enough and in good locations are beyond our budget. Do we want to be struggling to make ends meet the whole time? No. We want to have money for fun and travel! I guess we have to keep our options open. Another option is a short-term rental in the 7th. The owner is French, but she lives in Colorado. Dave is going to call her now.

7:06 p.m.

Wow. The owner said a year lease would be fine. She quoted Dave a monthly price we can actually afford. The apartment is small, but the location is great—in the heart of the 7th. We can even pay in American dollars from our U.S. bank account, which is a lot easier to deal with.

After a lot of discussions with the owner, we decided to do it. We signed a rental contract for six months, with her guarantee that we could stay on for the rest of the year—leaving our options open in case we found something better once we were there.

May 31

Had a nightmare last night that we arrived in Paris, and the apartment we rented didn't exist. We went to the address and found a hole in the ground. I am SO paranoid! It all seems legit, but you never really know! I can't help but imagine the worse possible scenario. Why am I like this??? I told Dave about my nightmare, and Mr. Confident says he's already checked the address on Google Maps. It exists. He confirmed that the owner is a Realtor in Colorado with a good reputation, and he even read reviews from people who have stayed in the apartment. I have to trust him and stop dwelling.

June 2007

Finally, after what seemed like an eternity but was really only two weeks, I opened the mailbox and THERE THEY WERE... three letters from the bilingual school in Paris addressed to Julia, Matthew, and Katherine.

June 2

Should I open them? Should I wait for Dave? I sat and stared at them. This could be it. We could be all set, or we could be in for a huge roadblock. I can't wait! I'm opening them.

I read the first letter. Julia was accepted. I read the second letter. Matthew was accepted. Wait, really? I read it again. Yes, they got in. They got in! I opened the third letter. Katherine was offered a place on the waiting list. Okay, that's not a "no," it's a "maybe." I immediately called Dave and read the letters to him, and he said, "Oh, that's great." Of course, he wasn't worried. He just figured they'd get in.

Next, Dave called his close family friends in Paris to ask them about the school, and if they had ever heard of it. SURPRISE! They told him that it was the same school their children had attended thirty years earlier. We couldn't believe it. Then, they told us that it was one of the best schools in Paris, and it usually had a long waiting list. We were incredibly lucky that the Adaptation Classes weren't full by May, they said. Yet another sign that this was meant to be!

Dave explained how our older two kids had been accepted, and that Katherine was on the waiting list, and they offered to write a letter of recommendation for her. We hoped it would help.

June 16

I just found a letter in the mailbox from the school addressed to Katherine. Yikes! Nervous! Opening it… read and re-read it to make sure I read it correctly. Yes, she's IN! Hmmm, I wonder if it was because of the letter of recommendation or if a spot just opened up? Well, it doesn't matter. A huge hurdle has been cleared. I'm so happy!

Things were moving along. We had all three kids enrolled in a great school, and we had an apartment in Paris. *Check and check.* We hadn't rented our house in Santa Barbara yet, because we were debating selling it. It was worth twice what we paid for it, but that seemed rash, since we were only going for a year. It also seemed like a daunting prospect to sell it. Hindsight being twenty-twenty, we definitely should have sold it then, as the market crashed right after we left. But the way real estate prices were going up, we thought we'd never be able to get back into the Santa Barbara market and honestly, there was a limit to what I could manage in the two months I had to prepare the family for the move. Renting it was the easiest and fastest option.

June 19

Just got back from taking kids to the courthouse to order their passports. She said they'd arrive in time without expediting. That's great news!

June 22

Next, we have to figure out what to pack. What do we need for a year in Paris? No idea!!! We don't have any "real" winter clothes, but I'll have to deal with that later. I found some huge rolling bags on sale and bought ten of them. Whatever we're bringing to Paris has to fit in those ten bags (plus five carry-ons).

I packed up all the toys that the kids don't use any more and donated them to charity. Moving has been a great opportunity to purge, because the kids suddenly develop strong, nostalgic affection for their old toys whenever a purge is suggested. This way, they didn't know if I was packing up the toys to bring them to Paris, or giving them away to charity. Haha!

June 26

Decided we're going to leave all the kitchen equipment in the house, the books on the bookshelves, and even our beds for the renters to sleep in, except the king, which we'll store in the garage with the new minivan. Ah geez, the new minivan... we just signed a two-year lease. What bad timing! I hope there's some way to get out of it, but I cannot deal with that right now.

July 2007

Summer went along as usual: camps, barbecues, beach days, and visits from friends and relatives. We told the kids that they could finally tell their friends we were moving to Paris, and we started telling people as well. We'd kept it a secret for a long time—from everyone except our parents—just in case it didn't end up happening. But it felt real now. It was happening. Our friends were intrigued. Moving to Paris? Wow! Some were congratulatory and some highly skeptical. Our parents were torn because they'd miss us, and they were worried we'd never come back.

July 12

*Spent the whole weekend packing. The kids were
really cute "helping," but I'm happy that they went
back to their camps today: All Saints Camp for
Katherine, Junior Guards for Matthew, and Tennis
Camp for Julia. I'm checking things off my list. I still
need to figure out which cookbooks to pack. I want to
cook a lot in Paris! I received an email from Helen,
who is my "Parent Partner" from the school. She's
very nice. She suggests I try to learn some French in
advance. Well, yeah, but how?*

While searching the Internet, I found a set of French language tapes called *Muzzy*,[3] which I bought for the kids. I was excited for them to start learning French. Muzzy, a large, amateurishly animated, French-speaking monster, and his French-speaking cohorts were entertaining, but the story line was sexist. All the male characters were either brave or clever,

---

[3] *Muzzy in Gondoland*, created by the BBC in 1986, acquired and distributed in other languages by DMP Organization

and the female characters were fat or beautiful, which was weird. The catchy, silly songs got stuck in our heads all day long. The kids learned some French words, but it was really more comical than instructive. It wasn't a complete waste of money, since we do have fond memories of the hilarity of it. But that was as far as we got with the French language preparations. I just figured we'd learn French when we got to France!

August 2007

I spent some time researching Santa Barbara rentals and determined the price we could charge for our house. We decided to leave it furnished, mostly because it was easier, but also because we could charge more. We just hoped that the renters would take good care of our things. I decided to start with a price I thought sounded high, but we'd see what happened. The day I listed it, we received many calls. A few groups came by, comprised mostly of college students. Everyone wanted it. Seemed we might've been able to charge even more, but we were happy to get so much interest. Everyone filled out rental applications, and I checked their references. I picked a group of college girls that all knew each other and seemed the most organized. A few days later, we signed a year lease and hired a property manager to take care of things while we were gone.

It felt like everything was done. We were ready to go. My master "things to do" list had been methodically checked off, item by item. Our five little blue passports were in hand, and we were going on the adventure of a lifetime.

August 21

Wow. All the bags are packed and sitting in the front hall. We're leaving in the morning on our eleven-hour flight to Paris. I dropped Barley off with Francie, who will bring him up to Santa Ynez when Leslee and her family get back from their vacation. Barley seemed happy as can be. He has no idea we are leaving him for a year, of course. I'm heading over to Lee-Lee's with the kids so we can say goodbye. This is going to be difficult. God-Grandma is going to miss the kids so much.

Dave called my cell phone when I was sitting on Lee-Lee's couch, drinking a cup of coffee.

"Can you come outside? I need to talk to you."

That was vague, I thought. I looked at Lee-Lee.

"Dave wants me to come downstairs," I said.

"Is something wrong?"

"I don't know." I started twirling my hair, a nervous habit I've had since I was a kid. Dave's voice sounded a little strange, which was unsettling. Maybe it was nothing... maybe just a surprise gift for the trip? Something felt wrong. The butterflies started flying around in my stomach. I walked down the stairs... so many thoughts going through my mind. What was it? Was it serious? Did someone get hurt? I saw Dave standing by his car. When he walked toward me, I knew something definitely was wrong by the pallid look on his face.

"What?" I asked. "Is everything okay?" Then he gave me the news.

"I just got laid off."

I remember staring at him, but not saying anything. Did I hear him right? I felt my body get weak, like I was going to faint. Maybe this was a joke? It was really not funny if it was. I looked into Dave's eyes, and I could tell he was serious. Dave, being Dave, seemed distressed, but not panicked. I searched for answers. I couldn't believe this was really happening.

How could they do this? How could ANYONE do this to someone? It was inhuman. We were leaving the NEXT morning, and our fifteen bags full of our life's belongings were packed and sitting by the front door. Everything was done. All the decisions and doubts were over. Our kids were starting school in one week in Paris, France. We had signed a year lease for our house in Santa Barbara. We had rented an apartment in Paris and sent a non-refundable deposit. We had made it through everything, taken care of EVERYTHING, and now this???

Dave continued talking and told me that when he got to work that morning, George came into his office and said, "There was an emergency board meeting last night, and they made drastic changes to the company strategy. The CEO has left, and the board gave the interim management team three days to decrease payroll by fifty percent. You have a decision to make: You'll have to cancel your plan to move abroad in order to stay with the company." George said he felt sick about it. He knew the timing couldn't be any worse. Dave told George we were going. He couldn't let the family down.

"We can't go," I said. "We can't move to Paris with three children and no job!" I was freaking out. Dave remained surprisingly calm.

"We're going," Dave said. "Everything will work out. I have severance that will cover us until Christmas, and if it doesn't work out after that, we'll come back then, but WE'RE GOING." Dave was assertive and steadfast. He would not even consider the idea of changing our plans. I know now that I needed him to be that way, because if he had wavered, I'm not sure we'd have gone.

In the middle of the night, I lost it. Panic overcame me, as problems always seem so magnified at 3:00 in the morning. My whole body started shaking uncontrollably, like those nights in the hospital after giving birth. (In those cases it was due to hormonal shifts that occur after delivery, but in this case, I was having a panic attack.) Dave was sleeping away, seemingly without a care in the world. I shook him. He woke up, and held me, and said all the right things. He made me chamomile tea with honey. I drank the warm tea and felt the panic slide away, and finally, I fell asleep for an hour or two.

In the morning we woke the kids up early to leave, and we tried to act excited. We didn't tell them what happened. We told Dave's Mom, who was driving us to the airport, but we asked her not to talk about it on the car ride. The kids slept, and we drank our coffees. An hour and a half later, Dave's Mom dropped the five of us and our fifteen bags at the curb of the International Terminal at LAX. It would have been laughable, if things weren't so tense. A very kind airport personnel man named Darrel did our curbside check in, meeting eyes with me when we got out of the minivan at LAX. In that one short look, I could tell he just knew. We were like the clown car at the circus—kids and bags kept coming out. I'm not sure how Dave managed to fit all those bags in the minivan, but he can make anything work. Dave's nickname is MacGyver, named after a secret agent in a popular American Action Adventure series in the 1990's, who solved all manner of problems using everyday items he had at hand—usually duct tape and a pocketknife.

Dave was harried, and I was still in shock. Normally we work as a good team, but I was not myself. Darrel put all the heavy bags on a cart and ushered the kids and me over to a separate area, where we waited. He and Dave handled the whole thing, somehow getting all the bags checked in and through security. Dave returned and became Superdad! He dealt with the kids, kept them engaged, and kept it all together. I was there, but I was no help. Normally, I'm an optimist, but I didn't know how to act in this situation. I wanted to be excited, pumping the kids up about how exciting it all was, but I felt like I was in a stupor. I wanted to believe it was all going to work out, but I couldn't get out of my head that we were moving our family of five to Paris, and Dave did not have a job. We gave Darrel a well-deserved, very large tip and said our goodbyes to Grandma. Dave grabbed my hand, which was very comforting at that moment. We took the kids up the escalator and out to Gate B22 to Paris.

Dave made some phone calls while we waited for our flight at the gate. He had to use my cell phone because he didn't have one anymore. He had to return his phone and laptop because they were company provided, and he obviously didn't have time to replace them in the few hours before we left. This was more than crazy. He called a couple of friends and old coworkers and told them what had happened. I think he wanted to pacify me by finding some consulting jobs right away.

August 22

I feel drained. All the excitement and anticipation I had for this experience has been replaced with a paralyzing feeling of powerlessness. Dave is not in

denial, but is somehow able to avoid negative thoughts.
I'm trying to put on a brave face for the kids, but I
cannot swallow reality as well as Dave can. I don't
know how he does it.

While Dave was on the phone, the kids and I went to look around the airport shops and get some breakfast. We had made the decision to go, so I had to stop dwelling. The kids didn't notice anything was wrong. They played around in the airport like kids do, and they kept themselves entertained. Finally, they called our seating area, and we got in line. We walked onto the plane and found our seats. Dave and I looked at each other. It was really happening. What would happen once we arrived was not so clear, but we were moving to Paris. The mood was not exactly as we had imagined it.

4:22 p.m.

We're on the flight now from L.A. to Paris. Yep,
we're moving our family to France without a job, with
our house in Santa Barbara rented out for a year, and
with a big deposit on a Paris apartment that's
probably non-refundable. Dave says he can do
consulting from Paris, no problem. I have to stop
worrying. If we have to move back before the year is
up, we can live at his Mom's house with her. There's
plenty of room there.

We arrived, jet-lagged, groggy, and irritable, at Charles de Gaulle airport in Paris. The flight had been an overnight red-eye, and, while we tried to sleep, only Katherine succeeded. She had stretched out on the ground beneath our feet, and since we covered her up with a blanket, the flight attendants didn't notice. It wasn't the safest place to fly, but on that huge plane, we figured it was fine. The rest of us tried our hardest to sleep, but nothing had worked, not even with the soft neck-pillows we bought at the airport. We watched movie after movie and ate a lot of airplane food. We wandered up and down the aisles with the kids, making friends with other non-sleepers in the standing sections of the plane.

When we finally landed in Paris, we retrieved our huge mound of bags from baggage claim and piled them on three carts. We exchanged our dollars for euros at the currency exchange booth. Dave went looking for a pay phone to call Franz, the property manager, to tell him we'd arrived. He was supposed to let us into our apartment. (My cell phone didn't work in France.)

August 23

The kids and I are sitting with the bags and waiting, not so patiently, while Dave curses at the French pay phone. I guess it isn't working. I'm deliriously tired, grumpy, and feeling like a fish out of water. I just want to see the apartment (and make sure it's there)!

Finally, Dave got the phone to work and talked to Franz. He'll meet us at the apartment. Now we need to get all these bags outside and find a big van that can fit us.

When we went outside, Dave found the pre-arranged van that our new landlord had ordered for us, and we had forgotten about. The French driver laughed when he saw all the bags. We were quite a sight—definitely Americans in Paris. Dave had to do all the talking, all the time, but he handled it very well. His French was really good. We fit everything in the van, barely, but the kids had to sit on and all around the bags. It didn't seem very safe, but the driver didn't seem to care at all.

Dave sat in the front seat and spoke French with the driver. It was fun for us to listen. *Wow, Dad can speak French*, the kids realized. We stared out the windows at a rainy, gray Paris, and I wondered what our life was going to be like. We drove in around the Arc de Triomphe, which was quite a spectacular sight. Even jet-lagged and sleepy, the grandeur wasn't lost on us.

It was an impressive way to enter our new life in Paris—encountering that magnificent, huge, and stunning arch.

We arrived at our new home in the 7th arrondissement of Paris after a forty-five-minute ride. Dave paid the taxi driver who left our fifteen bags and us on the sidewalk, in the pouring rain. I knew we had umbrellas somewhere, but they were packed away in one of the big bags, and I had no idea which one. We were getting soaked, and Franz was not there yet. I looked around in dismay. I hoped he was coming soon.

Dave noticed a covered courtyard next door, so we moved all the bags underneath. We had no way to call Franz, so we just waited, my irritation amplifying, second by second. Then we saw a man walking hurriedly up the street.

"Are you Franz?" Dave asked.

"Oui, oui, bonjour!" he said. He shook Dave's hand.

I felt my body relax as I took a huge sigh of relief. Franz was a friendly French man. He welcomed all of us to Paris. When he saw our luggage he almost collapsed. With a serious look of disbelief, we got our first *"Ooh la la!"* That was not a good sign. How small was this apartment?

Franz punched in the code to unlock the outside door, and we dragged our bags inside. I looked around. There were small mailboxes on the wall and a staircase with a pretty Persian rug running up it. There was a VERY small (maybe 3' x 3') elevator with a wrought iron cage around it. No way more than two people could fit in it, and I wasn't sure about the bags. They were really big and heavy. How were we going to get them up to the fourth floor? Each bag would have to make its own trip up in the elevator, it appeared. Our bags were taking up all the space in the foyer, but I was anxious to go up and see the apartment before dealing with them. Would it be okay to leave our bags downstairs and get a quick glimpse? Franz said yes. Dave and the kids ran up the stairs up to the fourth floor, and I took the elevator up in very close proximity to Franz. My personal space was slightly encroached upon, but I tried to make conversation to hide the awkwardness.

When Franz opened the door of the apartment, it looked okay, but I had no idea what an apartment in Paris would be like. It seemed small, but not tiny. (It was seventy square meters to be exact, which is about 800 square feet.) There was an entrance foyer, two small bedrooms, one bathroom, a main room, which served as the living/dining room, and a kitchen. The living/dining room had a modern glass dining table with six chairs, a white "leatherette" couch, a matching white "leatherette" chair, and a desk in the corner. Sliding glass doors led to a balcony above the street side of the apartment, and there were blackout blinds we could roll down at night. The kitchen was good-sized and looked fairly modern, with stainless appliances. There were bright red pans, hanging from a rack, which caught my eye and looked fresh and contemporary, and there was a small breakfast counter with two red stools. A large window over the sink looked out over a balcony.

It wasn't terribly special, but it was fine. "Fine" was not the feeling I was hoping for exactly, but at least we had an apartment, not a hole in the ground. It was somewhere to sleep, which was really all the kids could think about right then. The jet lag was hitting us hard. We thanked Franz, who told us to call with any issues, handed us his card, and left. Wait a minute! I just realized that all three of our kids had to fit in that one small bedroom! It wasn't even big enough to have two single beds side by side. "We'll get a bunk bed," Dave said, "and there's a trundle underneath that we can push in during the day. Matt can sleep in the living room on the pull out bed until we get a bunk bed." I didn't say anything. I just stared at him and at the room, trying to figure out how this was going to work.

Dave went down to drag up our bags, one at a time, in the tiny elevator, and I collapsed on the bed in our bedroom. Then it hit me. I started to cry. Was it the size of the apartment, the jet lag, the rain, or a combination of things? This apartment was so much smaller than it looked online. How could we manage to not kill each other, or go crazy in this cramped space? I didn't want the kids to hear me. I had to stop crying. At least we had an apartment. We were going to have to make it work (at

31

least for three months if Dave didn't get a new job). It would not be good for them to see me upset. They thought it was great. It was all new and exciting for them.

Julia turned on the TV. Katherine plopped down on the rug on the floor, and within a couple minutes, she was asleep. We let her sleep and the other kids rest, and I helped Dave bring up the bags. The bags were quite a sight—taking up pretty much all the free space in the living room. Where would everything go? We didn't even have any winter clothes yet. And where would these giant bags go after they were emptied? I only saw two tiny dressers and a small closet in the kids' room, and one slightly bigger closet in our bedroom. That was it for storage space! I didn't want to think about it. We decided to leave the bags in the living room and head out to find some food.

I found the umbrellas. We splashed some water on our faces, and we dragged the kids outside. I had no idea which way to walk, but thankfully, Dave did. The location of the apartment was fantastic. We headed over to a nearby street called rue Cler and found a little café. The kids kept putting their heads flat down on the table, trying to sleep. We tried to keep them awake, but they barely ate a thing. Matt asked for toothpicks to hold his eyes open, like he saw in a *Tom and Jerry* cartoon. We finished quickly, headed back to the apartment, and put them all to bed; Julia and Matthew on the twin beds (there was a trundle that had been pushed underneath, fortunately) and Katherine slept on our bed until we got the couch/sofa bed made up in the living room. This was definitely more of an adventure than I had planned on.

August 24

I just awoke to glorious Paris. Dave rolled up the blackout blinds, and the rain has stopped. The sun is shining, and I feel like a new woman. I'm ready to make the best of things. I'm going to get the kids up and dressed, and we'll head out to check out the neighborhood.

Around our apartment were at least twenty restaurants to choose from. There were bakeries, grocery stores, clothing stores, and everything else we could possibly need. We ventured into one of the bakeries and smelled fresh, hot bread baking. We bought a baguette that was still warm and broke pieces off to eat as we walked. We got the kids their first *pains au chocolat* (chocolate croissants) that were deliciously warm from the oven. They were buttery and crispy, and the chocolate melted in their mouths. They looked like they had tasted heaven.

We wandered toward the Champs-Elysées, across the Pont Alexandre III. The kids stared up, wide-eyed, at the gold-winged statues on top of the tall pillars. The bright blue sky and white clouds were sliding across the sky behind the pillars. Their first question was, "Is that real gold?" *Hmmm… we didn't really know.* We walked by the Grand Palais and the Petit Palais, which both seemed "grand" to us, and on to the famous Champs Élysées. It was a Sunday morning and very quiet. Nobody was out. We didn't yet know that French people do not go out early on Sundays, and since it was August, most Parisians were still gone on their *grandes vacances* (summer vacations). It was like we had Paris all to ourselves.

We pointed to the Arc de Triomphe at the end of the long, wide Avenue des Champs Élysées, and the kids' jaws dropped. It was quite a breathtaking sight in the distance. It drew us toward it. Everyone wanted to see it up close. The kids hazily remembered driving by it the night before, but walking toward it, none of us could get over how huge it really was. It was quite a long walk up the Champs Élysées to the Arc. When we finally neared it, I wondered how we were supposed to get over there. There weren't a lot of cars around, but I didn't see any crosswalks. It seemed dangerous to try to dash across the road. Then Dave remembered that we had to go under the street. We found the underpass, which was a long, cool tunnel. When we got up the stairs, we wandered around the giant Arc, examining the reliefs that were carved in the sides. The kids asked us about the reliefs, and we tried to explain as much as we could with our handy guidebook, neither of us being that knowledgeable about

French history. They saw the eternal flame burning by the Tomb of the Unknown Soldier. We explained (from the guidebook) that it burns in memory of the dead who were never identified, now in both world wars. "It burns forever?" They looked stunned. We couldn't go up to the top because it was closed, but it was an excellent outing for our first day in Paris. We went back underneath the Arc to the Métro Station Étoile and rode back to our neighborhood.

Everyone was hungry and tired from all the walking and the jet lag. We got *croque monsieurs* and *croque madames* (toasted ham and cheese sandwiches, with and without egg) at a café and relaxed for lunch. Then we headed back to our apartment to start unpacking. Walking up our street, we saw a little store right below our apartment, called an *alimentation*. The *alimentation* was a convenience store, like a mini 7-11, French style. We went in to check it out, and the man that worked there told the kids to take some French candy from the bins. We allowed it, saying to just take a little, and when we went to pay, he wouldn't allow it. That was a surprise. "Our *alimentation* man" (as the kids called him) was the sweetest man, although he did not speak a word of English, and his French accent was very hard to understand (maybe Tunisian). We bought a few items to tide us over for the next morning and went upstairs to our apartment.

For dinner, we headed to the crêpe stand we had seen on rue Cler the night before. Rue Cler, a cute, cobblestoned, pedestrian street, was just a five-minute walk from our apartment. The street was lined with produce stands, where men in aprons were bustling about, lining up their glistening summer fruit and vegetables in perfect rows. There were smelly cheese stores, butcher shops with dead animals hanging from the ceiling, wine stores, and popular restaurants. While we waited for the line at the crêpe cart to get shorter, we went into a honey store where they had "tasters." We bought a few bottles of our favorite flavors, and then we headed back to the crêpe cart. The kids stood together, watching the crêpes being made. The man poured batter on the hot plates and smoothed it in a circular fashion with a wooden tool. He had two crêpes cooking at the same time. He spoke a little English (since rue Cler is one of the most popular streets for Americans visiting Paris) and asked the kids what they wanted on their crêpes. "Nutella," they all said, and Katherine wanted bananas too. "Alright," we said. We wanted them to have fun, so it was going to be dessert crêpes for dinner!

10:45 p.m.

Just got back from a family walk along the Seine. We entertained ourselves by finding designs in the clouds and waving to tourists in the boats called Les Bateaux Mouches. We are not tourists. That's so WEIRD! Thank goodness we have these blackout blinds. I didn't realize how late it stays light here in the summer. Getting the kids to bed is very challenging. At 10:00 at night, it looks and feels like 3:00 in the afternoon. "But Mom, it's broad daylight," they complain. Then, we just roll down the blackout blinds and voila, it's nighttime!

The next day, we decided to take the kids to the Louvre. We walked through the Tuileries gardens and took funny pictures of the kids imitating the statues. They had a fun time. We waited in line to visit the Louvre at the main entrance by the glass pyramid, but we later found out about the secret entrance below where the lines are much shorter. It was quite overwhelming in the Louvre. We picked the wing with 13th-15th century Italian art, because it was on the way to the Mona Lisa, our ultimate goal (as well as EVERYONE else's). Every painting looked the same to us, except for Julia. Julia saw something different than the rest of us. I tried to keep everyone moving along, but Julia would stop and pull me back.

"Mom, did you see this?"

"Yes, already saw that one… moving on," but she wouldn't move on.

"Mom! Look at the woman's arm in this painting."

"Saw it Julia, moving on," but she still wouldn't budge.

She made us all go back to the painting we passed, and she showed us something interesting that we hadn't seen the first time. It reminded me of my experience going to museums with my mom as a child. It was fascinating to see that Julia has the same eye for art as my mom. Matthew, on the other hand, was NOT happy. Little Katherine was a great sport. She was up for anything, as long as she got a piggyback ride from Daddy.

August 26

We've been in Paris three days now, but it seems longer. I'm trying to be positive. During the day, I'm fine. It's at 2:00 a.m. that I freak out. Finally, Dave got the computer and the landline phone working. That's been a royal pain. The landlord set up a new system for us, so we were waiting for the box to arrive, which the building manager apparently took with him on vacation! Poor Dave was hunting around for it for three days.

We've unpacked now, and the kids are getting along so much better than before we left Santa Barbara. I guess it's because they are each other's only friends here. We've been eating a lot of crêpes, gyros (Greek lamb sandwiches served on a pita roll with onions and fries), and Asian take-out. These are the only fast food places we've found. We've definitely been spoiled by our fast, fresh Mexican food in Santa Barbara. "Fast food" choices are very limited here, and they're not exactly cheap. We need to get out of "vacation mode," and I need to start cooking!

August 29

The "Paris Intimidation Factor" is certainly getting the best of me when it comes to shopping. Dave is the interface between the outside, French-speaking world and me. Places like the outdoor market, butcher, and cheese store terrify me. How do you convert two pounds of meat to kilos? I have NO idea. Converting to the metric system is confusing enough, but even if I figure that out, I have to say it in French. Dave enjoys these outings, especially the cheese shop. All I have to do is intimate that I need something, and he is more than happy to go out and get it. But it's time to attempt the grocery store alone. We've been here for over a week, and I'm suddenly feeling courageous. How bad can it be? It's not even necessary to talk to anyone in a grocery store. I just have to walk up and down the aisles and pick things. I'm going for it!

There were a few different grocery stores near our apartment. I made my first attempt at Ed's, where Dave had gone before, but it didn't start out well. I couldn't figure out how to get the grocery cart out of the rack in front of the store. Even something as simple as that had to be complicated in Paris! I pulled; I pushed; I wiggled it; I tried to force it; but the stupid cart would not come out. I didn't want to attract attention to myself and make more of a scene than I already had, so, defeated, I walked across the street to Franprix, where the carts weren't locked up. I took a low-to-the-ground, plastic cart from the front of the store and pulled the handle up. That was a lot easier! *Never going to Ed's again*, I decided. I walked up and down the aisles and picked out some items. I was thinking, *Okay, this isn't so bad. I can do this!* I tried to find a few American products that we were used to, such as half-and-half creamer and cold cereal. It was funny that all the cold cereals had chocolate in them. I wondered about that, with all these skinny French people. Half-and-half creamer did not exist—at least I didn't know what it was called in French. Dave had bought something similar to half-and-half, but it was too thick, more like liquid crème fraîche. I looked at the French names for all the different kinds of milk, but I had absolutely no idea. It was overwhelming.

Why was it so hard to get some cream? Other things I could live without, but cream in my coffee was not one of them. I could ask for help, but I knew it'd be impossible for me to explain. I just had to guess. I picked out a small, plastic bottle called *lait entier* and hoped for the best. Then I went to check out.

I tried to make conversation with the cashier, which is normal behavior in the U.S. Whenever I went to Trader Joe's or another grocery store in the U.S., the cashier and I would always chat. He or she might ask me about my weekend plans or talk about the food items I'd chosen. At the very least, we'd say, "hello" and "how are you?" So I said, *"Bonjour."* She said, *"Bonjour."* If I stopped there, it would've been fine. But then I asked how she was. (I was pretty proud that I knew how to say, *"Comment ça va"* in French.) But that is not done. You don't ask the cashier how she is. You just say, *"Bonjour."* The conversation ends there. The cashier smirked but didn't answer. *Okay... rude*, I thought. She started ringing up the groceries, and I watched as they started piling up at the end. The line behind me was getting longer. I could feel the other customers' eyes making holes in my back, and I started wondering where the bagger was. I didn't know that I WAS THE BAGGER. I didn't know that I had to bring my own bags or a rolling caddy to pack my groceries in. (The mean cashier did have some plastic bags for purchase behind the counter, but she didn't tell me that.) Then she looked at my bag of apples and said something to me in French. I had no idea what she was saying. (I was apparently supposed to weigh all the produce bags in the produce area before coming to check out. How was I supposed to know that?!) I guess she realized I didn't understand, because she actually got up and went to do it herself. I could hear all the French people grumbling behind me.

When it came time to pay, my American Express card didn't work in the machine, and of course, I didn't have enough cash. (I later found out that I could've used my Visa card, but the cashier and I obviously were not able to communicate at all.) I was sweating at that point and completely clueless. Did Dave know about all this? Why didn't he explain things to me? It had taken me a long time to get all those groceries, and I really didn't want to leave without them! But what could I do? The cashier had already rung everything up and said something to me in French again. I panicked, left my groceries, and ran out of the store, home to Dave. I was completely traumatized, and Dave had to do all the grocery shopping for a while after that.

August 30

There's a silver lining to Dave not working full-time; having him around has been great! Everything would have been so much harder without him, and not nearly as much fun. And he did receive a nice severance package, so we're making the best of it—pretending like we're on a long vacation! School is going to start soon. We only have a few days left to play tourists!

Small things took some getting used to. For example: well-trained dogs pooped in the gutter, but all other dogs pooped on the sidewalk. It was a "dog poop minefield" on some streets, which was very annoying. We were told if you stepped in it with your left foot it was good luck. *Gross!* Public bathrooms were not available when we were out walking around—not in grocery stores, not in any stores really, and if we wanted to use one in a restaurant, we were supposed to eat or drink something first. Katherine's peanut-sized bladder meant she needed "to go" every hour on the hour. That required us drinking a lot of espressos. Of course, in an emergency, they'll let a child use the toilet in a restaurant, but they'll give you the "stink-eye." Katherine, the baby of the family, was the most particular and the most persnickety. Normally, her pickiness was cute and entertaining, as is usually the case with most third children. It seems like once you've been through things a couple of times, the third kid can do no wrong. Nothing seems as big a deal as it would've been with the first, or even second child. At five years old, Katherine was a happy girl, but she had a mischievous streak and could throw a big temper-tantrum. She was, and is still, perfectionistic, careful, inquisitive, and an over-thinker (like me).

She was also shy, which was interesting for us, because neither of our other two kids were remotely shy. Her nickname was "Velcro," because she would cling to my side as if stuck like a rhesus monkey. She could be difficult, compared to our other two easy-going kids, but I understood her. Since there were never any towels in the public bathrooms and usually no toilet seat, "Miss Picky" did not like to use the public toilets. But out of desperation, which was usually the case with her, we used them often. As I said, when Katherine had "to go" she had "TO GO!" Many bathrooms were unisex, and that took some getting used to. I had to shade Katherine's eyes while we raced by the naked male bottoms on the way to the toilet.

August 31

Living in this small, cramped apartment might be sustainable if we can find somewhere to take the kids to play. But otherwise, we may all go crazy. Today we took the kids down to the little park at the end of our street, but when Matthew started running around in the grass, kicking his ball, a policeman blew a very loud whistle. He came over and shook his finger at Matthew saying, "Non! C'est interdit!" which meant, "That's not allowed!" Poor Matthew. He picked up his ball and came over to us with such a sad look on his face. Apparently, the grass is just decorative. It's certainly not for kids to run and play on. No! The dirt is for that! This is bewildering and a bit maddening. It seems skinned knees and scraped hands are an inevitable part of the suffering that children must endure in Paris.

Finding a playground for the kids was urgent, so we started exploring other parks around Paris. One day we found ourselves in the Tuileries by the Louvre. Dave remembered there was a playground somewhere in the gardens. We wandered around until we found it. There was no grass, but there were some very interesting-looking pieces of playground equipment, like some futuristic blend of modern art and Pilates equipment, different than we had ever seen before. They were definitely more dangerous. The French are not worried about lawsuits like we are in the U.S. They don't have the same safety constraints. It's "play at your own risk," and you can't sue anyone if you get hurt.

We walked through the low metal gate to the park. The kids ran over to a large, flat, metal disc that went around and around. They jumped on, landing on top of one another in a big pile. It was sort of like a merry-go-round with no handles. Next, they tried the metal digging scoopers—basically manual backhoes with two handles. You pull on one handle while pushing the other one to move a pile of sand. It was challenging, active play. I liked that. Then they saw the giant metal dome. They watched the other kids first to see what to do. Momentum was necessary to make it up to the top. It took a few tries, but once they were up, they were king and queen of the mountain! There was also a tall metal pole that formed a circle at the top, and a girl around Julia's age was sitting on top. Julia came over to ask Dave for help up the pole. Julia has always made friends easily, kids and adults alike. She's funny, easy-going, and makes people laugh. She's also completely right-brained, artistic, messy, and disorganized. We have always said that Julia lives in "Julia-land" and it's far away, but a happy place. Dave gave Julia a boost, and she climbed up. The girl moved over to make room for her.

"What's your name? Where do you go to school?" the girl asked. Her name was Valentina.

Then Julia yelled down to us, "What's the name of my school?"

We told her.

"I go to that school too!" Valentina said. She had already been there for half a year and told Julia that she was going to love it. *Wow, how lucky to meet a girl Julia's age, from the same school, in the Tuileries playground*, I thought. When Valentina's dad came over, we all started talking. He was American, with a bit of an

41

accent I didn't recognize, and very friendly. The girls exchanged numbers and that night, at about 7:00 p.m., Valentina called to invite us to a picnic dinner at the Champs de Mars, the park in front of the Eiffel Tower. It was pretty late for us, and I was already preparing dinner. We were still on an American dinnertime schedule, so I hemmed and hawed.

"What time will they be there? Isn't it kind of late to head there now?"

"NO, MOM, PLEEEASE?" Julia begged.

I knew she'd be less insecure if she had a friend at her new school, so I gave in. Valentina's mom said they'd bring a picnic dinner for all of us. We just had to show up. So I packed up the dinner I was cooking to save for the next night, grabbed a bottle of wine, and we headed over to the Champs de Mars. When we got there, we saw a lot of people picnicking in the grass, with the Eiffel Tower panoramically standing at the other end of the park. It was quite a happening place! Valentina spotted us and ran over to welcome us. She introduced us to her mom and reintroduced her dad. We sat down and shared the picnic they had brought: delicious, fresh fois gras, cheese, olives, and a few baguettes. Valentina's mom, Sofia, was a beautiful Venezuelan woman who spoke Spanish to Valentina. (Julia was impressed that Valentina spoke Spanish too!) She told us she loved to cook and make jewelry, and she too was a stay-at-home mom. Valentina's dad, Gunter, had retired from the Foreign Service and now worked in Paris. He was a life-long expat. They had been there for six months and lived right near the Champs de Mars. The conversation flowed easily. They told us all about the school and life in Paris. When we left the park, they invited us to their apartment the next weekend for a spicy Venezuelan dinner.

September 2007

After hearing all about the school from Valentina and her parents, the kids begged us to go see it the next day. It sounded like a smart plan to map out the route before the first morning. We knew that Julia and Matthew's campuses were right next door to each other, but Katherine's campus was in a different location. Fortunately, from the Métro stop near our apartment, it was a direct shot to Julia and Matthew's school, but to get to Katherine's school would require one line change. Dave and I could divide and conquer to get them to school in the mornings (at least for now).

We went to find the older kids' school first. It was located in the 15th arrondissement, and we had no idea where that was. The 15th happens to be the largest arrondissement in Paris, but most tourists never venture there, and we hadn't either. When we looked at the map on the wall of the Métro Station, we saw that it actually bordered the 7th arrondissement, along the western edge of the Champs de Mars. Curiously, we headed up the stairs to exit the Métro station closest to the school and were pleasantly surprised when we looked around. It was a lively area, with cute shops and cafés everywhere. There was a big park right at the top of the stairs. We walked through the metal gate to investigate. Kids were playing ball and running in the grass. *I thought there was no running on the grass...* And what was that concrete table in the colonnade of trees? It was a ping-pong table! The kids were thrilled. The park was rectangular shaped with lines of perfectly cut, box-shaped trees running down the sides, cone-shaped bushes in the corners, and of course, the requisite metal benches around the perimeter for resting. Dave wanted to rest for a moment, but the kids couldn't wait. They were too anxious to see their new school.

We pulled out our map, the *Plan de Paris*, and headed out of the park to find the school. Delicious, mouthwatering pastries were lined up in the windows of the bakeries we passed. They were incredible looking. And, just like the other streets we visited a week or so ago, there were more smelly cheese stores, produce stands, and butcher shops. There were also some very Parisian-looking children's stores with exquisite, little baby outfits hanging in the window displays. I loved this area! It was so busy and so French! We walked along, taking it all in, until we found the school. When we arrived at the address, we saw the school name in large, metal letters up high on the wall, but big, locked gates kept us from seeing inside. From what we could tell, the school appeared to take up a good part of the city block. We saw a bell outside the gate, but we didn't dare ring it. We hadn't called, and we didn't think we should show up, unannounced, for a tour. The kids were disappointed that they couldn't go in, but it made the anticipation for the first day even stronger. At least we knew where the school was and how to get there. It would only be a few more days.

Next, we went to see Katherine's school. We looked at the map and saw that it was a direct route from where we were—just two stops away. "I love the Métro!" Julia said, as we handed each kid a Métro ticket, and they walked through the turnstiles. They were getting the hang of it. We plopped ourselves down on the green, molded plastic, bucket-seat chairs to wait for the next train. Our American feet were not used to so much walking. "Two minutes," Matthew said. He had already figured out how to tell when the next Métro car was coming. We stared around at the posters on the walls showing an ad for a department store I had heard of—the Galleries Lafayette, and a current Andy Warhol exhibit at the Grand Palais. A huge ad for Bueno (a chocolate covered cookie) was posted with a health warning, which read, "For your health avoid snacking between meals." *That was strange*, we thought, *promoting it, yet telling you not to eat it*. The Métro came through the tunnel and stopped in front of us. The kids raced to push the button that opened the door. We got in, rode for two stops, and hopped off. We raced up the stairs to the street where Katherine's school was and saw a fancier neighborhood. The street was very wide, tree-lined, and pretty. The school gates were a hundred feet from the Métro stop, and there was a little window in the metal gate to see inside. "Lift me up!" Katherine begged. I lifted her up to peek in. Her school looked much smaller, with a tiny courtyard. It didn't look as if anyone was there either. There was a note posted outside the gate describing the lunch menu for the first week of school. Were they serious? Couscous salad, Chicken Cordon Bleu, potatoes au gratin, pears and Camembert cheese were on the first day's menu. It sounded amazing!

We decided to walk around the neighborhood and check things out. Just around the corner was a small bookstore. Inside were French children's toys, puzzles, games, books, and all the daily newspapers. The man working there asked us, in French, if Katherine would be attending the school around the corner and Dave said yes. "You can bring me the school supply list and I will fill it for you," he said in French, and Dave translated. I looked at Dave. We had seen the supply lists, and they did look complicated. It sounded a lot easier than finding all the items ourselves, but at what cost? We were sure there must be a big mark up for that service, so we said we'd think about it. We didn't know how worth it ANY markup would have been... but I'll get to that later.

September 1

Today was such a fun day. After we left the bookstore by Katherine's school, we decided to stroll for a while longer. We found ourselves at UNESCO. I didn't really know what this building was, but I looked it up when we got home, and it stands for United Nations Educational Scientific and Cultural Organization. On the fence surrounding the building was a mind-blowing, gorgeous, photographic exhibit. Each photo was an enlarged aerial or satellite view of different places in the world: the pyramids of Egypt, a desert city alone at the edge of miles and miles of sand, a rain forest in the Amazon with swirling river designs, an aerial view of Mt. Everest in the Himalayas, among many others. Each image was visually stunning and captivating.

Okay, we randomly walked down a street and happened upon one of the most fabulous photographic exhibits I have seen in my whole life. No joke! I was craving something "more" in my life, but I wasn't sure what "more" meant. Now I'm here—one week into my new life in Paris, and I already feel like I'm finding it. I'm pinching myself, and saying a prayer that we can stay awhile.

The next few days we set out to do the boring, but necessary tasks we needed to do, such as getting French cell phones and a French bank account. These things are not easy undertakings in Paris. They're a "Catch-22." You can't get a French bank account unless you have the utilities in your name, and you can't get the utilities in your name unless you have a French bank account. This is the normal red tape and bureaucracy for pretty much everything in Paris. Bureaucracy means "making the possible impossible" and in Paris, they have mastered this. Everything is complicated. Nothing is easy. You must suffer. It's part of the culture. The one piece of paper you didn't bring is the one they always demand. A lot of people who move to Paris get quite annoyed with this aspect of living here, but it didn't bother me that much—not yet at least. True, Dave did most everything for us, but things weren't as difficult for him as our other friends complained about. He must've gotten our local French banker on a good day when he went in to open our account because he found it painless.

We had to get *Navigos* for the kids and ourselves. These are the cards used for all public transportation in Paris, instead of using paper Métro tickets all the time. Again, there was a lot of bureaucracy and paperwork, but it was worth it to not have to manage all the little tickets. Everything we did required passport pictures. *Aha! That's the reason for all the photo booths in the Métro stations,* I realized. *I thought they were just for taking fun photos with friends!* *Duh!* Slowly, I was figuring out things that everyone else already knew.

I needed to learn my way around Paris. I understood the Métro, but the bus and the RER (train) were a lot more complicated. Poor Dave couldn't accompany us everywhere we needed to go. Matthew had already memorized the entire Métro map—quite an accomplishment for an eight-year old—but that's the kind of thing Matthew liked to do.

"Name a stop!" he'd say, and he'd tell us which line number it was on and the color of the line on the Métro map. Matthew is our kid who loves a challenge. When he isn't challenged, he gets bored, and when he gets bored, he gets into trouble (similar to his mother). When he was a baby we called him the "Baby CEO" because he could always get other kids (and adults) to do things for him. One example I remember is how he'd sit firmly in the plastic baby pool at the club and throw a tennis ball out, onto the grass, pointing at it and saying, "BALL, BALL, BALL" until one of the other little kids went and fetched it for him. He'd do this over and over again, and the other kids would keep fetching it for him. Always responsible and mature for his age, he loved the older brother role and looked out for Katherine. Being the middle child meant that on one side he had Katherine, the little sister who complied with almost everything, but on the other side was Julia, the unaffected older sister, who had no problem ignoring him whenever necessary.

So, next, Matthew and I wanted to figure out how the Paris buses worked. The bus was the preferred choice of the locals, especially in good weather, and I liked it too. It was delightful to see the sights of Paris out the windows, and the extensive service meant that the waiting time wasn't ever too long. But the bus was definitely more complicated than the Métro. I have a terrible sense of direction—it's pretty much reversed—so we often found ourselves going the opposite way we needed to go when we took the bus. We found the RER even more confusing, but fortunately, we didn't need to take it when we weren't with Dave. Yes, it was a more direct route to some places, Dave would argue, but I didn't really care if my route took a little longer. I was in the "slow lane." When Dave was with us, we took the RER. He'd try to explain it to me, thinking it made sense to me when he said, "We want to go that direction, toward the blah blah blah, right?" He thought I knew where we were in relation to certain monuments, but I didn't know where anything was in Paris, so it made absolutely no sense to me.

September 2

Today we found a great playground in the middle of Luxembourg Gardens. This will definitely be one of our favorite weekend spots from now on. We hopped on a bus that ran along Boulevard St. Germain and hopped off just a few blocks from the park entrance. It was easy (because Dave was with us). I've noticed that everyone says "Bonjour" to the bus driver when they get on, and he or she says "Bonjour" back. I don't think people do that in America... do they? I can't remember. Anyway, I really like taking the bus here in Paris! It might not be as fast as the Métro or the RER, but it's definitely more scenic and relaxing.

When we walked into Luxembourg Gardens, we saw kids playing with miniature sailboats in the pond, just like we'd seen in pictures. We found the man in charge, paid a nominal amount for three sticks and three small, wooden boats, and we let the kids try it. They plopped their boats in the water and watched them slowly cross the pond. Then they walked around to the other side of the pond to push them back out, and the boats sailed back across. The kids gave each other some funny looks and asked us quizzically, "Okay... is that it?" Yep, it was a bit too slow for our kids. I wondered if there was something we were missing.

"Where's the playground?" Matt asked.

We returned the boats and set out to find it. There was a

line to get in and a small cost to enter. Dave and I noticed many parents stayed outside the perimeter of the park, kicking back on metal chairs that purposely leaned backwards for relaxing. Our kids ran straight over to the kid-friendly zip line: a fun, trapeze-like ride where they climbed up on a platform, grabbed a rope, and stood on a small tire to zip around until the cable until they hit the ground. That was fun in itself, but when two kids rode together, it was hilarious. There was really only room for two feet on the tire; the first kid jumped on, and the second kid held on to the first kid for dear life. The ride says you must be seven years old to ride, but no one appeared to be enforcing the rule, so we let Katherine do it too.

Later, we found a snack stand near the playground where we bought cinnamon and sugar crêpes for the kids and espressos for us. Then, a bell sounded, and we saw everyone scurrying. Where were they all going? There was a *marionette* show in the park theater. Sounded like fun, so we followed the crowd. Once we got to the theater entrance, we realized the puppet show was in French. (Of course it was, but we hadn't really thought about it!) Our family consensus was to hold off until a future time. Instead, we headed back to the playground, because with most of the kids at the puppet show, our kids could take ride after ride on the zip line without waiting.

We had been counting down the days until the Back to School Picnic, and the day had finally arrived. It was Saturday, a day and a half before school was to start, so we headed over to the Champs de Mars. All the new school families were invited to come and meet each other. "Peer leaders," who were *Première* and *Terminale* students (juniors and seniors), took the kids to meet their new classmates. We were surprised how many new kids there were. While each class played games and did icebreakers, the parents met and mingled. In the background was the awe-inspiring *Tour Eiffel*, as everyone called it.

At the picnic, we heard from the parent volunteers (current school parents) that it was practically unheard of to get three kids into this school all at once. *Whew!* They also said that getting them *into* the school was only the beginning. Getting them *through* the school was going to be an even bigger challenge. It was a tough school, and they'd be kicked out if they didn't do well, but luckily, not in the first year. They took it easy on "Adaptation kids," which Julia and Matthew were considered, but not Katherine. (There was no Adaptation in kindergarten, just full French immersion.) It was going to be hard work to learn French in one year, but it was necessary, they said, because if we decided to stay another year, they'd be expected to perform at the same level as the French kids.

Julia had always enjoyed school in the past and got better-than-average grades. However, she never really put too much pressure on herself academically. It sounded like things might have to change a bit for her to succeed at this school. Matthew was the opposite. He always put pressure on himself— to the extreme. For example: whenever he didn't get a perfect grade on an assignment, he'd go in after class to find out what his assignment was lacking. If he felt he didn't get the grade he deserved, he'd discuss it "ad nauseum" until either he agreed with the teacher's reasoning, or the teacher changed his grade. (Remember, he was only eight years old.) We figured he'd be fine! Katherine was just starting kindergarten, so we didn't have any idea how she'd perform. Her preschool had not been academic at all. Of course, the psychologist reported (after the testing the school required) that she'd do great in this environment, but honestly, she was five. I thought it was hard to predict.

September 3

Life is pretty confusing at this point. People ask me what grades my kids are in and I can't answer. They call the grades different names at different times. For example, Katherine is in "Grande Section," which they sometimes call "École Maternelle," but at other times, "12ème/Douzième." Matthew's grade has the most names: "CM1/Cours Moyen 1" or "8ème/Huitième," but they also call it "Adaptation," "A2," and "École Première," and somehow Julia is already in "Collège." What happened to junior high? (That is what they call junior high.) Her grade is also called "Adaptation," "A36," and "6ème/Sixième." Sixième seems to correspond, since Julia is in sixth grade, but it's the only one that makes any sense. It turns out they count backwards and start with twelfth grade for kindergarten, eleventh for first grade, and so on, until sixth grade when it matches up. Seriously, why does everything have to be SO complicated?!!

At the picnic everyone commiserated about the unbelievable demands of the Back to School supply lists. *Aha! I wasn't the only one overwhelmed by them.* These long, precise lists of textbooks, dictionaries, and notebooks—listed by paper size, line width, and page count, pens, paintbrushes, erasers, etc. were all in French, and not translatable, because there are no American words for these things. The lists were truly impossible to understand unless you had previously attended French school.

Each of my kids had a three-page list—we're talking size ten font! One list would make any American stressed out. Three lists were over the top. We tried to use an automated online translation program, but we ended up with descriptions like: "small colored notebook of simple paper in a book with a soft pocket, twelve trombones, and big clear files." *Trombones??? What the heck? That must be wrong,* I thought. The paintbrushes alone were overwhelming; each was very specific in terms of size, shape and type of hair for the brush. I had no idea kids' art supplies could be so painfully precise.

Getting all the school supplies was an exhausting experience. Had we known, we definitely would have taken the nice man at the bookstore up on his offer! We went to at least ten stores, all over Paris. It was very hot in the stores and we were harried, as were all the other sweaty, bleary-eyed parents, trying to find all the items on their lists. With trepidation I called Helen, my Parent Partner, to clarify what the instructions meant about labels and book covers. Dave thought it said that all the books and notebooks needed colored, plastic covers. That couldn't be. I doubted that they could really be asking that of us, on top of these insane lists of supplies. She confirmed that Dave was correct and at that point, I'm lucky I didn't have a nervous breakdown. Each of my kids had at least eight notebooks and eight books.

"All of them?"

"Yes," she said.

I cursed under my breath. She also said that each and every pencil and pen and every other item was supposed to have names on them.

"WHAT? They really are crazy! How do you put a name on a pen?" I asked her.

"With a label. You cut it and wrap it around it, and write really small." She commiserated with me, but she said I had to do it. Everyone did. There were also rulers, paintbrushes, scissors, art smocks, and lab coats! Everything needed a name on it—everything. And lest they make any part of this easy, we also had to sew in (not write with a Sharpie) the kids' names on their lab coats and art smocks.

September 4

Learning a lot about "La Rentrée"—what they call "Back to School" here. They take it VERY seriously. I hesitate to call it manic, because my new French friends might be offended, but it seems more than crazy how intensely they prepare for the new school year. The labeling exercise certainly seems extreme. TV and newspapers denote the summer days remaining with "R-13," "R-12" ("Rentrée minus 13" and so on). Parisian mothers are out IN FORCE buying their children the newest, best school supplies, fancy French shoes, and clothes. Everything must be perfect. I had to go shopping myself to buy the kids more new school clothes and shoes when I learned that "casual" (according to my lovely British Parent

*Partner) meant something different than we mean by
"casual" in Santa Barbara.*

Katherine and Matthew got their first haircuts just before
school started at a salon right down the street from our
apartment. The stylist asked what kind of cut the kids wanted,
and Dave tried to translate. We had no idea what they were
going to end up with. A female hairdresser cut Katherine's hair.
She called it the *Coupe Française*, which turned out to be a bob—a
very mature look for a five-year-old. Matt got the *Coupe Anglaise*,
which I guess meant a short cut since most boys in Paris had
longer hair. They both looked great. We also found ourselves
with some great-smelling, very expensive, French shampoo.
Dave didn't know how to avoid that part of the salon
experience, but it was worth it because it really smelled
incredible.

September 5

*I was up until 3:00 a.m. last night trying to finish all
the excessive labeling requirements for the kids' school
supplies, and I doubt I did any of it correctly. Today is
Day One of French school. Yep, they're really going!
Julia chose her outfit last night, trying to look as
French as possible. She talked to her new friends from
the Adaptation Picnic, Cristina and Jasmin, on the
phone to see what they were wearing. Matt wanted to
wear shorts and a tee shirt, but I said no. I made him
wear khakis and new shoes with a button down shirt.
Katherine wore a new outfit she picked out from
Monoprix, a French department store.*

Cristina and Jasmin were waiting for Julia at the school
gate when we arrived. They all looked great, but you could
definitely tell they were American. The French girls looked
French. They were casually chic, even at eleven and twelve years
old. The French girls were dressed simply, but they had that
French sense of style that is hard to emulate. Julia and her

friends did not fail to notice these things. Jasmin had a fancy backpack, the same brand as a lot of the kids had (her Mom had found this out in advance), but Julia and Cristina had their new American JanSport backpacks. The French girls did not use backpacks. They all had shoulder bags. A lot of them were the nylon, designer Longchamps bags.

At drop off, Matthew was relieved to see that the other boys walking in were dressed similarly to him. *Mom was right about something… Whew!* Dave and I said goodbye to Matthew at the gate of his school—no kisses were allowed. Then we went together to drop off Katherine.

We carried Katherine's backpack for her since it weighed a ton with all those crazy books (with plastic covers), dictionaries, and labeled school supplies. Walking up to the school, Katherine saw that everyone else was wearing his or her backpacks, so she wanted to wear hers too. She put it on and almost fell over. How were the other kids carrying those heavy bags? Little did we know then about *cartables,* a different style of backpack, wider and unbeknownst to Americans, much easier to carry and specially made for young backs. All the French kids had them.

Katherine wasn't at all nervous that first morning, which we were surprised, yet relieved about. I guess it was because she thought it would be like her old school, but she was in for a big surprise. She had always loved school, but she'd attended a small American preschool from two years old, with all her best buddies. This was going to be *very* different. We tried to prepare her, but we didn't want to scare her.

That first morning, we were allowed to accompany her into the school courtyard for the class assignments. That would be the only morning we were allowed inside. It was a small courtyard and as it turned out, the only outdoor play area for the children. How could that be, we wondered? There was no playground? We saw a hopscotch court and a couple of small tricycles, but that was it.

The blonde, female *Directrice,* who was Irish, but spoke perfect French, called one name at a time, and as she did, the child who was called went to stand by his or her teacher. Katherine saw two girls whom she had just met at the picnic—Alice, whose mom was French and dad was Swiss, and Colette, whose dad was French and mother was American. They both spoke English, but they also spoke French. Katherine was surprisingly brave when they called her name. I was predicting the "rhesus monkey-death grip" on my leg, but she went along with things and walked over to stand by her new teacher: a young and pretty teacher named Celine. Apparently, in preschool and kindergarten French children call their teachers by their first name. After all the children were assigned to their classrooms, the parents were asked to leave.

Katherine was used to getting out of school at noon, but here she wouldn't get out until 4:30 p.m. This was going to be a very long first day. I tried not to worry about her. Dave and I took the Métro home to our apartment and plopped down on the couch. Okay, we did it. Our kids were all in school in Paris. Wow. What should we do? I knew I needed to keep my mind busy, so I went to the grocery store and planned the kids' favorite dinner: lemon-roasted chicken with onions and homemade croutons. I cleaned the apartment. Dave did some work. We had a nice lunch together with a glass of wine, and we eagerly waited to hear about the kids' first day of school.

First, we picked up Matthew. He got out fifteen minutes before the other two. We arrived a few minutes early and saw all the parents waiting in a big crowd, also known as a French *queue*. (They never line up. They always bunch together—but never touching.) At 4:15 p.m. the *Directrice* and another woman, a stern-looking door guard, let the kids out—one by one—when they recognized the parent or nanny (which was fairly common at this school). Of course they didn't recognize us, but we finally saw Matthew and waved at him to come out. The door guard confirmed, and he came out smiling. Phew! He wanted to tell us all about his first day, but we had to get our other kids first. Julia and Katherine were both out at 4:30. I headed to the Métro to race over to Katherine's school, while Dave and Matthew waited for Julia outside her school gate, since it was right next door.

Everything seemed okay when I picked Katherine up. It was the same drill. Everyone waited outside the gate for the also-serious-but-a-little-bit-nicer-looking, female door guard and the *Directrice* to let the kids out, one at a time. All the other mothers seemed to know each other and were all speaking French. Their outfits were straight out of Vogue magazine. I looked down at my outfit: a pair of skinny jeans, flats, and a sweater. At least, I had thrown on the new scarf I had recently bought at Monoprix. No one spoke English, so I just stood there and waited until I saw Katherine come to the door. The door guard looked around, and I waved and smiled. She let Katherine out and directed her to me. Katherine was glad to see me. "It was kind of fun," she said, "but everyone spoke French the whole time, except in the English class." *Okay*, I thought. *She wasn't upset. That was a good sign.* We headed down the stairs to catch the Métro.

While we waited for the Métro, Katherine told me the names of the other kids she recognized from school and pointed them out to me. Elena and Charlie were twins, and they were in her English class. They were munching on snacks. Apparently, all the Moms welcomed their kids with a snack after school. I thought kids didn't snack in Paris! Just as Katherine started telling me that she was starving, Charlie walked over and offered Katherine a cookie. *How sweet was that?* I thought. French kids seemed pretty friendly! The language barrier didn't seem to matter. Things were going well. We hopped on the Métro and headed home.

Matthew was the first to talk when we walked in the door of the apartment. He told us all about his class, which was a fourth and fifth grade combination. There were kids from all over the world. He recounted the make-up in as exact detail as he could: one Chinese girl, one Korean girl, one Russian girl, one German boy, one Irish girl, one Canadian boy, one Greek/French girl, one Finnish girl, one African boy, four French/American boys and girls, and one British boy. The rest he couldn't remember. All the new, non-French, fourth and fifth graders were in his class, and most all of them did not speak French either, which made him feel better. But some of the kids could speak multiple other languages. Matthew told us that one of his new friends, Abdel, was from Sudan. "He has been to so many places," said Matthew. "I want to go to more places!" He was more than impressed. It was quite eye opening for our highly competitive, academically over-achieving child. He was not the top of the top. He was behind. What was going on? He wanted to know why everyone else was ahead of him, knowing all these languages. Aha! He was feeling a bit like an underachiever for the first time in his life.

He said he liked his teacher a lot, even though she was pretty strict, but "in a good way." She did not speak any English in the classroom. There was no field to play on at recess, just a concrete courtyard. In the middle of the courtyard was a small fenced-in area covered with fake grass where they were allowed to play ball. They also played tag or a game called *fille-garçon* where the girls tried to trap the boys, and the boys tried to trap the girls. Boys and girls played together. In America, fourth grade boys and girls did not normally play together.

"Lunch was delicious," he said. Matthew is our foodie. He loves food and watches all the cooking competitions on TV. There were four-courses, including an appetizer (salami), couscous, steamed vegetables, and fish with cream sauce, cheese (he wasn't sure what kind of cheese it was), and fruit for dessert. They could drink milk, Candy-Up (a flavored milk drink), or water.

Julia loved her first day of school. She told us about the things she found funny: they played ping-pong for *Sport* (what they called P.E.) "Seriously, ping-pong is not a sport," she laughed! How much exercise can you get playing ping-pong? She really liked her science class, because the science lab was huge and brand new. They all wore their lab coats (with the SEWN-IN labels) and were told they were going to do some impressive experiments. Science was in English, which she was happy about. Her Math Class—Geometry—was all in French, but I think that actually made Math *more* stimulating for Julia, since Math in English was not at all interesting for her. In her three-hour French class they did role-playing, with lots of pictures and cartoons to go along with it. She thought she actually understood what was going on. She didn't necessarily know what she was saying when she read the French words, but she used as strong an accent as she could. It worked for her. I would say she got all A's in self-confidence.

There was a play they acted out, which was very French and very edgy—almost inappropriate by American standards, but Julia loved it. It was all about love and kissing and "it didn't seem to embarrass anyone," she said. She had a homework assignment to memorize a long, French poem, but she didn't know when it was due (typical Julia). Dave looked at it and said it was, of course, about love and suffering, as most French poems are. It seemed quite difficult, but Julia wasn't at all concerned about learning the poem. She liked it.

Katherine didn't have too much to say about her first day. She also liked the lunch, and they too had a four-course meal. It was incredible to me—that even the littlest school children in Paris eat lunches like that. She said they told them to push in their chairs so close they were practically sitting on the table, to sit up straight, and to use the fork and knife properly. They only spoke in French, but her new friend, Alice, translated for her. She learned her first two French words, *exactamente* (exactly) and *maintenant* (now). The words sounded so cute coming out of her mouth with a perfect French accent.

She liked her English class the best, of course, but it was only for one hour per day. Her English teacher had a "funny" accent (Scottish), and was very sweet. She also liked her French teacher, and thought she was pretty, but she didn't speak a word of English all day. She said that the only play area in the whole school was that little courtyard where they'd received their class assignments. There were some giant Legos and two bikes, but other kids were always playing with them, so she just stood around.

September 6

Yay! They all made it through the first day of French school! And it went well—better than expected,

58

actually. Julia and Matthew really liked it, and Katherine didn't mind it. No one speaks English in Katherine's class besides her new friend Alice, who translates everything for her. I wonder how long they'll let that continue. Some kids in Katherine's class went home for lunch and came back afterwards. She asked us if she could do that too, but we said no.

Matthew said for Sport they took a big, fancy bus— like a rock-star tour bus—to a pool, and he was quite surprised that his teacher got in the pool and swam laps with them. He was also happy and relieved that I sent a Speedo with him, even though he told me not to. (It was on the list, and, of course, the nametag was SEWN IN.) No trunks were allowed—all the boys wore Speedos. (Ha! Mom isn't totally lame!) He took a swimming test and was very surprised to see that some of the kids in his class couldn't swim.

Julia and her new Adaptation friends, Cristina and Jasmin, are already inseparable. Jasmin grew up in Atlanta, Georgia. She moved to Paris with her Mom, Farah. They are Persian. Cristina is from Colorado, and she can speak Spanish fluently too, like Valentina, Julia's other new friend, who is not in Adaptation. Her mom, Maria, is Colombian and her dad, Jim, is American. I met both moms at the New Parent Picnic, and I like them both very much.

Julia is now saying she wants to learn French AND Spanish! This is so motivating!!!

Katherine's school experience was not nearly as positive as Julia's and Matthew's, who had a much "softer landing" into the French system. Her school was exactly how one would imagine an exclusive private school in Paris to be. All the parents and kids were super-fashionable. Many kids arrived in black cars with drivers and nannies, and it was all very French. Everyone in her class spoke French except her. The novelty wore off quickly, and the early weeks didn't go well. Katherine did NOT want to go to school. She cried and threw temper tantrums and had to be forced in the school gate each morning. Remember, we were never allowed inside. It broke my heart. She wet her pants every day at school the first week, because she didn't know how to ask to go to the bathroom in French. It was highly distressing. I did not want to give up, but it really became too stressful for me after a few weeks, so Dave had to take her to school in the mornings.

September 7

I received a phone call last night from Amanda. She's in Paris for two nights with her mom and sister, but she has to head back to Geneva tomorrow. She brought a big bag of Eden's hand-me-downs for Katherine. We can't get together this time, but she left the bag for me at the front desk of her hotel. I'm going to head over there now.

Later

Oh my gosh! All the clothes that Amanda brought are gorgeous and so French looking. How lucky are we that they moved to Geneva a few years ago and have a daughter who is just a little older than Katherine?! There are wool sweaters, dresses with matching hats, Mary Janes in blue, black, and patent leather, and the cutest coat ever—it's light blue wool with a navy-blue velvet collar, navy-blue buttons, and a matching hat. It's seriously straight out of the "Madeline in Paris" book, a story Katherine loves. She wanted to try on everything (a girl after my own heart), and it all fit perfectly! She's very excited. She's having such a hard time. I think these beautiful European clothes are just the thing to give her attitude a lift.

School days were very long. The kids were gone from 8:30 to 4:30. This meant Dave and I had a lot of time to enjoy Paris together. Mornings were a mad dash, but the rest of the day was relaxed pleasure. Lunches were gastronomic ventures. We tried all *les plats des jours* (the meals of the day) at our local cafés and bistros: chicken with morels and morel cream, duck *confit* with sautéed potatoes, fresh fish and skinny green beans, desserts such as *crème brulée* or *tarte tatin* (an upside-down tarte made with carmelized apples and sugar) and cheese, delicious cheese. Of course, we didn't always eat out. At home we prepared ourselves big salads for lunch with side items such as the popular French *salade des carrottes râpées* (grated carrot salad) or the curry couscous salad, which were just everyday items in the Paris grocery store. We added fresh vegetables and cooked chicken, rosemary ham and *Comté* (Swiss) or *Roquefort* (blue cheese). Our kitchen always smelled like stinky cheese because a round of *Camembert*, which seemed so innocuous on the shelf at the grocery store, could smell up a kitchen like a room full of dirty socks. That didn't stop us from keeping it stocked though. We loved it. (We just had to buy some gas masks!)

September 10

Dave and I have so much alone time, it feels like we're on a long second honeymoon. We've been taking leisurely naps in the afternoons. I've never been a nap taker before, but it's miraculous what a little wine with lunch can do. And no early pick up from school helps a lot too! (That 2:20 pick up at Santa Barbara Junior High nearly killed me!) Naps are actually possible when the kids aren't home until 4:00 or 5:00 pm.

The Velib rental bikes are so much fun! We rode all around the city today. What an invigorating feeling it is to ride a bike on a crisp, sunny day on the streets of Paris! I just ride along behind Dave (since I have no idea where we're going). He points out things and acts as my personal tour guide.

The "work thing" is still hanging in the air. Dave has found consulting work and tells me not to worry so much. "Things will all work out," he keeps trying to reassure me. I'm trying not to dwell, but I can't help it! I agonize about Katherine—will she ever like her new school? And I'm anxious that Dave won't find a job that will allow us to stay in Paris for the year!

When I wasn't with Dave, I hung out with my new friends, mostly Maria and Farah, who were always up for anything. We were a happy trio. Sometimes we'd get coffee or tea, sometimes go on a walk. We'd go shopping and to museum exhibits. Farah was an art historian whose knowledge about history and art made the exhibits fascinating. Both she and Maria were quite funny and kept me laughing all the time. Farah was planning to stay in Paris for a while, probably until Jasmin finished high school. Maria was there for just a year, on sabbatical, with her husband and two kids. Her husband, Jim, was an astrophysicist who traveled a lot for his job.

Dave made some friends too, but on days when we weren't hanging out together, he mostly tried to get his consulting work done, so he'd be free when the kids got home from school. While he was busy, I ventured out into the beautiful Paris fall. Many days, after dropping Katherine at school, I'd skip the Métro ride and walk home instead. After a while, I didn't need to look at my map, which for me was very exciting. As I said before, I have a terrible sense of direction, but I felt like I knew the general direction I needed to walk, so I'd just walk that way, taking different routes each time to see different things.

September 12

*I feel such a sense of freedom walking in Paris. I
always have my Plan de Paris with me, but I try not
to use it. I just walk and walk, and I eventually make
it to wherever I'm going. There's no hurry. I have
nowhere to be and all day to get there. I put on my
iPod and listen to music, or go without it if I want to
let my mind wander. What a different feeling than
sitting in my car all day, being Mom, the chauffeur.*

Besides the difficult time Katherine was having, we were off to a pretty good start in our first Parisian fall. We didn't know it at the time, being such newbies, but each season had a different feel in Paris. From the colors the Parisians wore, to the food they ate, and even their attitudes—each varied with the seasons. The weather at that time was crisp and cool. There wasn't a lot of color to be seen. Mostly everyone wore gray, charcoal, black, or navy blue clothes, and everyone wore scarves. Dark colors suited Paris at that time of year. Color was for vacationing and frivolity, not for fall in Paris. The French people were typically in good moods in the fall. Their summer tans were not yet faded from their skin or their memories. Everyone went around asking each other about their summers, and they seemed to be chattier with the neighbors and local vendors. We were strangers and observers, trying to get a grasp on the way things worked, and to fit in with the cool, chic Parisians.

On the weekends we played "tourists." We took the kids to see all the famous sights. We also decided it would be fun to dedicate one or two nights a week to finding our favorite pastries in Paris. (Otherwise, the kids wanted them every night.) Wednesdays and Sundays were denoted "Pastry Nights." Dave and the kids would go out to a *pâtisserie* (bakery) and pick three pastries, bring them home, and after dinner we'd cut them up to share: *éclairs*, *profiteroles* (cream puffs), *mille feuilles* (sheets of puff pastry layered with whipped cream), almond croissants, and apple tarts; they tasted and judged and became quite the experts.

The main attraction of Paris for the kids was the Eiffel Tour, and they wanted to go up to the top as soon as possible. But every time we went to the Champs de Mars, the lines of people waiting to go up were too long. "We live here. We can come back when the tourists are gone," we told the kids. We picnicked at the Champs de Mars practically every weekend, so we really could see when the lines got shorter. We'd bring a blanket and a picnic basket from home and usually stop at a sandwich stand to get freshly made baguette sandwiches of ham and cheese, chicken, or salami with *cornichons* (tiny, tart, crisp pickles made from gherkin cucumbers). We'd find an open spot in the grass, plop ourselves down, and eat our picnic lunch— maybe even with a glass of wine (hey, everyone else was doing it), and the kids would kick a ball around, jump rope, or play with juggling sticks. Then, we'd head over to the playground or to the old-fashioned carousel that had the metal ring game, which Katherine loved. The metal ring game, we learned, is a children's reenactment of a medieval game where knights speared rings with lances. On the Champs de Mars carousel, kids were handed wooded batons, and every time they spun by the metal rings, which dangled enticingly on a block, they tried to hook one on their baton. There were also dual-action, sea-sawing swings, pony rides, and little bikes for the kids to rent.

We even learned how to avoid the gypsies and their begging: "Speak English? Speak English?" If we said yes they'd hand us a piece of paper that explained their sad sob story asking for money, but if we said no, they'd leave us alone. We found it amusing when we answered, in perfectly good English, "No, we don't speak English," and they still left us alone. They also had a bizarre ring trick, which confounded us: They would drop a gold ring on the ground in front of us, then pick it up when we saw it lying there, and ask us if it was our ring. When we said "No" they, for some reason, thought we should give them some money—that day it was for a sandwich—and also let them keep the ring. We never did figure out how it was supposed to work, but "Money for a sandwich? Money for a sandwich?" became our family's inside joke.

September 14

I am seriously loving this new unscheduled lifestyle,
where we take family walks and daydream together,
not feeling like we have to rush off to some sports
practice every day. But it does still feel like we're on
vacation. I wonder when it will kick in that this is
home for a year.

Running errands on my own was my next big challenge.
One errand a day was a huge feat, and sometimes it took the
whole day. Matthew needed swim goggles. Where could I buy
them? How would I get there? What was his Euro size? Is that in
centimeters? Katherine, Miss Particular, needed new tights—
without seams on the toes. Seams were her nemesis, which made
them MY nemesis. Every morning was a temper tantrum. Where
could I find tights with no seams in Paris? How would I get
there? What was her French size? Everything was so
complicated! When I finally found tights for €20 per pair at Le
Bon Marché, it was the most gratifying €20 I'd ever spent. If
someone would have told me (before we moved to Paris) that I
would happily spend that much for a pair of tights, I never
would've believed them!

September 15

We have not set lofty academic expectations for the
kids, and we told them that. We know their grades
won't be great, but we want them to enjoy this
experience, and grow, without more pressure than there
already is to learn French and adapt to the new
culture. This is not about academics. It's about life
lessons and character building. No one will care about
their grades from French school when they get back.
They probably won't even be able to read them! I found
a great quote: "A bad grade is just one letter in the
Essay of Life."[4]

Our lackadaisical attitude made it much easier for the kids, especially Julia, because she wasn't the kind of kid who put too much pressure on herself to get good grades anyway. She did her homework the best she could, and she absolutely loved French school. It was so different. It was engaging and social. I think her relaxed mentality helped her learn French. It came fairly easily for her, as did making lots of friends and a great social life. After a very mediocre fifth grade in Santa Barbara, it was just what she needed.

September 16

Matthew was having a hard time making friends at school, but not anymore. There weren't enough balls at school, so he brought one from home. He was told "non" by the "serveillants" (school security personnel), but they said he could bring a ball if it was soft. We found one at Decathlon, the big sporting goods store in Paris. The next day he brought it to school, and all the boys played with him. Good for him! He figured out a way to make friends—boys and balls.

There was a Back to School Night for Matthew's Adaptation Class after a few weeks. We met his teacher and learned that she had been teaching Adaptation at this school for thirty years. We were happy to hear she had so much experience. She said she could teach non-French kids to be completely fluent in a year. *Wow! Quite an astonishing feat*, I thought. I was interested to hear how she did this. Unfortunately, she spoke in French for most of the meeting.

It was complete immersion in her classroom, where Matthew attended most of the day. She wouldn't speak a word of English, unless it was totally necessary. Sitting there at Back to School Night, and not understanding much of anything, gave me a lot of empathy for what my kids must be going through. When

---

[4] Lee Drake

she said that History/Geography was all in French, I was pretty sure Matthew was in trouble. Math is numbers, so that seemed possible, but History and Geography? She explained that they started out with Geography, which made sense because she could point to the map. But after Christmas Break, they'd switch to History because, by then, they'd understand more French. There were three hours a day of French language instruction on top of all the other classes in French, and there was one hour a day of English, taught by a different teacher whose native language was English, thank goodness. And science was in English.

We went to see the Science lab, which was the same lab that Julia used. Julia had told us about some crazy, seemingly dangerous experiments she was doing in there, such as an experiment pouring acid and bleach. I don't think they'd ever be allowed to do this in sixth grade in America. It was too dangerous. But here, they let them do it.

While the French teachers would typically be described (by Americans) as strict, in certain areas that was the case, but in other areas—things that Americans are strict about—they were more relaxed. The Science teacher explained *Le Cadre* theory to us, which is a model for teaching—not just in school—for all things. *Le Cadre* means "the frame." The frame is the boundary, and kids live within the frame. The boundaries are essential to their safety, but within the frame there is a lot of freedom. It made sense to me.

Physical autonomy builds self-reliance and inner resilience, the French believe. Related to this, we learned that starting in *Sixième* (sixth grade), French parents normally let their kids go to and from school alone. Of course, if it isn't possible for the kids to go alone (if they live too far away or for some other reason), then they'd continue to take them. But in general, they believe in giving kids as much physical autonomy as possible, at as early an age as is reasonable, and sixth grade is one of the milestones.

They also believe in emotional autonomy. That's why French parents don't praise their kids as much as we Americans do. They believe that children's self-confidence should come from within, not from others building it up for them. Kids should develop the capability to work hard without approval or acknowledgment for everything they do, my French friend told me.

> *September 23*
>
> *Hmmm. I'm dwelling on all the "Americanisms"— especially the parental behaviors that I am guilty of, such as "meritless praise." I remember saying, "Good try" after Julia mistakenly scored a soccer goal for the other team last year. Hmmm... I do praise my kids a lot—maybe too much—because I do it even when they're undeserving to make them feel better. Sometimes what I really should be saying is, "You need to try harder." On the other hand, in Paris, they focus on the negative TOO much. It should be somewhere in between. Katherine gets "frownie" faces on some of her assignments and Julia's teacher actually called her "null," which means "nothing." Julia thought it was funny and didn't take it too seriously, but eventually I'm afraid those kinds of comments will wear on her.*

Luckily, it was normal for Adaptation kids to get accompanied to school, even in sixth grade, because we enjoyed it. None of us Adaptation parents knew or realized that the rest of the French kids were going on their own at that point. Dave would take Matthew and Katherine. Julia and I would meet up with Cristina and her Mom, Maria, on the street between our two apartments. We lived only a block away from each other, so we rode the Métro to school together in the mornings. Then, after drop off, Maria and I would get a coffee with Farah, Jasmin's mom, at the café by the school. After school, we'd wait together for the girls, outside the school gate, and then we'd all walk over to the café and have tea and a crêpe or a *pain au chocolat.* The café was on the same street as the school, so I just left everyone for a few minutes to pick up Matthew when he got out, and I'd bring him over to join us.

September 24

Dave was finally able to meet with Katherine's teacher, Celine. She had no idea that Katherine can't speak French, and she can't speak English! Huh? What? I guess even though it's a bilingual school, the homeroom teacher doesn't necessarily have to speak English because there's an English teacher for that (for one hour a day). Wow. Apparently Katherine hasn't said a word in class, so Celine didn't know there was a problem. Well, we learned our lesson! Never assume anything.

September 29

We took the kids out to Nuit Blanche last night (the yearly "White Night" festival), when all the museums and gardens of Paris stay open all night and are lit up with fire and light displays. We went to the Tuileries Gardens and the Louvre with a group of our Adaptation friends. It was a little scary keeping track of all the kids in the dark, with all the crowds, but it was a great time. We stayed out until midnight. When we got on the Métro to go home, it was full of ROWDY, French rugby fans, all worked up about France's win in the World Cup. It was a crazy evening!

September 30

Today we went out to the big science museum on the other side of Paris, called Cité des Sciences et de l'Industrie, where there is a planetarium, a submarine, and an IMAX Theatre in a giant geode. Apparently it's the biggest science museum in Europe. Unfortunately, right after we bought the tickets, we realized that everything was in French, with no translations. We decided to skip it because it was pretty pricy. Dave tried to return the tickets, but "non" was the answer once again. "Non" seems to be the word of choice here. Argh!

October 2007

October 3

Shoot! Matthew found out about the other kind of "carte de sortie" (his school I.D. card)—the one that allows him to leave school on his own. Some of his friends have it, and they walk out of school by themselves and play handball against the wall until their parents come. He's begging me to change his card, but I'm apprehensive. I told him we'd think about it.

The kids needed cards for everything. They needed a card to ride the Métro (called a *Navigo*), a card to get into school (the *carte de sortie*), a card to buy lunch (the *carte de canteen)*, and a card to get out of school (the *carte de sortie* again). The schools were very strict about these cards. For example, the guard at the front of the school would not let them in or out without their card. If they forgot a card, they got punished: fifteen minutes with the *Directrice* the first time, half an hour the second time, an hour the third time, and if it happened a fourth time, you don't even want to know what would happen. (Luckily, that never happened!)

October 5

Katherine says she misses all her friends from home and her dog and her fish and her grandmas and grandpas… Ugh. That makes me sad.

October 10

I've never seen so many black shoes in my life. I find myself looking at shoes often, since nobody looks directly at you on the Métro (at least not when you can catch them).

I still have to bribe Katherine to go to school every day. Every single day, I buy and hand-wrap a small present for her to unwrap if she goes to school. Usually, it's a plastic animal figurine or animal family from Le Bon Marché, which I buy for around €5-€10 each... yes, every day! We've even resorted to bigger presents some days. Today Dave bought her a new scooter. We're desperate and determined to stick with this.

On days after school when we moms didn't go to the café with the girls, Julia and her friends wandered around by themselves. They'd go shopping on the streets near the school or hang out at the Champs de Mars. One of their friends would bring his guitar and play, or they'd just sit in the grass and talk. They all had *Navigo* passes for the Métro, so they could go wherever they wanted, whenever they wanted. Julia loved being independent and getting herself around Paris. We too were enjoying the "French autonomy" philosophy. It was good for them to be so independent, and for us not to have to chauffeur them around all the time.

In retrospect, some problems occurred as we may have taken the "low pressure for academics" idea a little too far. It would've been helpful to know a little more about the French educational philosophy, which is very different than ours. In America, external methods are emphasized, meaning homework is assigned and graded, and parents are notified if something is amiss. In the French system, students are assumed to be responsible for their own learning. Minimal daily homework was assigned, and it was never checked, so Julia just didn't do it. She didn't know that the other kids were keeping up at home, especially on the weekends.

We weren't notified that anything was wrong—when in fact, there were problems. There were quizzes she said she didn't do well on, but again, we assumed we'd be notified if some kind of intervention were necessary. I knew she was assigned a long, complicated, French novel: Victor Hugo's, *Hunchback of Notre Dame*, but this seemed absolutely ridiculous. *How could they give a kid who just arrived two months ago such a book to read? They couldn't really expect her to read it,* we assumed. Turned out there was a youth abridged version of the book which was a lot easier, but we didn't know about it because Julia lost the paper that explained it, and Dave bought the book from Canadian Amazon while he was in Santa Barbara. Anyway, without Dave's help or looking up every word in the dictionary, it wasn't possible for Julia to read the book. And, because of Julia's personality, she preferred not to do it at all. So she just didn't, and we didn't know enough to worry about it.

Matthew didn't do too badly, even at the beginning, or we would have heard him complain. Matthew does not like to get bad grades, so we knew he was doing fine. He worked hard and learned all the French verb conjugations. (There are a lot of them!) I'm pretty sure most Americans wouldn't learn all of them until high school or maybe even college. He was definitely challenged.

October 16

Today I went for a tour (in English) of the Musée Bourdelle with a group of parents from the school. I had never heard of this museum before today. There are so many museums in Paris, it's incredible. Most people only visit the famous ones. But now, I get to go to all the lesser-known museums because I've already been to all the well-known ones. In addition, there are no crowds.

The tour included the apartment where Antoine Bourdelle lived and worked. My favorite thing was the

*progression of his most-famous sculpture called
"Hercules the Archer." The progression demonstrated
how he made the archer look stronger and stronger each
time. It was brilliant. (I just love the word brilliant!
My British friends use it all the time.)*

October 21

*Mornings are getting easier. Today, Katherine went to
school without a bribe... finally! I don't really know
why. I think she is starting to understand more
French, even if she doesn't realize it. She also said
they're doing "something fun" in her English class
today. I truly believed she'd start liking school
eventually, but it has been such an exhausting struggle
going through this process. If not for Dave taking her
to school, I don't know if I would have persevered. I
can see now why so many people give up in this
situation. I feel an overwhelming sense of relief today.*

October 22

*Julia's first Midterms (called "Les Compos") are
coming up, and she just brought home the study guides.
Uh oh! Now we realize how far behind she really is.
She is very upset. Dave is in Santa Barbara, which is
a huge bummer. I'm trying my best to help her study,
but most of it is in French, so it's almost impossible for
me. We heard that the teachers are extra nice to
Adaptation kids... let's hope so! Julia is going to have
to work a lot harder from now on! She sees that now.
Another one of my favorite quotes fits here: "Adversity
introduces a 'girl' to herself!"[5]*

---

[5] Albert Einstein "Adversity introduces a 'man' to himself."

October 23

*The kids sure do get a lot of vacations here! Every six
weeks they get two weeks off. We had no idea about
all the extra vacations, so this is a big bonus. We can't
go crazy, however, since Dave is only consulting. He
doesn't have a "real" job. But still, we want to make
the most of these breaks—on a budget. We made a
list of our top destinations that aren't too far away. It's
a big job for me—planning all these family vacations,
and it's especially complicated because everything is IN
FRENCH. Wait! Challenges are a good thing!!!
Challenges make me stronger!!! (Sigh)*

The kids' first vacation, called *Toussaint* (the French name
for All Saints' Day), was just after *Les Compos*, from the last week
of October through the first week of November. All Saints' Day
is when the French honor their deceased relatives. We took this
to heart and said some prayers for our relatives, and then headed
to San Sebastian, Spain. San Sebastian was pretty close to Paris,
just over the French border, and an easy ride on the TGV—the
super-high-speed train. The kids were excited for their first ride
on the TGV. It took five hours, but it was a fun, luxurious ride.
The kids loved walking around the train. There was a café that
served snacks and drinks, and they played Nintendo with other
kids they met on the train. We were passing Bordeaux, pointing
out the tall, skinny Cypress trees with tops that looked like mini
Christmas trees, when Dave said, "Do you realize we're going
around a turn at over a hundred miles an hour right now?" We
couldn't even tell. It was crazy how fast we were going.

I thought I'd be a big help as our interpreter in San
Sebastian, but that did not turn out to be the case. I'd studied
Spanish in America and became fairly fluent in it for a while.
Surprisingly, however, the Basque people did not understand my
Spanish at all. Or, from my point of view, they were pretending
not to understand it, because Basque sounded pretty similar to
Spanish to me. All of us were amused by the "th" sound that
they used instead of the "s" sound. Even after we heard

"*Grathias*" pronounced thirty times, it still sounded odd. Dave kept us in stitches with imitations and jokes like: "Doeth he have a thpeech impediment?"

October 30

San Sebastian has a similar architectural feel to Santa Barbara. It's "beachy" with surf shops lining the streets. But the similarities end there. Downtown, where we're staying, is "party-central." Apparently, dinner is served at midnight, happy hour at 2:00 a.m., and then nightclubbing at 3:00 a.m. Restaurants don't even open until 9:00 p.m. Poor Katherine. It's 8:00 now. She's sick and wants to go to bed, but we have to keep her up to go to dinner.

"The Basque food is the best in Europe! The whole city has a cocktail party with finger foods!" That was what we'd heard. It sounded like so much fun—until we were there, trying to get food in dark, smoky bars with cigarettes dangling dangerously at kid level everywhere we looked. *Pintxos,* what they called their appetizer-sized finger foods, were served in every bar in San Sebastian at dinnertime. We'd take a *pintxo* off a communal plate and hand it to the kids. They'd of course ask, "What is it?" and we had absolutely no idea. Everything was salty and greasy, and we all ended up with terrible stomachaches. The *pintxos* didn't work for us, but the *sangria* did (for me and Dave, that is). It kept the buzz going as we tried to drown out the sound of our children saying ever more emphatically, "I'm hungry."

"Have another sausage and salami... or a beef cheek or a lamb hip... Yum!"

October 31

It's Halloween in America, but it isn't celebrated here, and the kids have accepted that (surprisingly). Our (my) great plan for tomorrow was to rent a car and drive to Biarritz, but I didn't realize tomorrow is the actual All Saints' Day and all the car rental companies are closed! Argh! My other plan was the Guggenheim Museum in nearby Bilbao, "one of the most admired works of contemporary architecture," but that, too, is closed tomorrow. Okay, I should've done better research, but how the heck was I supposed to know that everything would be closed on All Saints' Day?!

November 2007

Instead of Biarritz or Bilbao, we woke the kids up the next morning and took a family walk along the four-mile, oceanfront, San Sebastian promenade. We found an old, rumbling funicular, which took us up the hill of Mount Urgull. There we found a sketchy-looking, ancient, (abandoned?) amusement park. Of course the kids still wanted to go on the rickety, old rides, but they, too, were closed. *(Heavy sigh)* At least the funicular was kind of like a ride!

Later, we headed to downtown San Sebastian and had a yummy Italian lunch. We were already sick of the greasy Basque food and the not-so-nice Basque people. For example, when I went up to the counter to order a Coke, the bartender said in an exasperated, rude tone, "What do you want?" After lunch, we decided to walk around downtown, but everything was closed. What? Was it still the holiday? No, it was just time for their naps! In the middle of the day from 2:00-4:00 p.m. everything closed down and metal gates were lowered and locked on all the shops for their daily Spanish *siesta* (our prime touring hours on our short vacation). What else could we do? This vacation was not going as well as we'd hoped! Surfing? No, the surf shops were also closed for naptime—no way to borrow boards or wetsuits for a while. Dave and the kids decided to take a dip in the freezing cold ocean, in honor of Dave's deceased, surfer brother for All Saints' Day. At dinnertime, we tried to go to a real restaurant instead of the bar scene, but, without reservations, we couldn't get in anywhere. We tried at least five restaurants in the neighborhood of our hotel. Frustrated and tired, we decided to go back and try the restaurant in our hotel. Turned out it was Vietnamese, and it was delicious. The kids announced that Vietnamese was their new favorite type of food—another fortuitous discovery!

Unforeseen circumstances, such as what we encountered on this first trip, with me—the naïve and inexperienced vacation planner—were the cause of many McClintock family "misadventures," which later became the norm. No vacation was complete without at least one mishap, and on this trip there were too many to count.

When Dave went to check out of the hotel the next morning, he asked the front desk clerk to call a taxi for us, and we went outside the lobby to wait. No taxi came. We waited and waited, checking our watches, and growing more nervous and impatient by the minute. When the taxi driver finally arrived and saw five of us, he drove away, shaking his head. We even tried to hide Katherine behind us when he pulled up, as we've been refused service before with five people.

Dave went in and asked them to call another taxi (a bigger one this time). We waited again. We were getting precariously close to missing our train. Finally, the taxi arrived, and the driver agreed to take us. *Whew!* We weren't going very far but there was unanticipated traffic. Our train was scheduled to leave 11:24 a.m. It was 11:18. We had six minutes. The train station was in clear view, but there was no way to get there. My stress level was through the roof. We made it to the train station at 11:22. (We had TWO minutes to get all our luggage and ourselves onto the train.) Dave paid the driver, grabbed the bags, and screamed at the kids to RUN to the train right outside the station. We were pretty sure it was our train, but not positive. As we jumped in, the doors closed. It was so close that Matt's jacket actually got caught in the train door.

"Is this the train to Paris?" we asked hopefully.

"Sí." (Oh, thank God!)

November 3

We are learning so much about family travel.
Flexibility is key. There's a lot of stress when you
almost miss a train and there are no others that day.
Long plane flights are draining, and spending money

dangerously is worrisome. Spontaneity is NOT always a good thing, especially when everyone is hungry, grumpy, and you don't have reservations! BUT, even with all the problems we've encountered, Dave and I are realizing how much we love traveling with our kids. Seeing things through their eyes gives us a whole new perspective.

November 4

Today is Katherine's 6ᵗʰ birthday. We took the RER train out to Marne-la-Vallée (Disneyland), the coldest—whoops—I meant the happiest place on earth! A bunch of our new friends met us there. The day was spent as any other normal day in Disneyland is spent, waiting in lines and searching for "barbapapa" (French cotton candy, which translates as "grandpa's beard"). The main difference here was that we also had to avoid frostbite. It was SOOO cold. The food was expensive, but it was definitely better than California Disney food. The French will only go so far with the American theme. All in all, it was very similar to the experience at American Disneyland "butt" colder (Dave's joke), and that was just what Katherine needed—a little America back in her life.

When we got back to Paris, we had homemade chocolate cake with strawberries. Katherine opened her birthday presents and was very happy. Her last gift was in a giant box, sent from her grandma, which arrived while we were gone. It was a gorgeous, light-green, silky, heavy blanket for her bed. Katherine took off all her clothes, wrapped herself all up in it, and rolled around in bliss. The other kids joined in and rolled around with her. (All of them were on a major sugar high from too much Coke and cake!)

It was not until mid-November that Katherine actually started liking school and wanting to go. But she also got sick a lot. She was young, without a strong immune system, and all the French germs were new. Plus, all her stress at not knowing how to ask for simple things—like going to the bathroom—definitely did not help the situation. Being inside so much in close quarters, such as the Métro during cold season, we could understand it, but it seemed like her nose was always running. Kids were not allowed to miss three days of school without a doctor's note, so we had to visit the doctor often.

Medical care is probably one of the biggest fears of a move abroad. But with this being an "expat school," the Parent Group published an updated, yearly guide called "The Survival Guide to Paris" for all the newcomers. Along with doctor recommendations, there were all the emergency phone numbers for fire and paramedics, school contact numbers, useful websites, recommended books, and extracurricular activities for kids. There were even explicit directions for emergencies. "Just dial 18 for an emergency," everyone said. But no one explained that after you dialed 18, you most likely needed to speak French. The Survival Guide had translations for describing different types of emergencies in French.

The doctor whom we chose for the kids had his office right next door to the school. He was also a parent at the school. Unfortunately, his English was not great, which complicated things, but we liked him a lot. I learned things from him about fevers and medications that had never been explained to me in the U.S. Despite the difficulties in our communications, I understood his diagnoses—sometimes even better than when my doctor in the U.S. spoke to me in English. He drew me a chart that described fever movements that characteristically indicated viral or bacterial infections. He explained why French doctors believe that different pain relievers work better for throat infections than work for ear infections, which I had never heard before. At €40 a pop, no matter how long we were in the doctor's office, I was happy to visit whenever necessary.

November 11

Ah, the Paris Métro… it's fabulous when it's running… but today all the transit workers are on strike AND when there's a strike, it's pretty much impossible to get a taxi. That means we have to get everywhere we need to go on foot or by scooter (a foot scooter, not the motorized kind)… fun, fun! And of course, it's raining.

Survival as an inexperienced expat in Paris required endurance. According to Webster's Dictionary, expat is short for expatriate: a person temporarily or permanently residing in a country and culture other than that of the person's upbringing. In addition, I had left my home country for the first time to live in a foreign country after living in a mono-cultural environment my entire life. Everything was literally foreign to me, but I was surrounded with more experienced expats who could provide guidance and advice. Most of the kids with parents who worked in the international embassies went to this school. These families were often relocated every two years. Many were experts at adaptation to new cultures.

We learned that the school we had chosen was one of the top expat schools in Paris. This particular school had been creating successful French students from other nations for over half a century. Countless people had done this before us, and we could've gained a lot of perspective in advance if we'd done some research. There were also many books and websites about expat life, but ours was such a spontaneous last minute idea, I hadn't read anything, nor had I ever heard of this lifestyle.

November 12

I feel so lucky to have made such wonderful, new friends here in Paris. I just read a book I checked out from the American library about expat life. It says, "Not only adapting, but also enjoying a new culture is the most desirable outcome of a move to a foreign country." [6] This is not always easy. But for us, having found such a "giving" parent community has made it very pleasurable.

My Parent Partners were always there to help me with issues that came up: Helen, who is British and married to a French man, was chosen for me because her kids were the same ages as mine, and also in the same order - girl, boy, girl. She had arrived in Paris one year prior. Her two older kids were at the same schools as Julia and Matthew, but her younger one was at the other primary school campus. She emailed me in the summer to answer all my questions before we arrived. Then, she invited me to coffee the second week of school, and we immediately hit it off. I also got a second Parent Partner, Anna, because her younger girls were at Katherine's school. She and her husband were originally from Lebanon, but they'd lived in Paris for many years. She also was very generous with her time, inviting me to coffees, and Katherine to play with her girls. I got to "give back" too: Anna liked practicing her English with me, because she rarely got the chance.

That part of the experience, having a "sponsor" (or two, in my case)—meaning an expat or local person who was knowledgeable about my new home and willing to help me with my transition, was vitally important.[7] Every experience at the beginning of the year was intense. The barriers to success all seemed magnified, and I felt as if I'd never figure some things out. I was very lucky to have so much help during that adjustment period.

The same teenage Peer Leaders who helped at the Back-to-School Picnic also oversaw the new kids' adjustment to school, and acted as their liaisons if they needed help. They did activities with the new kids weekly and helped them by being mentors, guides, and friends. Struggles were common in the first few months, but this school really tried to ease the transition.

[6] [7] *The Expert Expat* by Melissa Brayer Hess and Patricia Linderman

Behavior expectations were tough. Bad behavior was not tolerated, not that our kids were badly behaved; they just weren't trained the same way as French children. They were expected to be very quiet and to stay very still—no wiggling, whispering, or playing when it was not playtime.

November 13

Today I saw a group of the most well behaved children, sitting, lined up on a wall, for at least twenty minutes. They couldn't have been more than three or four years old. Every single one of them sat perfectly still. Not one tush left the wall, not a wiggle, not a poke. I was so in awe I stayed to observe, pretending that I was reading a book. It was remarkable! Were they sedated? No, just French! My kids had better learn to be good French children, and quick!

The kids also had to learn to write their numbers and letters differently than they learned in the U.S. They also learned to write with fountain pens with erasable ink, not pencils. Pencils were only used for drawing. Even math was done using an erasable fountain pen. In the French education system, children are not taught to think creatively. Apparently, that's an American concept. They're taught information, and they're to learn it the way it's taught. There is no room for "personal expression" or for thinking "outside the box." French school is a disciplined and rigorous education system that focuses on negative reinforcement and little encouragement. But for some reason, my kids liked it.

Because the school was set up for short-timers, they held lectures on adaptation and culture shock to help us deal with our expectations. A woman named Clare spoke at an evening meeting at the school, organized by the Parent Organization. Clare, a highly energized British expat, had three older children at the school. She and her family had already been at the school a few years. She valiantly headed up a team of like-minded volunteer parents to work with her on a 'Parents in Adaptation" team. She was determined and dedicated to doing everything she could to help new families adjust to the school and to life in Paris.

We learned in her speech that culture shock was a very real thing and we were in the middle of it. Culture is defined as a system of shared beliefs, concepts, and values. It is learned, rather than instinctive. It is something caught from, as well as taught from the surrounding environment, and it is passed on from one generation to the next. So, when one moves to a new country and tries to adapt to a new culture, they have to change the way they behave, dress, eat, and speak to fit in with the people around them. French people take things for granted that are part of their culture, just like we take for granted things that are part of our American culture—things we are used to—such as ice in our drinks, smiles from people we don't know, and conversations with grocery check-out clerks.

Culture shock is the name given to the stages one goes through while trying to adapt. They are sometimes called the Honeymoon Stage, Negotiation Stage, Adjustment Stage, and Mastery Stage. Knowing the stages in advance could prepare us, we were told. In Stage One, the Honeymoon Stage, everything is seen in a romantic light. This time was filled with observations and discoveries. In Stage Two, the Negotiation Stage, we'd start to make a lot of comparisons between our new life and our old one. She said we'd probably find ourselves getting irritated over minor things and being critical because people do not do things the way we do them. In Stage Three, the Adjustment Stage, we'd start knowing what to expect, and things would start to seem normal and make sense. In Stage Four, we could experience an end to culture shock if we realized we were foreigners, spending just a portion of our lives in this new and different place. We'd realize by then that we didn't have to act just like the French act, but we could exist and participate happily in the new culture if we accepted things as they were.

November 14

The Honeymoon Stage is over, so I guess I'm in Stage Two—the Negotiation Stage—also known as "the hard one." Why can't I wear my workout clothes all day? I REALLY want to. It's such a pain to get dressed up every single morning and try to look perfect before I leave the apartment. Even when I do feel good about my outfit, I don't look half as good as the French women, so why even try? How do they do it? It's so annoying. Today, for example, I wore my new, black Lulu leggings and matching jacket. I thought I was quite well-dressed, but enough people asked me if I was on my way to exercise that I won't wear that any more. I would also like to keep speaking English and not worry so much about learning French. Almost everyone here can speak English!

I have to keep reminding myself that we chose NOT to put our kids in The American School of Paris or the International School of Paris because both of those schools, while very good, are not French schools. We wanted them immersed, not only in the French language, but also in the French culture, and since we're their parents, we too should make the effort to adjust to the French culture.

Okay, okay, I have to listen to the advice of the experienced because they know what they're talking about. They know how to make this a successful experience not only for our kids, but also for us. This school has an extraordinary track record of creating children who excel, and who are open and intellectually engaged. It isn't just immersion. It's a well-thought out and effective process, including this wonderful Parent

Organization, dedicated to helping us adapt. We are lucky!

They said at the meeting (and I have the hand-out here to remind me) that "taking the initiative to learn French, lowering my expectations, and trying to keep my perspective positive will help me enjoy the differences in my new environment instead of challenging them." Okay, I'm going to try.

That is not to say that it was easy, by any means. But it was comforting having others around who had experienced the same emotions I was experiencing and gotten through them. There was a light at the end of the Adaptation tunnel. Clare told us that she went down to the basement to cry at night when she and her family were new and having a hard time. She said how important it was to put on a brave face at all times, and to be positive and supportive to the family. That is a very British trait, but it reminded me of a bumper sticker I'd seen in America: "If Mama ain't happy, nobody's happy." What she said made me feel better.

We were used to things being easy, and nothing in Paris was easy. But that was okay. I wanted challenge in my life and I was certainly getting it. We ALL had to learn to adapt. If we were thirsty, we had to sit down in a café to order a glass of water or a *carafe d'eau* (a small pitcher of water). Same for coffee: we had to sit down and order it—except in the areas where new Starbucks were popping up—a sacrilege to the Parisian café mentality, but popular with tourists and the younger generation. We were all used to immediate gratification in America and that was one of the toughest things to adapt to. My kids were constantly asking me for water when we walked around and I'd say, "No, you'll have to wait." What? Wait? Yes, wait—a new concept for us! Water bottles were too heavy to carry around when you were walking everywhere.

Paris was not a "to go" kind of place. I remember going to a café on one of our first days there. I'd barely eaten any of my dinner, so I asked for a "to go" container. The waiter replied, *"Non."* I laughed, thinking he was trying to be funny. We waited and waited. Finally Dave said, "Okay, everyone, let's go."

"But I haven't gotten my to-go container," I said.

"Toni, he isn't bringing it."

I couldn't believe it! "Yes, he is. Isn't he? No? Really?"

"Really." Dave said.

November 16

I'm definitely in Stage Two, and NOT happy. I really cannot believe they didn't have ANY to-go containers at the restaurant last night. I mean yes, I do know that plastic and Styrofoam pollute the planet, but they could use paper "to go" boxes. There are alternatives. But any attempt to persuade a French waiter of this is dismissed or ignored, especially if you don't speak French!

November 17

I need to vent! How do French women run around in high heels with such ease? I don't understand how they do it! Today, once again, I tried to wear my new heels—the expensive ones I went out and bought after seeing all the French women prancing around so effortlessly—but I lasted about an hour and a half and then I had to hobble home and take them off. My feet were in SO much pain. There must be some special French footpads or techniques that I don't know about... And how do they all (French men and women) keep their shoes so PERFECT? They can't wear brand new shoes all the time, can they? Do they polish and shine their shoes every night?!! GEEZ!!

It seems everyone (in Adaptation) has a plan to learn French except me. I just want to wander around Paris aimlessly, smiling at all the people, and enjoying the pleasant buzz of "background noise" (French). I don't want to spend my short time in Paris in a classroom! But I must learn French somehow. That's becoming evident. Dave found an online program that has a free trial period called Rocket French. I think I'll try it.

November 18

I can only do Rocket French while the kids are in school. Solitude is completely impossible in this tiny apartment, and the kids all listen and make fun of my accent. (They're "méchant" (mean)—my children!) I just heard about a private tutor who can come and teach me. I'll see how that goes…

November 19

The tutor is very nice, but not effective. I have to cancel her. She wants to meet at coffee shops and walk around different neighborhoods to make it more stimulating, but I am too A.D.D. to learn that way. There are too many captivating things to look at, and I cannot focus. I can do the same thing with one of my new French-speaking friends for free. I'll just keep using my kids as my mini-translators. I see no problem with this plan.

November 20

Dave got a job. YES!!! Just in time for our expensive Thanksgiving dinner out! The company he was consulting for in Santa Barbara wants to hire him

*full-time, and they're willing to let him finish out the
year in Paris! (Yay, yay, yay!!!)*

All our American friends wanted to celebrate
Thanksgiving together, so thirty of us made a plan to meet at the
Paris Hard Rock Café in the 9th arrondissement, where they
advertised a "traditional" Thanksgiving dinner. It turned out
there was a *grève* (a transportation workers' strike) that day, so the
Métro line to the Hard Rock was not running. We finally got a
taxi after waiting in a long line at the taxi stand, and crawled
through traffic at a snail's pace. We probably could have walked
faster. We arrived very late, but everyone else did too. All the
adults sat at the bar and ordered mixed drinks, a novelty because
mixed drinks are crazily expensive in Paris—we're talking twenty
euros for a drink: five for the juice and fifteen for the alcohol.
None of us cared though, after the huge hassle of getting there.
The kids all wandered around the café and checked out the
American memorabilia on the walls until everyone arrived.

All the adults sat at one table and the kids at another.
American music was blasting so loud we couldn't hear each
other. The food was terrible, and there was no stuffing!
Seriously, how could they call it a "traditional Thanksgiving
feast" without stuffing? The turkey was dry and the gravy was
unappetizing, to say the least. Well, I had not tasted bad food in
Paris before this, but I found a meal that French people cannot
make… finally something! The kids thought the night was
fabulous. They loved the loud American music, Shirley Temples,
and sitting with their friends.

For the New Year we started planning a trip to Venice. It
was a city I had always wanted to visit, and Dave had never been
either. Just for the record, January is not when most people
would choose to go to Venice because it's unbelievably cold
there, but when we were offered a fabulous apartment, on the
Dorsoduro—a peninsula just across the Grand Canal from San
Marco—and we didn't know how long our stint in Paris really
would last, we felt we had to seize the moment. Our friend
Valerie's parents owned the apartment, but they required an
"interview" with our kids beforehand. *Yikes!*

Nervously, we instructed the kids to be on their best behavior. We went out to their house in St. Cloud, about a twenty-minute ride on the train. Isabelle, our friend's mother, picked us up from the train station in her car. She drove us, in the pouring rain, up to a grand gate, which opened, and then down a very long driveway. The kids were wide-eyed. The house was like a château. We were a bit nervous when we got inside, because there were expensive-looking things everywhere. We met Dario, Valerie's father, who was very friendly and funny. He told us all about his family and showed us pictures of Venice and his apartment. Venice was obviously very special to him, and he loved it very much.

November 27

We just got home from Valerie's parents' house in St. Cloud. Her parents are so friendly and funny, and they loved our kids. They're going to let us stay in their apartment in Venice, and I bet it's going to be gorgeous! Dario gave us all sorts of advice, but most importantly, that getting lost is the best way to see Venice.

November 30

Dario came all the way into Paris to bring us a hand-made book of pictures, maps, and a guide to Venice in English. He called me to ask for our door code and left it in our mailbox. I can't believe he made that for us! Wow is all I can say.

December 2007

I joined a weekly French/English Conversation Group with twelve women from the kids' school. We took turns hosting the group at our apartments. We'd serve coffee, tea, and some goodies. We spent the first hour speaking in French and the second hour speaking in English or vice-versa. The English speakers got to practice their French and the French speakers got to practice their English. In our group, we didn't choose a topic, although some of the other groups did. We'd just talk about our weekends, our vacation plans, or events happening in Paris.

December 1

I'm definitely the token beginner in my Conversation Group, but they always insist I take a turn, and they are very patient. I can't really speak any French, but they help me get at least one sentence out. The rest of the time I just listen, and I'm starting to recognize a few words. Dave also joined a group (a different group). We both agreed that joining the same group wouldn't be good. I know I'd look to him for help (or he'd help me when I didn't want help). We both really look forward to our weekly groups.

In my Conversation group we had one Parisian, Lucy. She was a "storehouse" of knowledge on everything about Paris. Her English was perfect, but she enjoyed the camaraderie, and said she didn't get much of a chance to practice her English since she left the working world. Another new friend in my group was Emma. She was in Paris for one year with her husband and her three boys from Canada. She was an English major in college and had an awesome vocabulary that made even the English part of our conversations a growth experience for me. She also had a lovely singing voice and said she'd sing for us someday.

My group was all women, which was not the case in all groups, but I think that lead us to more cohesiveness and openness. Clare, the head of the Parent Association, was also in my group. She used lots of fun British words. We laughed a lot and constantly argued the American (correct) versus the British (wrong) pronunciations of words. One of the funniest things was hearing the difference when the French women tried to speak English with an American accent versus a British accent, and I didn't feel so bad about my French pronunciations!

December 2

It would be an understatement to say that there are certain things that are scary about not speaking French and living in Paris. One is getting a haircut, and I NEED a haircut. I have put it off too long! But even when you speak the same language as your hairdresser, sometimes you can't put into words exactly what you want. And when you can BARELY speak the language, it can be really stressful. Dave's just going to have to come with me, and hopefully he will explain it right. (Fingers crossed!!!)

Cooking in Paris required a massive learning curve. First of all, I didn't have any American measuring tools, which all my American recipes called for. I looked everywhere in the stores, but nobody sold them. Our apartment had perfectly good French measuring cups and spoons, but the conversions to use them were complicated math problems. You can't understand how complicated this really was unless I describe it in more detail. For example: French measuring spoons are called *cuillère à soupe* (15 ml) or *cuillère à café* (5 ml). Basically, a soupspoon is one size (an American tablespoon) and a coffee spoon is the other size (an American teaspoon). That's it for the spoons. The liquid measurements are called for in milliliters and the solid ingredients in grams. Just try to figure that out when you're mid-recipe!

It was almost easier to just use French recipes and French measuring tools (but that meant I couldn't read the directions, and I often didn't know what the French ingredients were). There were many meals where the ingredient conversions were obviously off. Dave would eat anything, no matter how badly it turned out. He would say, "It's not bad, really Toni. I think it's good!" He seemed genuinely sincere, but my kids were not as understanding.

December 3

Need to vent again about French perfectionism and really, do there have to be twenty different kinds of sugar? How different can they be? Seriously! A French recipe that calls for sugar can stump even the most competent American baker (which I am NOT). There is "sucre glace" which is powdered sugar and "sucre cristal" or "cristallisé" which is granulated sugar. There is also "sucre en poudre," which is also granulated sugar, not powdered sugar, as one would think, right? And there's "sucre semoule" which is also granulated sugar, but apparently the crystals are a little bit finer. WAIT! There are still more, MANY more! There is "sucre en morceaux," "sucre en grains," "sucre vergeoise," "cassonade," and "sucre de canne complet." I'll stop there, but I'm sure there are more.

I have messed up so many recipes because of the wrong sugar. It's very frustrating. I forgot to mention that all the sugar is sold in paper bags or boxes—not clear plastic bags where you could potentially see the sugar and get a hint. No, that would make it too easy! You wouldn't have to suffer! (Have you ever tried shaking a

sugar box to try to guess what kind of sugar it is?
Well I can tell you, it doesn't work very well.)

We hadn't been to Montmartre yet, so we took the kids there on the weekend. Montmartre is a Bohemian village in the eighth arrondissement of Paris, famous for cabarets *Le Moulin Rouge* (with the famous red windmill) and *Le Chat Noir* (with the famous black cat). We took the funicular (basically a big cable car on an escalator) from the Métro station and arrived at the summit where the big, white, Roman Catholic basilica, the Sacré-Coeur sits. The Sacré-Coeur, with its giant, round dome and two smaller domes on either side, sits at the highest point in the city of Paris. Dave pointed out all the distant landmarks to us from the scenic lookout point. Cruising around the basilica, we came across a mime with his whole body painted white, standing perfectly still like a statue. When we walked by him, Katherine was intrigued but very unsure. Walking slowly, and watching him very carefully, we tried to get by while he appeared to be staring out into space. Then right when we were passing him, he stuck a rose right in front of Katherine. It scared the heck out of us.

Next to the Sacré-Coeur was the artist-filled square called Place du Tertre. We thought it would be fun to get the kids' portraits done. We strolled through the rows of artists sketching portraits of tourists in different styles and mediums. Some were a little pushy, but we wanted to find the style we liked best. We chose an artist to draw Julia who used dark red pastel on cream-colored paper—it was kind of an old-fashioned style. The artist we chose to sketch Katherine told us that he had been working there, in that same spot, for thirty years. Wow! He used black, grey, and white pastels on light gray paper. We could tell he was popular because there was a line of people waiting for him and many people watching. He started with Katherine's eyes and took the majority of the time on them, but he was finished with the whole portrait in about twenty minutes. It was a remarkable resemblance. I was surprised Katherine was able to stay so focused and still. A similar portrait would cost hundreds of dollars in the U.S. but it was only €50—quite a deal! Matthew wanted a cartoon caricature instead, which only took about two minutes and cost €25, not quite as good a deal, but it turned out to be pretty funny.

After the portraits were done, we wandered into an art gallery in the square where the kids got their first look at art by Spanish Surrealist, Salvador Dali. We probably should've done a run-through without the kids first, as some of it wasn't very "kid-friendly," but they were definitely mesmerized. Art no longer could be described as boring after seeing Dali's weird skeletons and melting clocks, kind of like a disturbing, hallucinogenic dream. At one point I looked over at Julia. Her head was tilted sideways and she had a confused, quizzical look on her face. We couldn't provide any explanations. There was really no way to know what Dali was trying to say.

After gelato and a coffee break, the kids wanted to take one of the long stairways down. We passed the famous, ornate carousel and meandered through the narrow, village-like streets of Montmartre, buying a few souvenirs, and a few, gorgeous fabric pieces for a tablecloth and sofa pillows I intended to make. When we came upon the Moulin Rouge cabaret theater with its red windmill, Julia, Katherine, and I high-kicked our best can-can for Dave and Matthew (which was pretty bad).

Then it was time to plan our first Parisian Christmas. The celebration in France starts on December 6th when all the kids leave a pair of shoes by the fireplace at bedtime, and *Père Noël* (Father Christmas) comes and fills them with treats. Katherine, Miss Picky Girl, didn't want treats in her dirty old shoes. That would be gross! So we bought her a pair of new shoes. Ok, spoiled, I know, but we were really feeling bad about her having such a rough time, so we thought a little spoiling was okay at that point.

December 15

We went out to get a Christmas tree today and found that they're all tabletop size—no big trees to be found. We asked if there was somewhere to get a big tree and the answer was, "Non, ce n'est pas possible." (It's not possible. Argh!!)

Whereas most Americans will not take "no" for an answer, "*non*" was a very popular word in France. The French are very practical people and even though we Americans know it is not practical to get a big Christmas tree, it's just what we do. The French normally don't. And if it's not reasonable, it's apparently impossible. I guess I was finally in Stage Three of culture shock since I was learning to accept these kinds of things. So, we got ourselves a tiny little tabletop tree and decided to celebrate Christmas *à la française*. The only decorations I found were paper chains and gold tinsel, so we decorated our tiny tabletop tree with tinsel and paper chains. It didn't look too bad. It kind of reminded me of Charlie Brown's tree in the Charlie Brown Christmas movie.

When it came to dressing the Christmas tree, the French decorated haphazardly, at least the French friends I had. It was funny, given their uniformly perfectionistic behavior in practically everything else. It seemed to be of no importance to them, another one of those strange French contradictions, or a "cultural irony." *(I didn't yet know about the giant department stores such as Galleries Lafayette where whole floors were dedicated to Christmas decorations. My learning curve improved with time.)*

It was very festive on the winter streets of Paris during this time of year. All the store window displays had elaborate, Christmas-themed designs. Chestnuts were roasting in big tin barrels on the street corners by the Seine. They smelled delicious (actually, much better than they tasted). There were outdoor markets with twinkling lights, and Christmas music was playing. People bustled about everywhere. We got bundled up in our warmest coats with our scarves, hats, and gloves, and wandered around the Christmas markets, buying gifts and enjoying the festive mood. We drank hot-spiced wine and hot apple cider, and had our first taste of *marron glace* (sugar-glazed chestnuts).

"Who wants to go ice skating at the Hotel de Ville?" Dave asked after we finished dinner on Christmas Eve. What a fun idea! I was surprised it was open on Christmas Eve, but Dave said he had checked.

A resounding "Yay!" came from the kids.

An outdoor ice rink was set up at the Hotel de Ville. We took the Métro over and arrived to see a huge, noisy crowd of mostly French teenagers, and the music was blasting—not my favorite scene. I don't love crowds or loud music. I decided to sit out the ice-skating, and instead tried to find some hot chocolate for everyone. Dave and the kids got their ice skates on and headed out to the ice. They found that Parisians skated like they drove. They didn't believe in following the rules. When I arrived with the steaming hot chocolates, Matt was worked up. He had almost been barreled down by a bunch of French teenagers. Dave said it was fun, but actually quite dangerous.

The kids and I participated in "Love in a Box," a Parisian Christmas tradition organized by the American Cathedral in Paris since 2001. Each child at our kids' school was asked to bring in a wrapped shoebox filled with items that a needy child could use and would be happy to receive for a Christmas present. This program served around two thousand kids every year. We made a couple of boxes ourselves, but we also volunteered to work at the American Cathedral, filling boxes there. I brought the kids with me, and we made many boxes. The required items were: a pair of mittens or a scarf, a bar of soap, a new toothbrush, toothpaste, and a book. The rest of the box was filled with small stuffed animals and small toys, which were all donated by people and businesses in Paris. We put together the boxes and gift-wrapped each one. This gift was sometimes the only one the child who received it got for Christmas, and this experience was a major eye-opener for my kids.

Katherine was an angel in the Christmas pageant at the American Church of Paris; reminiscent of our annual Christmas pageants back in Santa Barbara. The kids all liked going to the American Church because it was the only place in Paris where people spoke English. White holiday lights twinkled and sparkled on all the trees along the Champs-Elysées, where we took our

Christmas card photo on a blustery, freezing night. *"Merry Christmas from the City of Light"* read our holiday card.

Even with our tiny, badly decorated tree, Santa Claus found us at our apartment in Paris. Julia was delighted that he had brought her a cell phone. We were also happy about it, because with all her newfound freedom, we'd be able to find her. She also received some new clothes, scarves, and French perfume. Katherine got a stuffed *Marsupilami*, a yellow, polka dotted, French cartoon character who was known as "royalty" in Paris. (I think this was because of what they charged for him.) Our kids were well versed in French cartoons since we couldn't get any TV programs in English. That made it easy for us to allow them to watch as much TV as they wanted. It was an enjoyable way for them to learn French. Of course, their favorites were the cartoons with no words, such as *Oggi et les Cafares,* about a little blue cat and three bugs, but they also liked the cartoons that were in French.

Matthew received some board games, which were badly needed in the cold, dark, and long Paris winter. His favorite was a French *Wheel of Fortune* game, which he was obsessed with on TV, and was actually pretty good at. I'm not sure if it was their "Vanna White" (who was a good-looking, well-endowed blonde), the Jack Russell terrier, which had a permanent seat on the show and was always making quizzical looks at the camera, or the competition of the game, but Matthew loved it. We equally enjoyed seeing his fast growing vocabulary of French words. For Matthew's last gift, he opened a wrapped box within a box, within a box, within a box, and finally he saw his *jaune carte de sortie* (that sought-after yellow card which allowed him to exit school alone). He couldn't believe it! It was the best gift ever!

December 26

Katherine lost her first tooth. Finally! It took for-e-ver! Honestly, I have never seen a tooth take so long to fall out. It must've been loose, really loose, for over a month. Luckily, the Tooth Fairy made it all the way

to Paris, and we learned about another French myth:
The French Tooth Fairy is a mouse. "La Petite
Souris" (the tooth fairy mouse) left Katherine €1 and
a little plastic Becassine doll, another French cartoon
character Katherine has become fond of.

In our family, the Tooth Fairy had a history of paying as many dollars as the tooth number lost. That year, Julia lost tooth numbers fifteen, sixteen, seventeen, and eighteen. It was an expensive year for *La Petite Souris!* With the euro conversion to the dollar at around $1.50 to €1, the Tooth Fairy Mouse was going broke! You'd think being such a good traveler, she could've figured out the exchange rate and adjusted for it. But I guess she felt sorry for the American kids relocated to a foreign country and didn't think that would be fair. Thank goodness for the International Tooth Fairy Hedge Fund… (Not!)

December 31

It's New Years Eve, and we just arrived in Venice…
a lot of planes, trains and boats later! When we were
on the plane, we popped up through the clouds, the sun
was shining, and Julia screamed, "We're in heaven!
Oh my gosh, Mama, are we?" I will always remember
this.

To get to Venice we had to take the Métro to the RER, then the RER to the airport. At the airport, we took the Roissy train (similar to an amusement park ride with no driver) to the terminal and boarded the plane to Venice. We arrived at Venice Marco Polo Airport on the Italian mainland at sunset and still had to take a boat, called Ali Laguna, for an hour boat ride to Zattere, the closest stop to the apartment. We were pooped when we arrived on the shore of Venice.

It was very dark. The five of us walked along the canal, dragging our suitcases on the cobblestone and marveling at the sparkling reflection of the moon on the water. When we arrived at the apartment, Tony, the caretaker, let us in. The apartment was gorgeous: marble floors, antique furniture, and colorful glass chandeliers. The ceilings were hand-painted and etched with flower designs. All the furniture looked hand-carved. Tony didn't speak a word of English or French, and we don't speak a word of Italian, but he described everything in the apartment in great detail, and we got the gist of it. Very important, we could tell, were the boots that we'd need if the Acqua Alta (flood waters) came in. Tony made a siren sound, which we understood meant that we'd hear a siren if the water was coming, and he pointed to the boots. Apparently, it only gets a few inches deep, so everyone has to walk around in these boots, but there is no telling when it will happen. Dario had also explained this to us, but it seemed a little scarier when Tony animatedly explained it in Italian—with the siren sounds and all.

The kids' beds were down in the basement, which Dave pointed out was actually below sea level. As soon as they saw their beds they crawled in them. "No fireworks?" we asked them, but they weren't moving.

Dave and I stayed up to see the fireworks. We poured ourselves some red wine that Tony said Dario left for us (at least we think that's what he said) and relaxed on the couch. When it was getting close to midnight, we heard firecrackers and people laughing, so we went outside to check things out. The fireworks were going off over the canal right in front of our apartment. It was magical with the glittering water, the fireworks in the sky, and our kids sleeping below sea level in a fancy apartment in Venice. Who would ever have thought we'd have such an experience? We sat down on the edge of the canal just outside our apartment and toasted to the New Year, 2008.

January 2008

January 1 (New Year's Day)

*Today is sunny and gorgeous, but still VERY cold.
We made some coffee in the apartment and we're
heading out in search of breakfast. Then we're going to
wander around and try to get lost, as Dario told us to
do.*

No one was out and empty champagne bottles were
strewn everywhere. We felt as if we were the only people awake
in Venice. We bought some pastries at a stand near the
apartment—not as good as Paris, but very good. We walked
over famous bridges and ended up at Piazza San Marco where
we finally saw some people, as well as lots of pigeons. Pigeons
were everywhere and people were letting them land on them. We
never saw anything like it before. The kids wanted to try it, so we
bought some corn from a vendor. Sure enough, the pigeons
landed right on the kids' arms and even on their heads. At first it
was horrifying having pigeons land on us, but we got used to it,
and it was very amusing. Even Katherine didn't mind the dirty
birds.

When we got back to "our" apartment there was a little
microclimate of sunshine outside the front door. We decided to
bring some chairs outside and relax for a while. Dave brought
out the Prosecco (Italian champagne), and we sipped it as
Matthew read a book, Julia drew a picture in her drawing book
of the church on La Guidecca, on the island across the lagoon,
and Katherine relaxed (brought out her pillow, her "blankie,"
and even her stuffed animals). Basking in the sunshine, we
actually felt warm, and started shedding our jackets and shoes.
Dave observed that the general sentiment of the passer-byes in
their heavy coats and scarves had gone from envy to downright
resentment. A few people smiled and admired Julia's drawings,

but the other looks we got were hilarious. There was definitely some envy for the family basking in the sun, sipping Prosecco outside "their" apartment along the Venice canal. January 1, 2008, in our shirtsleeves in the glow of the Venice sunshine. We raised a glass to life and for yet another special experience.

January 2

Today we took the vaporetto, the waterbus, out to Murano, a little island off the coast of Venice. It was really fun. We went to a glass factory and watched a glassmaker make objects in the same way they've been doing it for thousands of years. Metal poles with balls of glass were held in the fire with careful cutting, spinning, and blowing. We visited shop after shop on the little island, everything made from the famous Murano glass: colorful chandeliers, vases and statues. But our favorite items, by far, were the little glass-animal families. The kids are obsessed with them: tiny snails, frogs, dogs, swans, and penguins. They spent all of their Christmas money on them.

Dave and I wanted to sit down and relax in a café after about five of the glass shops, but we must've gone into at least ten more. Finally, we talked the kids into exiting the glass menagerie by bribing them with gelato. Dave and I decided to switch to wine at that point. We sat inside, while the kids ran around bothering everyone outside (like the high-spirited, American children they are), and we ignored them.

We took the vaporetto back to Venice and went on a tour of the Peggy Guggenheim Museum. It was too cold to be outside, and it was very close to the apartment. We learned that Peggy Guggenheim was an American modern art collector and socialite who moved to Venice after World War II. She donated her house on the Grand Canal, and much of her collection was on display there. The highlight for the kids was a picture of a weird, four-boobed, pregnant, mutant, male frog. The kids guessed the artist right away: Salvador Dali!

Back at the apartment, we cooked a big spaghetti dinner, accompanied by hot garlic bread and a Caesar salad. The kids unwrapped their glass families, to our chagrin, since they'll have to wrap them all back up again when we leave, but we let them enjoy their purchases.

The next day we bundled up and went out walking again. We came across several, exquisite, Italian paper stores where I bought stationery, fabric-covered drawing books, writing books, and gorgeous, Italian wrapping paper. The kids wanted to take a gondola ride, but it was too cold for that (and too expensive)! We came across a Ferrari Store that looked warm, so we went inside. Who would've thought that there'd be a Ferrari store right in the middle of the narrow streets of Venice? It was cozy and warm inside the store, so we didn't want to leave. We pretended we were interested in buying a Ferrari. Matthew pointed to the black Ferrari in the middle of the store, and the salesperson looked over at Dave who quickly said, "Oh, should we buy another one?" The kids couldn't keep a straight face, so no one believed us. We ended up buying Katherine a stuffed bear in a leather Ferrari jacket. It was all great fun, but we all agreed we should come again when it's warmer. *(Footnote: Paris is not as cold as I thought, when compared to Venice, but it was still definitely worth coming, even in January.)*

January 5

As our luck goes, we had another "mis-adventure" on the way home—there's never a dull moment! Julia left her brand new camera on the boat that was headed back to the mainland. She realized it just in the nick of time for Dave to run back to the boat, which had just left the dock. He jumped about three feet from the land on to the boat—which they were not very happy about—and found the camera. It was like a movie scene.

When we got back to Paris, we found the kids' grades in the mail. Julia's weren't that great:

"Results unsatisfactory. More effort needed. Julia is not trying."

"Julia, you must try to be more consistent. Need more effort to produce quality work. Let's go, Julia!"

"Pupil is distracted. Pay attention at all times and participate in class!"

Their blunt remarks were not something we were used to, but it wasn't as bad as we were expecting. Her grades weren't THAT bad. Maybe her grades didn't show it, but we felt she was learning a lot, and she was definitely having a good time. Matt's grades were pretty good, and Katherine's were great. The little perfectionist was meant to be in French school! I'm happy. The truth is, I was skeptical when I heard that most of their schooling was going to be in French. I wondered if they'd really learn anything in school this year. They didn't know A WORD in French when we got here, and yet, they all appeared to be having success (at least in our opinion).

January 7

I'm trying to make some resolutions, but instead I've decided to do "New Year's Deep Thoughts" (and some not so deep ones):

"After you've walked a miles in our shoes be sure to check for dog sh*t."

"People like to praise the French for their cooking, but how much of it is good cooking, or is it that you are so famished by the 9:00 p.m. dinner hour that everything tastes like it's from Le Cordon Bleu?"

"Wine goes with everything." (Yep, deep, huh!?)

"Steak frites… yummm."

"Now I get the scarf thing! It's not just for fashion! It's to keep your neck warm!"

A fun French tradition we experienced for the first time was the *Galette des Rois*, the King's Cake, traditionally eaten on the 6th of January (Twelfth Night or Epiphany). It's made of puff pastry and can have different fillings, but marzipan is the most popular. There's a trinket (called *la fève* in French) hidden somewhere inside the cake. Traditionally, it was a bean, but nowadays, different items are baked into it. The youngest child sits under the table and gets to decide who gets each piece of cake as it is cut. The person who gets the trinket in their slice gets to be the king (or queen) for the day. They get to wear the paper crown that comes with the cake, and they get certain privileges—whatever the group decides upon.

We were invited to our friends' house (Matthew's best friend Martin's family) to share a *Galette des Rois* with them. Katherine and their youngest son, Louis (the two youngest from each family) sat under the table and chose who received each piece of cake. We all started carefully eating our piece, hoping to be the lucky one to get the trinket in our slice (and I was also hoping not to crack a tooth on the trinket). But Julia was the lucky one who found *la fève*—a little framed picture of a queen. So she put on the paper crown. No one was sure exactly what her privileges were, but we said she could boss everyone around for the rest of the night. As one would imagine, that did not go over well with her siblings.

The holidays ended, but it still felt like we were on a long, extended vacation. When would Paris start feeling like home? I wondered. Things started slowing down. The weather became colder and colder. We had to buy even warmer coats, and when we went out, we had to layer with wool sweaters, warm socks, gloves, and hats. That was just before *Les Soldes* began. *Les Soldes* (The Sales) happen bi-yearly in Paris, once in summer and once in winter. In fact, sales are not allowed at any time, besides the two, six-week time periods known as *Les Soldes*. This regulatory practice goes back over a thousand years. In light of the current economic crisis, the government was loosening up on the regulations a bit. But, we soon learned that if you live in

Paris, you wait for this time of year to shop. Unfortunately, I heard about it too late.

January 8

I am more than a little upset to see all the clothes I just bought on my recent shopping spree all marked down to half price. No wonder the stores were so empty! The salespeople were so helpful! They let me try on as many things as I wanted in the dressing rooms! Duh!! I should have realized something was wrong!

It was also around then that I finally wanted to start learning French. It wasn't always possible to drag Dave or a French-speaking friend along whenever I needed to speak. I had to stop ignoring the ringing phone, and just imagine trying to return clothes! That's not even fun in English. As I said, the French do not take returns without a theatrical performance, and that was one thing at which Dave drew the line.

Sometimes when I came home, I was tired and just wanted to take the elevator up to our apartment, but I was too scared I'd end up with one of my neighbors in the elevator—because then I'd have to talk. I was humiliated early-on when one of my neighbors joined me in our tiny, two-person elevator, and I couldn't even say, "Sorry, I don't understand." I just stared at her, nodding stupidly, hoping she'd realize I didn't understand a word, but she kept talking until it finally got uncomfortable. After that, I avoided those situations by convincing myself that I needed the exercise of five flights of stairs. A few times I got away with saying *"Bonjour"* and then suddenly having my attention be absorbed by searching for something hugely important in my purse. When it was time to get out of the elevator, I'd only have to say *"Au revoir"* (goodbye) or *"Bonne journée"* (have a good day). I mean, the French don't really expect you to talk, but if you do, and you open up the line of conversation, then... well... you've opened up the line of conversation!

So finally I decided to learn French. The free online program Dave found had different conversations each week, but they were more appropriate for singles out partying, or tourists visiting Paris, not for really learning the language. I learned how to say things like "What's your sign?" I even tried to learn French using the kids' French textbooks. I made flash cards and put them all over the house, but I still wasn't learning fast enough.

At that point, I think I was somewhere between Stage Two and Stage Three of Culture Shock. I was missing some American things badly and getting irritated by many French things, but I was also starting to adjust to and even enjoy some things.

January 11

Things I want:

A big cup of American coffee—NOT a tiny espresso, and NOT a "café crème"

A big American comfy couch (Hmmm… noticing that big is a common word for American things)

Spray and Wash—none of the French products work as well

Trident chewing gum—blue (peppermint) and green (spearmint)

Hot sauce and good salsa (Tapatio, Green Tabasco, Herdez salsa), fresh tortilla chips, and tortillas

Fruit by the Foot and/or Fruit roll ups

I want to wear my running shoes and my Ugg boots when I go out!

Julia wants… no… actually said she NEEDS a bean and cheese burrito

A tan

New things I like that I never liked before:

Scarves (well, I liked them, but never wore them)

Rugby

Al Jazeera News

Dressing up (sometimes)

Cold weather

Small cars

Erasable pens

Commercials (they are actually entertaining here)

Explicit advertising (also quite entertaining)

Black and gray

The unbelievably low prices of pharmaceuticals

La politesse: the kids saying "Bonjour, Madame or Bonjour, Monsieur" to all adults

There were also things I was getting used to or figuring out, such as the perfect walking speed that worked with all the other walkers around me. This was very exciting. One day I was in perfect speed with all the other walkers. This probably sounds weird, but it was actually quite challenging on a crowded sidewalk to figure out the right walking speed to stay with everyone else, and not get in anyone's way.

I was learning more French beliefs about things that were not reasonable or possible, and starting to agree with some of them. Coats made from small animals were reasonable. Living in Paris, I understood this one for the first time: it took living somewhere REALLY cold and seeing how warm (and chic) those brown mink coats looked to understand. Unfortunately, I couldn't afford one... therefore it was impossible for me. *Oh well!* Having more than two errors on a *dictée* (where the teacher dictates in French and the kids have to write what she says) was not reasonable. Forgetting things over and over again (a kid forgetting his jacket, for example) was not reasonable. "To go" containers were definitely not possible, and spending less than an hour and a half for lunch was not reasonable. (You have to love that one!)

January 19

It is NOT okay to eat on the Métro. Today I learned this the hard way. I bought a sandwich on my way home from Conversation Group, found a seat on the Métro, and had pretty long ride home from Clare's in the 16th. I unwrapped my sandwich and took a bite. Everyone was watching me. I tried to chew slowly, barely moving my mouth at all, and trying painfully not to make any chewing sounds, but it was very awkward—a cultural faux pas. No, I'm never going to do that again.

In Paris, you sit at a table to eat. It is not well regarded to eat on the Métro or while walking down the street—the exception being that it's acceptable for children after school for the one and only snack time, called *le goûter*. *Le goûter* usually consists of a *tartine*, a piece of a baguette with butter or chocolate, or for younger children, a *pain au chocolat* or Nutella sandwich. French adults are not supposed to snack at all (with the exception being people with increased nutritional needs like pregnant or nursing mothers or the elderly). The government is constantly reminding everyone about healthy ways to eat. All snack food or sugary drink advertisements on television, radio, and billboards contain one of four warnings. They are:

"For your health, eat at least five fruits and vegetables a day."

"For your health, undertake regular physical activity."

"For your health, avoid eating too much fat, too much sugar, too much salt."

"For your health, avoid snacking between meals."

I thought of a new one: *"For your health, just don't eat!"* That's more like it. I tried my hardest to acclimate to the French principles of gastronomy, but my loud, grumbling stomach wouldn't comply. It was hungry and angry. I gave myself permission to snack when the kids snacked, just once a day for *le goûter,* but truly I felt as if I was starving most of the time.

We learned that Paris is a safe city (besides pickpockets on the Métro and people grabbing iPods and phones out of your hands), but there is hardly any violent crime. We were happy to learn that we could let our kids walk around by themselves, play in the park, and take the Métro alone. We heard stories and even saw a few people get pick-pocketed on the Métro, so we learned to always zip our bags and make sure the kids did too. And not to worry, Parisians would tell us if we ever forgot. In a way, it was nice to know that they were looking out for us, but sometimes they were rather bossy and had no qualms about telling us what we should and shouldn't do.

I learned that the best map (the only map) was the *Plan de Paris,* a small book with a page dedicated to each arrondissement in Paris. It was indispensable. I learned about two weekly pamphlets, *Le Pariscope* and *Les Spectacles,* that the locals bought every week for thirty-five *centimes* (cents) at the corner magazine stands, which contained all the weekly events going on in Paris. We learned to always carry an umbrella in our bag. It started raining out of the blue, and it rained hard. We learned to remember door codes for buildings and to always hit the *lumière* (light) button when we walked in—if we didn't want to end up standing in the dark. (This was before the iPhone and iHandy flashlight came to Paris.)

We learned how to push our way onto a crowded Métro, usually by entering backwards, but no matter how much we pushed, we were never to say a word. This was unsettling for me, because we Americans are normally friendly with strangers, unlike the French. We smile at people and say hello, even with people we don't know. If we touch or push someone, our normal reaction is to say, "I'm sorry" or "Excuse me." The French don't. They say, *"Pardon"* (excuse me) in other situations, but getting on the Métro does not require that. Getting off the Métro, on the other hand, they do say, *"Pardon"* because they want you to move out of their way. They don't smile or talk to strangers, and they rarely get their feathers ruffled, no matter how much you push them. That was a lot of things we had learned about our new city!

Winter in Paris was when the residents reclaimed the city for themselves. The tourists were gone, and the city was quiet. The kids went back to school the second week of January. We were all feeling pretty confident with the Métro by that time, but once the kids were comfortable, they stopped being careful… and with our kids on the hyperactive, competitive side of the spectrum, they liked to sprint to the emptiest car when people were getting off. They spread like little bugs.

"THIS ONE'S the emptiest, NO, THIS ONE!" they'd yell at each other.

"Where's Matthew? Did he get on?" My "Mama Bear" panic inevitably kicked in.

Once inside, they'd fight over who got to push the button to open the door. Oh, what fun! A nice long visit to the Louvre was a great threat to get Matthew to behave. He never wanted to go back there again, so that worked very well!

Sometimes, when the Métro was crowded, we'd get separated into different cars. At those times that panicked feeling would come over me. We realized we needed some guidelines, and we tested the kids with questions such as: "What do you do if the door closes and we get on, but you don't? Should you stay and wait for us to come back or get on the next Métro and come to us?" We decided the best plan was to stay put and we'd come back for them.

January 25

Today, I received a call from the Directrice of Katherine's school. She wants us to come in for a meeting. That doesn't sound good. Just when I was thinking how well things were going...

January 26

Just got back from the meeting. The Directrice was very nice, but she told us we have to get Katherine a tutor. She hasn't said one word in French, and by now, she should have. Shoot!

All the evidence we read on bilingualism says that children can learn two or more languages naturally and effortlessly if they need them to communicate, and Katherine definitely needed French to communicate. But Katherine is a perfectionist. Unlike the other kids, who were willing to try (and get things wrong), she wouldn't try. I started looking online and found a wonderful, young, and very French tutor named Mathilde. Katherine was NOT happy about this. She hid from Mathilde when she came over, but Mathilde was not offended or discouraged. She brought her favorite picture books—without words—and had Katherine describe the scenes to her (in French). It was brilliant! Mathilde told us, "It's all in there," meaning that Katherine could understand everything, she just wasn't confident speaking yet. We arranged for Mathilde to come back every few days for lessons.

January 31

Just got back from Franprix. Bought some sugar for a recipe and was sure it was the right kind. Opened the box and found... SUGAR CUBES! Ahhh!!!

Decided to have a "sugar cube smashing party" with the kids at the kitchen table.

Later

Found the smashing of sugar cubes a very satisfying exercise for anger management due to the wrong sugar purchase, once again. Used improvised mortar and pestle (the back of soup spoon on a plate). Sugar cubes promptly exploded and flew to the dark corners of kitchen that only the French mice can find. Oh well! I feel much better!

February 2008

February 2

*Mathilde works patiently and steadfastly with
Katherine. Katherine is starting to speak French. I
have to hide in the next room to hear her little voice.
She has a perfect accent! It's soooo cute!*

Dave and I made a decision to take the kids to only one
museum per month. We didn't want to burn them out on too
many museums. The first Sunday of the month was Free
Museum Day in Paris, so we decided that would be our Museum
day. We soon found out that Free Museum Day was also the
most crowded day at all the museums (obviously), but luckily,
families got preferential treatment, and we were usually able to
move to the front of the entrance lines.

The Picasso Museum was our first Sunday of the Month
trip for February. We learned about all of Pablo Picasso's
different artistic stages, and I was surprised to learn that he did
naturalistic, fine art at a very young age. In fact, when Pablo was
a teenager, he could draw and paint as well as the masters. His
more experimental type of art was all I'd ever seen. The kids
drew their own "Picassos" in their fabric-covered drawing books
from Venice. It was a great museum experience until I almost
got mugged when we left. A gypsy woman started freaking out
in front of me and threw her baby into my arms. What was I
supposed to do? Drop the baby? Turned out it was just a doll,
but it scared me! Then a gypsy child tried to take my wallet.
Dave caught her, but it definitely freaked us all out.

Everything was starting to feel more normal and
understandable until February, when the kids got homework
assignments related to Mardi Gras. I didn't understand that the
assignments were related to Mardi Gras though, since our kids
had never celebrated it before in school. I just thought they were

getting some strange homework assignments. Mardi Gras was originally a French celebration, brought to the United States by the French who immigrated mostly to New Orleans. Mardi Gras means "Fat Tuesday" in French. It is the day after the weeklong celebration of the "Fat Days" or "Carnival" and the beginning of the "days of fasting." The name came from the ancient custom of parading a fat ox through the streets of Paris to remind people that they were not allowed to eat meat during Lent. Nor were they to eat sugar, fat, eggs, or dairy products.

Matthew's assignment was to bring three crêpes to school on Monday morning, made from a French recipe the teacher game him. Crêpes apparently are traditional for Mardi Gras, but that was not explained in the assignment. Obviously, we were just supposed to know that... again, only obvious if you're French. We had never made crêpes before. His teacher said that if we couldn't make them, we could buy them. *Hmpf!* I thought it was probably a good idea to practice before Monday morning, but it was Sunday and all the grocery stores were closed. That was something we still had not gotten used to. Luckily we had all the ingredients except the eggs, which we borrowed from a neighbor who thought Matthew's homework assignment was *super* (another favorite word of the French).

Here is the recipe the teacher gave him that we were to follow: (Note: The English translations were not provided. Babbelfish, a free translating program, was my best friend in those days.)

Crêpes

250 g. de farine (flour)

25 g. de beurre fondu (melted butter)

3 oeufs (eggs)

1/2 litre de lait (milk)

25 g. de sucre en poudre (powdered sugar, I think)

Verser la farine dans une jatte (Pour the flour into a bowl)

Faire un puits au milieu et ajouter les oeufs (Make a well in the middle and add the eggs)

Remuer avec le fouet (Stir with the whisk)

Ajouter le lait au fur et à mesure. (Add milk gradually)

Ajouter le beurre (Add the butter)

Laisser reposer (Let stand)

Some things we didn't understand, such as "let stand"... for *HOW LONG?* Or "make a well"... *HOW DEEP?* French people think these kinds of things are obvious... they're obvious to French people only! Matthew said he was supposed to flip the crêpes in the air (must be a reason for this, but again, it was lost in translation).

Then I found a letter in Katherine's school bag that said she was to "come disguised" to school. (At least I thought that was what the letter said. It was in French.) The *déguisement* was meant to be a mask for Mardi Gras, but I didn't know that then. I wondered why she needed to wear a costume to school. It was nowhere close to Halloween, and the French don't celebrate Halloween anyway. I had NO idea where to find a costume in Paris. Finally I saw a sheep mask at Monoprix, the local super-store, so I bought it for her. Katherine would have been all set with the mask (because that was all they meant by "disguised"), but I dressed her up in yellow pajamas, added a cotton ball tail and sewed an oval, fleece spot on her belly, and Katherine went to school as a sheep. I crossed my fingers that she wouldn't be the only one dressed up. Turned out she pretty much was. Everyone else just wore masks, but all her friends loved her costume. I'm sure her teacher had a good laugh about that one!

February 13

Just when I thought this winter cabin fever was going to be the end of us, someone in my Conversation Group told me about a giant park for the kids. Geez! Why did it take us six months to hear about this?! It's called the Jardin d'Acclimatation and it is well known to all Parisians. We don't care how cold it is, we're going this weekend.

February 14 Valentine's Day

*Julia received a dozen red roses from a boy at school
that she carried around all day. Oh, those French
boys—they start young! She acted nonchalant about it,
and tried to pretend like it wasn't a big deal. It was
pretty cute.*

We all put on our warmest clothes and went out to investigate the Jardin d'Acclimatation the next weekend. It was on the western edge of Paris, in the 16th arrondissement—about a twenty-five minute Métro ride from our apartment. Then we had to walk about four blocks from the Métro stop and pay a small admission charge to go in. Near the entrance was a mirror maze with distortion mirrors. We were all giddy and laughed uncontrollably. (We definitely needed to get out more often!) There was a playground with a huge replica of the Eiffel Tower—at least two stories tall—built with connecting steel cables. Everyone's hands were frozen, but that didn't stop the kids from climbing it. Dave followed Katherine up because I was nervous about the height, but luckily no one fell. There was also an area with carnival rides: bumper cars, flying swings, games, a place to ride horses and even a puppet theater (with only French speaking puppets). We were so thrilled to have found such a great park!

More cultural differences were becoming evident to me. I saw it at the parks, and I saw it in other places. French parents had a different way of doing things than we Americans did. They weren't at the constant service of their children and they didn't feel at all guilty about it. Their kids, in turn, didn't have expectations of that kind of attention. French rules for parenting were set in stone, unchanged for generations, and the job of parenthood was to impart these rules, along with autonomy and good manners. They called it becoming *bien elevé* (well brought-up), and it appeared to work well for them. French children were very well behaved. The French also believe it is society's role to be involved in bringing children up, whereas most Americans I know typically do not like anyone telling them how to do things.

It was not just French families I was observing. I was surrounded with a diverse international parent group of many different cultures, all of which were compelling to learn about and observe. The extent of their influence for me went beyond helping with the adjustment to life in Paris. They also became the weekly, sometimes daily, tour guides. Clare, the tireless overachiever, who was also my good friend by then, wrote a weekly blog in which parents from the school could join or volunteer to organize events. There were potluck lunches and dinners, museum and neighborhood tours in French and English, visits to châteaux, hikes through forests and towns outside of Paris, cooking demonstrations (some by professionals and some given by parents)—often with tours to the places to shop for the ingredients, chocolate tours, cheese tours, wine-tastings, and movies in French or English with discussions afterwards at nearby cafés. *How could I sit in a classroom all day? We'd be gone in a year (we thought), and I wouldn't need French then anyway, right?*

At least once or twice a week, there was something fun to do listed on the school blog. To give an example: one of my favorite tours was a trip to the IFF (International Fine Fragrances) perfume creation department. A mom from the school (who worked there) hosted the tour. Some of the world's most renowned scents for perfumes and colognes are created there, such as Eternity, Polo, Drakkar Noir, Tresor, Dolce and Gabbana's One, Beautiful, White Linen, Red Door, Happy, and Carolina Herrera, to name a few. It's a two billion dollar American company, located in Paris, and the only American company of the Big Three leading fragrance creators. Not only do they create the scents for perfumes, but also for shampoos, gels, cleaning supplies such as Tide and Mr. Clean, scents for drinks and yogurts—basically everything that has a smell. The tour was fascinating and highly informative.

A monthly event I loved attending was the potluck lunch or dinner. For my first potluck, I decided to make a classic: Quiche Lorraine. I had already seen that there were pre-made crusts in the grocery store. Unfortunately, I hadn't looked closely enough, because once I went to buy one, there were many different crusts to choose from. There was *pâte sable, pâte brisée, pâte fine...* and all the pictures on the packaging looked like quiches. I had no idea which one to use. "Eenie, meenie, miny, mo." I picked one out and brought it up to the register. I asked the cashier if he spoke English, but, of course, *"Non"* was the answer. I said, "Quiche?" He nodded in agreement. I crossed my fingers that it was the right one. With barely enough time to make the quiche for the potluck, I rushed home. (I have a bad habit of not leaving enough time for things.) I mixed the ingredients together and popped it in the oven. I went to my room to get dressed, and when I came back in about fifteen minutes, I looked in the oven. What I saw did NOT look like a quiche.

"OH NO!" I yelled. Dave came running in. He was working from home in our tiny apartment.

It's "PUFF pastry! Get it out!" he said. (Puff pastry takes fifteen minutes to cook. Quiches take about forty minutes.) The crust looked as if it had exploded—it was puffy and burning. The middle of the quiche was still runny. I took it out of the oven, covered the crust with foil, and stuck it back in the oven for another twenty minutes. Fortunately the crust didn't burn too badly, but it was not pretty. I had nothing else to bring to the potluck, and I was out of time, so I put a towel around it, and took it on the Métro. I walked into the potluck with my head hanging low. I set it on the table reluctantly and took the foil off. *Voila!* I looked around and no one laughed. They all were very sweet about it, and luckily it tasted better than it looked.

February 18

Conversation Group was today, and I learned why we were supposed to flip the crêpes for Matthew's homework assignment. Apparently, legend has it that if you can flip a crêpe successfully while holding a coin in your writing hand, your family will enjoy a

prosperous year. I just love my Conversation Group!
I'm always learning such interesting things.

Our six-month lease was almost up when a friend told us he had an apartment that we could rent. It was his wife's aunt's apartment. He and his family were staying there, but they were moving at the end of the month. We debated whether it was worth it to move, with only six months left of our year in Paris. We had gotten used to our little apartment. It wasn't the greatest situation, but we were making it work, and we loved the location. It would be a BIG pain to move, but we thought we should at least look at it. It was also in the 7th and not too far from our apartment, so we took the kids and walked over.

In ten minutes we were at the apartment. The building was very pretty. We entered the code, pushed the heavy, green door open and went into the courtyard. Cars were parked inside, and a four-story, square apartment building surrounded the courtyard. To the left were glass doors that led us up Persian rug-covered stairs to the apartment on the third floor, where our friend let us in.

It was a big, traditional, Parisian apartment with high ceilings and the classic, hardwood, parquet floors. The walls were painted grey-blue. It had floor-to-ceiling windows with cream, linen curtains and two kitchens. (The apartment could be divided into two apartments, but we'd be able to use all of it.) It faced the street, providing wonderful light. There was a pretty apartment building across the street with grey-striped awnings over the windows, little, potted, mini-cyprus trees in the windowsills, and dormer windows up on top.

There was also a *guardienne* downstairs in an apartment near the front door. Our friend told us that she cleaned all the non-private areas, such as the stairwells and the courtyard, and she would deliver all the mail and newspapers to our door. The street outside the apartment was cleaned twice a day (only once a day in our current apartment). We could even have a parking spot in the courtyard, if we wanted to get a car. *Hmmm… almost made me want one!*

Feb. 20

We're definitely moving. We can appreciate everything about this new apartment so much more than if we'd started there. Things we would have taken for granted before feel like such a luxury now. There are THREE bathrooms. No more yelling out, "I'M FIRST" before we race to the toilet. Dave will have an office—with a door he can CLOSE! There's even a twin bed in the office for a guest. And, there are three other bedrooms! The apartment is not a rental property. The owners keep it vacant for their friends and family, and when they're in Paris, they stay in the other side of the apartment. It has all the extravagances and frills one would imagine a luxury apartment in Paris to have. The furniture is silk and linen with pale cream rugs. It's all in impeccable condition (and we'll have to keep it that way). We can use their china and silver. Julia will get her own bedroom and bathroom, and Matthew and Katherine will share a very large room with floor-to-ceiling, built-in shelves that they can fill up with all their new French knick-knacks, books, toys, and games. We've collected a lot of stuff already! French stuff is so cool!

Moving in Paris was not an easy undertaking, even though we were moving less than a mile from one furnished apartment to another. We rented a van—not realizing how hard it would be to find a parking spot on the street while racing up and down to the apartment... and of course, it was raining. At the new apartment, the *guardienne* opened the big, metal doors for us, so we could park inside the courtyard, but at the old apartment we had to find parking on the street. We didn't want to leave the van unlocked with all our stuff in it, so it was quite a circus, with both of us running up and down. We had originally moved to Paris with fifteen bags, and now we had around fifty.

We made five trips back and forth, with a stuffed van each time. It was worth it though. Our new apartment was gorgeous.

March 2008

One of the first mornings in our new apartment, we were awakened by yelling in the street. It was a *manifestation* (a protest demonstration). They marched right down our street, chanting something in French that we couldn't understand. We stared down from our apartment windows at the parade. *Manifestations*, we learned, are an essential part of the French culture. They're usually civilized (but not always), and they're always organized in advance, so that the police can be present. All classes of people protest in Paris. Just like the importance of clever conversation, protest is a morally important form of expression to the French.

I had heard of the protest demonstrations in the United States in the 1960's, and knew they were common in France, but I had never seen one in real life, and not on my street. At first, we were concerned that it might be dangerous. The police were wearing riot gear, but no riot ensued. Mostly, the police didn't seem to be paying attention. They stood around talking and laughing amongst themselves. We later observed many *manifestations*, a noteworthy part of the French culture we became accustomed to, and another display of how passionate the French are about their beliefs.

We noticed that while the French did have a lot of rules, they also had a certain disdain for rules. They loved to make rules, but they also loved to break them. We learned that a French person does not consider the law an absolute. It can be ignored if circumstances justify it. A good example is when you try to return an item to a store in France: "*Non*" doesn't mean no, it means, "convince me." It is a challenge and another example of the right to protest, but alas, you must be able to do it in French. (They wouldn't even consider it otherwise.) A theatrical performance is usually necessary to convince a French worker to give a refund, but even then it is not guaranteed. The customer is always wrong, as opposed to in America where the customer is always right. We also found it interesting that French vendors can speak English pretty well when you're buying things, but when you want to return something, they can't speak a word!

French kids are made aware of their right to protest at a young age with popular French puppet shows such as *Guignol*, who is famous for taking on the French police with a stick. He amuses children with his humor, but he also entertains adults with his sharp wit and linguistic verve. The French love to glorify the spirit of defiance. It embodies the general feeling that laws are necessary in society, but it is considered an act of liberty to stand up for one's personal beliefs.

We were starting to learn some of the French ways—learn them, but not necessarily understand them. Some we liked, such as the right to protest, but some made no sense at all—like the way they recycled bottles. Here's how that worked: There were giant, plastic containers with a hole in the top, surrounded by rubber flaps. The procedure is to drop each bottle in and let it fall, making a very loud crashing noise as the glass breaks on the bottom of the container. The crash and bottle breakage is unavoidable no matter how carefully one tries to drop the bottle through the flaps. The recycling containers were in the courtyard of our apartment building. Usually at bedtime we'd hear the loud, crashing noises of our environmentally friendly neighbors, who always did their recycling after their 9:00 dinner or early on weekend mornings. Maybe this method was a ploy designed to keep everyone's drinking in check, since all the neighbors could count how many bottles of wine you've drunk when you recycle the bottles.

Another irrefutable rule we learned is the French adult's demand that children's jackets always be completely buttoned or zipped up, never left open, not even partially. It does make sense in the winter—I get that—but my friend Rhiann was actually called in for a meeting with her daughter's teacher in the fall, when it wasn't even cold, because her daughter had a habit of walking around with her coat unbuttoned. The teachers and administration were very authoritarian, and held as much authority as parents in matters of dress, as well as matters of education.

We debated going to Morocco for the next, two-week, school vacation (Spring Break). Our friends were going there, and it sounded warm and exotic. Hopping across the Strait of Gibraltar was an easy trip from France, they said, but we also didn't want to miss the chance to ski in Europe. It was hard to decide. Other friends told us about a resort called Flaine, in the French Alps, where they were going. Their parents were actually the developers for the resort in the 70's. They said it was easy to get to, and there'd be no need for a car once we got there. There was also a climbing wall, an ice-skating rink, and the ski runs were walking distance from the hotel. It sounded way too easy. The ski mountain had a lot of advanced terrain (for Dave), and our friends invited him to go with them and their guide if he wanted to. That was all Dave needed to hear. Plus the TGV had a route directly there in five hours from Paris. It was decided. We booked the ski vacation.

March 3

NO ONE warned us about the thirty-minute, hair-raising bus ride around hairpin turns that was part of the deal to get to Flaine! Two honks alerted oncoming buses that we were coming around each blind turn—inches away from the edge of the cliff. I kept looking for seat belts, but of course, none were provided. I truly thought we were going to die today, and I think Dave did too, by the look on his face, but we've made it to Flaine alive. Whew! The kids thought it was all great fun.

Later

It's almost too easy now that we're here. The hotel is really more like an apartment complex with a common area for families, including pool tables and other games. It's right next to the slopes. There's a kitchen in our room and a bathtub, which is nice, albeit a mediocre substitute for a hot tub, which is conspicuously lacking. Ski lockers, included with the room, are located on the ground floor ten yards from the rental shop next door. There's a grocery store and a pizza parlor right down the street. This hotel situation is apparently a common style of housing for French families on vacation. It's all very convenient. Ski vacations seem to be the one time that ease and comfort are actually part of the French vocabulary.

Some background on our past ski experiences may help provide some perspective here: For the past nine years, we'd taken the kids to Dave's family house in Snowmass, Colorado— the same destination we were headed to when the famous Road Trip List was written. Snowmass borders the more-well-known town of Aspen, full of luxury hotels and a fantastic, expert level ski mountain, frequented by millionaires and billionaires. Snowmass is also a ski hill, built next to a mall and six hundred homes and condos, where the skiing is excellent, but also very expensive. Don't get me wrong. We love Snowmass and Aspen, but we do kind of feel like the poorest people in town when we're there. The classic story we always tell people is when the *"Got Milk?"* campaign was popular, we found tee shirts in the souvenir stores that read: *"Got Money? Aspen, Colorado."*

Flaine, on the other hand, was much lower key with a severe case of "concrete-itis" (70's style architecture). The first thing we noticed was that there was no flash or fancy Bogner outfits. The kids might even be wearing hand-me-downs or last year's style, which is something you'd almost never, if ever, see in Aspen or Snowmass. It's actually hard to identify your kids in Flaine, as every other kid is wearing the exact same, one-piece ski suit purchased at Decathlon or Go Sport, the two large sporting goods stores in Paris.

"Oh look, there's Kate! Oh, no, that's not her… but there's Matt—Hi Matt… Oh, oops, that's not him either…" You get the

idea. It was quite refreshing, frankly. Apparently, everyone skies in France, not just the wealthy. It was also amazingly affordable to put our kids in ski or snowboard lessons. For a week of lessons in Flaine, the price was the same as one day of lessons in Aspen/Snowmass.

So there we were... ready to "crack it" on our first day. But NO... there was a *grève* in Flaine! YES, a strike, just like the Métro and airline strikes. The lift workers were striking. We couldn't believe it. What did that mean? No skiing? Turned out it meant only a forty-five minute delay in the opening of the mountain, so it was really more of a "coffee break statement" to send a message to the French president that he better not cut benefits for seasonal workers as he had proposed, or he wouldn't get his presidential twenty-five days of skiing in.

Of course, there were even more "bumps in the runs" as there are never a shortage of them in our family travels. After getting our rentals and ski passes on the first day, we lost our keys to our room and ski locker, which had Matthew's snowboard in it. Since this was France, the front desk of our hotel was closed for their daily, two-hour lunch. Dave had to do a "MacGyver maneuver" (every McClintock family vacation included at least one per trip). He noticed the locked, ten-foot locker was open on top. So, after stacking two locker room benches on top of each other, he climbed up and tried to fish out Matt's snowboard with his ski pole. But even with the ski poles tied together with a camera strap, it didn't reach the boots. So he sent in Agent Matthew, who was very "stoked" with his mission. He climbed into the locker, over the top, then down the boot rack, and handed up the contents: his snowboard, boots, etc. Then he climbed back out over the top onto Dave's back and clambered back down the two benches. Mission accomplished! Matt had missed his snowboard lesson though, so we all skied together for the afternoon.

Our first day in Flaine was sunny and warm, with perfect snow. We were all having a great time until the end of the day, when we decided to *après ski*. After hot chocolates for the kids and cold beers for us, we went over to pick up our skis and snowboards from the nearby rack… but Julia's snowboard was gone. We walked around the rack a few more times and realized it definitely was NOT there. Really? Could anything else go wrong on our first day? There was a snowboard left in the rack, but it wasn't the one we rented. We were sure of it. Someone had taken Julia's, probably on accident (we hoped), since the other board was left there…

March 7

Our luck has returned. There was a knock at the door this morning and Julia's lost snowboard came back. Just as we thought, a girl had taken it and thought it was hers, but when she tried to return it, she found out it wasn't. Then, when Dave went to the hotel reception desk, they had recovered our lost keys! It turns out we (Dave) had left them in the ski locker door, and they found them, and kept them for us… Phew!

March 8

We were half an hour late picking up Katherine from ski school today, and the instructor left her standing alone in the snow! No, he didn't bring her inside the office… he just left our little, six-year-old girl out there alone. That would NEVER happen anywhere in the U.S., EVER! They were good teachers though, and all the kids enjoyed their lessons. You can count on the French to have an organized plan of teaching and to make sure it happens—just don't be late to pick up!

Despite Dave not verifying the time of our departure until after everyone was in bed, and then finding out it was three hours earlier than he remembered *(ugh!)*, we sailed home with no hitches. All in all, the skiing/snowboarding experience in the French Alps was enjoyable, with some distinct differences from the Colorado Rockies experience. The French ski instructors yelled at the kids (if they dropped a glove or let go of the poma too soon). In Snowmass they'd never yell. In Snowmass, they dressed up like a big, friendly bear and carried the kids around on piggyback. Not in France! Kids carry their own equipment, and they walk like good, little, autonomous children. The mountain was comparable though, and the skiing was excellent. It was fun to experience skiing in Europe.

March 10

We're back in Paris, and today I had a terrible mommy moment: I was with a group of my friends and all the kids at the La Motte-Piquet - Grenelle Métro station, heading to a park to hear some bands play. The Métro arrived, and we were about to get on, when I looked around, and Katherine was gone. There were tons of people coming through the station, but I didn't see Katherine anywhere. I yelled for everyone in the group to NOT get on the Métro! We split up. My friend Maria went one way, and I went the other way. Then I saw Katherine. An older, French woman was holding her hand, waiting for us to find her. She didn't speak a word of English, but she didn't need to. Katherine said she had just kept walking with the crowd until she realized we were gone. I thanked the sweet woman and hugged my girl. We will ALWAYS hold hands from now on!

We had settled into our new apartment by that time, and we all liked it very much. The neighborhood was great. I loved walking down by the Seine. It was only a five-minute walk from our apartment to the Pont de Solferino, the bridge that led straight into the Tuileries. We frequented our cozy, neighborhood café. The waiter there always wanted to discuss American politics with us. Barack Obama was running for President, and while most French people loved him, our waiter was a Republican. He'd give us free wine on occasion, and wave at us when we walked by the café, making us feel like locals.

An impressive, neo-gothic church, called Saint Clotilde was at the end of our street. After school, all the neighborhood kids played in the park outside the church, and older people sat on the benches to rest. The playground was a virtual fashion show of French, designer, baby clothes. The little babies played and fought in the sandbox, and the nannies and moms basically ignored them. They'd mess up each other's sandcastles and throw sand in each other's faces, and no adult ever intervened. They just carried on their conversations until a baby came up to them, crying with sand in his or her eyes. It was so interesting to observe such a different way of parenting.

The winter months were the quiet time in Paris. There was privacy about it that no other season gave us. Some winter days I'd go down to Saint Clotilde and sit in the silence, staring up at the stained glass windows and tall arched ceilings. It was always warm inside the church and unbelievably peaceful. Outside we were often alone on the streets of our neighborhood, especially on weekend mornings. One of my favorite things to do in the early mornings was to walk along Boulevard St. Germain near our apartment and look in the store windows. (*Side note: Window-shopping (lèche-vitrine) is translated as "licking the windows" in French – a translation I find very humorous.*) The modern, designer, furniture stores, bathroom stores, and kitchen stores were like art museums. I fell in love with modern furniture. There was a toy store with a giant, plastic *Marsupilami* ride in front of it (the yellow, spotted, cartoon marsupial that Katherine loved). We frequented the local bookstore on the corner—even though all the books were in French—it was still somewhere to go that was nearby and warm. When Julia came out with me, we'd head to the nearby *perfumerie* to try all the French perfumes and to the American Sunglass Hut to try on sunglasses.

March 15

Today we headed out on a family walk and happened upon Deyrolle, a famous taxidermy shop. I had never heard of it, but Dave remembered it. Downstairs, it

*looked like a small gardening shop, but when we
ventured up the stairs… Surprise! It was a secret
museum. There were collections of shells, leaves, insects,
birds, and rocks. There was also a room full of large
animals—including a white tiger and a giraffe, stuffed
by the taxidermist. The kids loved it!*

*Our new neighborhood is fantastic! And coming home
to our warm, cozy, beautiful, Parisian apartment is so
inviting. The long, quiet stretches of time inside are not
something we were used to, but I'm savoring them now.
We're getting the hang of the indoor, winter lifestyle
and enjoying it. Life here is so different. The change is
really the restoration my mind and body was craving.*

I decided to have a cocktail party for my thirty-ninth
birthday. Thirty-nine was a better year to celebrate than forty, in
my opinion, and who knew where we'd be the next year—
probably not in Paris. We had this fabulous apartment with two
kitchens—perfect for a party. I had to take advantage of it. I
could hire the kids and their friends to pass appetizers around to
the guests, as the apartment came with quite a few silver serving
trays. I invited fifty of my new, favorite friends, and they mostly
all said yes. I was so excited.

I went to get my hair cut early on the day of the party.
The stylist, a tall, skinny, flamboyant, Asian guy named Yugi,
pretended to understand what I was saying.

"I know *exactly* what you want," he said, in his strong
French accent.

Oh God, does he? I thought. I really wasn't sure. He then
made a cut to my bangs that were halfway up my forehead. I
gasped. *Holy #*%*! I looked like Captain Spock from Star Trek.*
From then on, I knew there was no hope. I just sat there in
silence, my eyes wide with fear of what he'd do next. I held back
the tears. I didn't know what else to do. I knew he didn't
understand what I was saying, but he acted as if he did. When he
finished, I stood up. He got my coat from the closet and helped

me into it. I was really trying to hold it together, and I was worried if I said anything I would lose it. But I was too quiet. He asked me if I liked it.

"Yes, thank you," I said. *Really, I wanted to strangle him.* I walked out the door and straight up to Maria's apartment, which was right above the hair salon. When she answered the door, I started crying.

"Oh my dear," Maria said. "Do you want some tea?"

"Maria, loo, loo, look at my hair!" I blubbered.

"It's not so bad." Maria tried not to laugh. She was so sweet, but the look she gave me made me start laughing too. Jim, her husband, was taking a nap in the other room and he said he heard me, but he didn't want to come out. Once we started laughing, he had to come and see. Genuinely, he tried to tell me that it looked nice. Maria and I just started cracking up.

"Oh well. Tonight is your party," Maria said. "Maybe you could wear a hat?" I tried not to think about it because I had fifty friends coming over that night. I took the bus home and the kids, Dave, and I prepared food for the party. We made loads of mini pancakes, then put the kids in an assembly line to add smoked salmon, a dollop of crème fraîche, and a sprig of dill. They were little masterpieces. I put together a big platter of cold cuts and cheese, so people could make sandwiches on fresh baguette slices. We put the crystal wine glasses out and got dressed up. The kids were in black and white, ready to serve the guests.

My friends arrived with other appetizers, wine, and desserts. Clare brought my favorite cookies, her signature raspberry financiers: little almond-flour cookies with a raspberry in the middle that I first tried, hot out of the oven, when she hosted our Conversation Group at her house. People brought me gifts and cards. I couldn't believe I had made so many great, new friends in our short time in Paris. I cried when I made a toast to everyone, and added a bit about my bad haircut experience. It was a fabulous night.

When everyone left, I gave each person a CD of French music that Dave and I made as a party favor. We included songs such as *Au Champs Elysées*—the song that the kids had all sung while skipping down the streets, arm in arm, on *Nuit Blanche*; *Quelqu'un M'a Dit* by then First Lady, Carla Bruni; *Mona Lisa* by Natalie Cole; and other fun songs by French artists such as Georges Brassens and Coralie Clément.

Easter was then upon us. Easter is an important celebration in France, and there were a lot of French customs we learned about. For example: bells play a major role in the French Easter celebration. On the Thursday before Good Friday, all the church bells are silenced. Children are told this is because the bells have flown to Rome to see the Pope. On Easter morning, when the children wake up, they all look for hidden, decorated Easter eggs, which were brought from Rome—where the bells had also gone—and when the chimes ring out, it means that the bells have returned to France and brought the eggs with them.

All the candy shops sell chocolate bells, called *cloche volant*, chocolate eggs, chocolate fish, and chocolate bunnies, and since the French are known for their great attention to detail, all the Easter designs looked more like works of art than anything edible. The kids all cut out paper fish, called *poisson d'avril*, and stuck them on each other's backs. Matthew said it's like their April Fools' joke.

The French allotted an extra vacation day for the Easter holiday, and everyone got an automatic three-day weekend. We decided to head south to Provence. Provence, known for its brightly colored fabrics, lavender, and olive oil, also has the best-preserved Roman monuments of any region in France. I have cousins (on my Dad's side) who live there, in a town called Fayence, and they invited us to stay with them for the Easter weekend. Nicole and Gerard are French. They speak French, but in the south of France, they speak more slowly than they do in Paris. They also speak English. Dave and I knew them already, because we stayed with them on our first trip to France just after we were married.

March 22

*We took the TGV down to Aix-en-Provence, where
Nicole and Gerard picked us up and drove us to their
house. They have a huge Bernese mountain dog, named
Scoop, who the kids have fallen in love with. They lie
on top of him like a blanket, and the dog lets them.
He is sweet and mellow. Nicole cooked us a big
Provençal-style dinner with many courses tonight. We
sat at the table for two hours and spoke mostly in
French. It's so much fun to hear the kids speak
French. I'm surprised I can actually understand a lot!*

The Easter bunny found his way to Nicole and Gerard's house in Provence the next morning. The kids were surprised when they awoke to hear Nicole say (in English), "The Easter bunny has hidden surprises for you outside in the yard." The cold, windy morning wasn't going to keep them from searching for chocolate eggs and candy. They raced to put on their coats and hats, and hunted around the frosty yard until they found everything. Then, when it warmed up a little, we all took a scenic two and a half hour hike to Mons, a medieval-looking village, perched up on a rocky spur, where we saw an old castle called Beauregarde, which was built around the 1500's. We saw part of an aqueduct, built by the Romans, that was almost two thousand years old. Provence was like a living continuation of medieval times with old, unchanged farmhouses scattered around and century old château forts.

We sat down to a two-hour feast again that night, all cooked for us by Nicole. But what the kids remember most was dessert, the Tarte Tropézienne, a giant cream-filled cake, which originated in St. Tropez. We had tried this cake in Paris, but in Provence, everything is bigger. Provençal croissants were twice the size of Parisian croissants and the Tarte Tropézienne was enormous, almost two feet in diameter. We ate some of it each night for dessert.

It was cold in Provence—with the Mistral winds blowing—so driving was the only way to see Provence on our third and last day there. Our local guides and cousins, Nicole and Gerard, drove us around and told us all about the region. The hills, soaking in the sun, were full of majestic olive trees—their strong, knotty, trunks thick to withstand the violent Mistral winds. Tall, slender, Cypress trees all leaned in the same direction from the wind, and rows and rows of dry grape vines ran along the side of the road. Nicole told us that the vines had not woken up yet. (The French have such a way with words.) Some of the trees were in bloom: such as the white, flowering, almond trees and the pink cherry blossom trees. We drove down to the Cote d'Azur (the coast), passing one little hillside village after another. Down by the water, we drove by the seaside towns of St. Tropez, Grimaud, Cogolin, Agay, San Raphael, and Frejus. It was a great weekend with lots of French spoken. We said goodbye to Nicole, Gerard, and Scoop and thanked them for the memorable and delicious Provençal experience. Then we headed back to Paris on the TGV.

April 2008

April in Paris was STILL cold. When would it warm up? The trees were still bare and the cobblestone still wet. I was ready to pack away my boots and heavy coats, looking worn by then. I was ready for spring, but it wasn't ready for Paris. We kept waiting. We discovered the covered passages—shopping arcades, which provided shelter from the cold and the rain. We spent a lot of time in the American library and the English bookstores, Shakespeare and Company and W.H. Smith, where it was dry, warm, and cozy. We drank a lot of hot tea.

April 2

We finally gave in and took the kids to Aquaboulevard today. We have purposely avoided it until now, but we are totally desperate for weekend entertainment. It was expensive, and now the kids will probably want to go every weekend... but oh well! There were eleven giant water slides, a huge rope swing, indoor and outdoor Jacuzzis, and even waves made by a wave machine. It was worth it and quite entertaining for me, watching men of all different shapes and sizes yelling in French and running around in their Speedos.

We checked out the Paris "underground" too. Paris has a whole network of tunnels under the streets. There was a catacomb tour and even a sewer tour. We were told the catacombs weren't scary, so we took the kids. We learned that millions of Parisian remains were moved down into the catacombs for sanitary reasons in the late eighteenth and mid-nineteenth centuries. It was weird to be down below the streets of Paris. The guide told us which streets were directly above us. It was cool, comfortable, and clean, and it didn't smell bad, which was one of the things we were worried about. We walked through dark tunnels with walls made of skulls and other bones. Layers of skeletons were piled high in a very organized, very French fashion. It was artistic in a morbid sort of way. We also heard about the network of underground tunnels that we couldn't see, where people held secret rave parties. (I saw Julia take note of that for later.)

And then Paris finally started to recover from winter. The trees—which had been gray and leafless—all of a sudden were full of leaves again. It felt like it happened overnight. After seeing only shades of gray and black clothing for what seemed like forever, I spotted the first burst of color—a woman walking across the street wearing a bright red skirt. After that I saw more colors—a blue scarf and a yellow blouse. It was as if someone had taken out colored pens and started coloring in a coloring book.

April 3

The colors announce that spring has finally arrived! Everyone's behavior seems different too. There's a spring in our step and everyone's in better moods. Rain showers come out of nowhere, but they don't stop anyone from walking outside in the sunshine—we just have to keep an umbrella handy at all times. I stop on the sidewalk and close my eyes to soak in the sun's rays when it streams in between the buildings. I can actually feel the Vitamin D re-entering my long-dormant, white, white skin. (It's really shocking how white my skin is.)

April 14

It's time for yet ANOTHER two-week vacation from school. I can't believe it. Again? These French people really know how to live. We've decided on a "stay-cation" as we call it in America. Most people would die for two weeks in Paris in the spring, right?

Actually it's more that we don't have any money to spend on another vacation right now. Plus we figure how bad can a two-week "stay-cation" in Paris be?

April 26

Okay, I read (in a book I received as a bon voyage gift) that you have to be bored in a city to really get to know it. Well... on this "stay-cation" we've all gotten to that point... and beyond!

Two weeks with no school, all our friends gone on vacation in exotic places like Mauritius and Tunisia, and lots of unanticipated rain gave us all a little too much time on our hands in the long, light days of spring in Paris (without black-out blinds, the only amenity our new apartment lacked). But... there was a silver lining to this boredom: Paris inspires people, in many ways, and the long days gave rise to our creative sides.

Every time the kids said they were bored, I handed them a piece of white paper and the watercolor paints or pens. We had quite a family art collection started! Matt and Julia read at least twenty books each, and we had some very stimulating discussions about them. We played many, many games in our apartment while it rained outside. And when it wasn't raining I walked or jogged around the Tuileries and down by the Seine. Sometimes I left Julia and her drawing book parked next to a sculpture in the Tuileries, and I ran laps around the park (and her) while she drew. We took the kids to the famous, old covered passageways, where there were wonderful toy stores, restaurants, art galleries, and even a wax museum. We would have never done all these things if we hadn't had all that time to get bored.

Finally, the kids were going back to school and Dave and I planned to go on a *randonée* to Vaux le Vicompte with the school parent group. Spring was the best time for *randonées*—what the French called hikes, but what we, Santa Barbarans, would call a long, flat walk. A French woman, named Monique, had the role of *randonée* planner (group hike coordinator). She organized a walk once or twice a month to get anyone (who signed up) out of the city and into the fresh country air. Normally Dave or I would go on a *randonée* separately. I worried about us both being away at the same time, if one of the kids got sick or something. But the kids were healthy and well adjusted now, and this hike wasn't too far from Paris, so we decided to risk it and go together.

Monique's directions, in French of course, were usually difficult to translate, but Dave said he understood the plan: Meet at the Gare de Lyon train station early in the morning, take a specified train, called MOFI, to Melun, around three miles from the Château of Vaux le Vicomte, then walk through the town and the woods for three miles to the Château. Once we arrived at the Château, we'd all eat our picnic lunch together.

Things don't always go perfectly when you don't speak the language or understand the French train schedules that well. This was one of those times. First of all, we couldn't find the group when we got to the train station in the morning. The train—the one Dave thought we were supposed to take—arrived.

"What should we do?" Dave asked me.

"Let's just go and hopefully we'll meet up with the group once we get there," I said.

We weren't even sure we were going to the right place, and of course we didn't have a map or anyone's phone number. Monique wasn't the type to post her cell phone on the website (and we didn't have smart phones at that time anyway). I had left the planning up to Dave, and he obviously didn't realize how confusing this would be. Dave's response was, "Well, it'll be another adventure." *(Ugh!)*

We got on the train and sat down. I was kind of irritated, so I was quiet. (I was also probably a little stressed about us both going.) After around forty-five minutes, we arrived at Melun. We had made it to the right stop. One step in the right direction... the Château of Vaux le Vicomte was nearby! Unfortunately, the school group was not there either.

140

"Let's take a taxi to the Château and see if we can catch up to the group," Dave said. Okay. Sounded like a good plan. We wouldn't get to hike in, but hopefully we would find the group and hike out with them afterward. When we arrived at Vaux le Vicomte, we didn't see anyone we recognized. Dave and I decided to take the audio-guided tour of the Château and after, we sat down on the grass to have our lunch, when all of a sudden we heard familiar voices.

"*Bonjour*! What are you two (silly Americans) doing here?"

"Uh, we, uh, got a little confused about the train," we explained.

Turned out we had taken the slow train and the group had taken the fast one, which was direct and only took twenty-five minutes. So they were just a half an hour ahead of us. But, to give Dave some (but only a little) bit of credit, Gare de Lyon is a confusing train station, and there really was no one around to ask. Anyway, we didn't know that MOFY meant "fast train," nor did we know that there was a "slow train" going to the same location. Our French hiking guide made a lot of assumptions that non-Parisians knew these kinds of things.

They laughed when they heard about our travails, and we joined them for the rest of the tour of the Château gardens, designed by the famous French landscape architect, André Le Notre. We headed back to the train station—via taxi again, with a few other parents—to make it to school pick-up on time. We didn't get any hiking in that day, but some of the other people thought Dave should be the guide in the future, because the taxi *randonée* sounded like a great idea instead of all that unnecessary exercise.

May 2008

May 1 (May Day and La Fête de la Muguet)

Outside, the flowers are blooming, and Paris is in all its spring glory. Our year abroad is almost over, and the thought of leaving is too much for me to endure. I can't stop thinking how badly I want to stay another year. The kids' French is getting really good. Everyone in the family seems content here. I feel like we're just getting the hang of things.

4 mai (see I'm even writing the date the French way)

Today I instinctively walked to the far end of the Métro station to get in the last car and realized I am no longer a tourist. I know which end of the Métro train to be on because I know which end the exit will be on when I get out. Those details take time to remember. And I must be starting to look more French because people ask me for directions all the time, and I know the answers—sometimes even in French! I know that 22:12 is 10:12 p.m. without even thinking about it, and I discuss the weather in Celsius now. It's becoming automatic. I know which musicians will come into which Métro cars, and I know on which line the deaf beggar rides. I know his routine: he walks up and down the aisle, handing out his little sheets of paper that say he's deaf and has a family. Then he walks back to collect the sheets and any money people give him—which usually isn't any, poor guy. I do wonder if he's really deaf. I'm pretty sure he is because Matt makes loud noises to see if he

can startle him, but he never startles. I know where
we'll see the Peruvian band, the chamber orchestra,
and the woman with the flute playing underground in
the Métro walkways. I finally feel like I don't have to
try so hard all the time, and I'm starting to understand
how this "Paris game" is played. I've learned a lot.
I've gained an intuitive sense, and it feels good.

It was the first Sunday of the month of May—Family Museum Day again! Dave and I decided to finally take the kids to the Musée D'Orsay—just a three-minute walk from our apartment. There were so many other small museums we wanted to check out first, but the time had come. The Musée D'Orsay is probably the second-most-well-known museum in Paris, after the Louvre, and it must have at least fifty percent of all the world's most famous Impressionistic art.

So how does one keep three young kids interested in this much art? We'd been in Paris eight months, and we'd visited a lot of museums. We were getting the hang of it and had learned a few tricks. Such as: it's a very good idea to do some research beforehand. But if you don't, you need to get a children's guide to the museum. If there isn't one at the entrance, you can go to the museum store and find one. These are usually take-home keepsakes, but they are even better as guides. They will tell you which are the most famous and important pieces of art to see.

The Musée d'Orsay had a guide called "On the Trail of the Impressionists" where our kids followed clues on a "mission of discovery." It included fifteen of the most famous pieces in the museum, and fifteen was enough in such a big museum. It also included a map that showed where each painting was (Matthew's job to find them), and a small puzzle-piece-sized clue, which was part of the painting. When we found the painting, the kids tried to find where the puzzle-piece fit. There was also a short description about the work and about the artist—just enough for kids.

Another important element of a long museum day is to take a break for lunch or tea. After seeing eight pieces of art, we debated continuing on and finishing before lunch—while our hungry kids complained—or stopping for a break and coming back refreshed. We opted for the break and then finished after lunch. We determined that an hour and a half without a break was long enough, at least for our family. We even opted for a second snack break, because we ended up at the museum for five hours, and that was for just fifteen pieces of art. Lastly, we let the kids pick out some small souvenirs, such as a refrigerator magnet or a poster and *voila*, the perfect family museum experience.

May 5

Matthew's two quotes of the day were worth noting: The first one this morning was, "I'm never going to make MY kids go to any museums," and the second quote later was, "Well, that wasn't as bad as I thought it was going to be." Ha! We're making progress... finally!

May 6

I cannot bear the thought of leaving Paris! I am NOT ready. Dave says we can stay. It won't be a problem. How is he so sure? I don't know, but I guess I'll just believe him because I CANNOT leave yet. I guess we should see how the kids feel about it though.

Dave and I asked the kids about how things were going for them, and if they wanted to stay in Paris for another year. Julia said yes without thinking twice. She told us how fun and entertaining school was, and that she definitely wanted to stay. Julia is very observant, always picking up on the humor and nuances of things. She told us a story about how badly behaved the French kids were in her classes. What? We were surprised. She said, "The French girls paint their nails in class, throw erasers across the room, just to make the teacher mad, then make up excuses for it, and they completely zone out and the teacher has to whack them on the head with a binder because screaming at them doesn't work." (We had heard about French teachers hitting the kids, but didn't believe it. I guess it is true in the upper grades, at least!)

Julia said that she had learned a lot about French fashion—at least teenage, French style—which she described for us. Apparently, there were different groups of girls at school, and they each had their own fashion style: The group that always studied at lunch wore sweatpants or jeans that were a bit too short and wide, which made them look skinny. There was the group that all wore fancy, black jackets, hair pulled back in a headband, and they wore skirts and ballet flats or shiny, high boots. Then there were the super-stylish girls, who wore expensive Montcler jackets, in all colors, but they also *adored* (popular word the French use) Hello Kitty parkas—Julia *detested* them (another popular word the French use, and one of Julia's new favorite words. She was starting to sound very French.) Lastly, the older girls were all very "high fashion," wearing fur coats and high heels to school. Julia's group wore jeans and scarves, and they were starting to look more and more French.

She said how much she loved having friends from all over the world—French, Korean, Chinese, Irish, English, Venezuelan, Colombian, Russian, Latvian, Polish, Spanish, Italian, Persian, Swiss, Greek, Japanese, Egyptian, Sudanese, Finnish, and she was sure there were even more, but she couldn't think of them. It was astounding that she could think of that many! *And how cool is that?* I thought. She said that she had come to love some new food, such as quiche, cornichons, Chicken Cordon Bleu, French pastries, macarons, and stinky cheese.

Matthew said he too wanted to stay. He was feeling like he could understand French more and more, although he still thought it was pretty hard. His nine-year-old description of Paris was that "life here is unlike other places because they eat snails here, they have really good manners, they don't celebrate Halloween, and they smoke." He said that he couldn't get some of his favorite foods, such as Mexican food and Tapatio (hot sauce), but that was okay, because he loved French food now. He liked taking the Métro everywhere, but the Métro workers went on strike a lot, and since we didn't have a car, he often had to walk to school, which was pretty far… so that was a pain. He said school was fun, but some kids were bullies. He thought the school lunch was a lot better than in Santa Barbara. He explained the four-course meal that was served every day: appetizer, main course, cheese, and dessert, which, to his dismay, was sometimes "just fruit," but on good days was a doughnut. It was almost as if he was weighing his decision, and debating whether Paris or Santa Barbara was better. First, he described what he liked and then there was always a "but" to say what he didn't like.

He did not want to leave his new friends or his school. Once again, in the "Matthew manner," he explained every detail to us. (He never wants to leave anything out, and he wants to make sure we understand what he tells us.) He rambled on about his school soccer team… (I know, I know. I said no after school activities, but we were loosening up a bit since there was a bus that took him to and from practice, and I didn't have to do anything. Parents didn't even come to watch. We weren't even told where the games were! Plus it was only on Wednesdays–which were half days.)

Matthew described how much he loved traveling: "A good thing about my school in Paris is that we get more vacations here. I've already been to a lot of places. All the countries are close together (he learned that in his French geography class), but I still want to go to Switzerland and Germany." Matthew is the kind of kid who keeps a checklist. The number of countries visited was a competition amongst his friends (because everything is a competition with boys). He once asked why we couldn't just drive over to Germany—so he could just put his feet over the border—then we could come right home.

Katherine said that her favorite thing about Paris was definitely the Eiffel Tower. She said she had to stay in Paris because she still wanted to eat dinner up at the top, as some of her friends had. She explained, "When you're up at the top you can see lots of stuff, maybe even all of Paris!" She also mentioned how much she loved the Champs de Mars, the playground at Luxembourg Gardens, and getting *barbapapa* (cotton candy), especially when she didn't have to share it with her brother and sister.

"I love the zip line thing at Luxembourg. You get on, and hold on tight, because it goes fast, and at the end, it's really funny because you get really low, and your bottom hits the ground." *I thought this was a very cute six-year-old description.*

She also said she had lots of new friends, and she wanted to play with them more, so we needed to stay longer, AND that they didn't speak that much English—but she could speak some French now. *Oh, that killed me! We were staying!* Then she said, "I like seeing other parts of the world, and taking pictures, because then I'll have good memories when we go back home. I've been to Spain, Colorado, France (which I'm in right now), Venice, Italy, and Mammoth." *The Mammoth part was funny. It's interesting what kids remember.* "But I miss all my friends from home, and I miss my dog, and my fish, and I miss my grandmas and grandpas. I love my new friends, and I love my teachers, and I really like the food here. I like our apartment, and I love my room, and I like cooking, painting, drawing, reading, and writing in French." It was a classic six-year-old consideration of two sides of the coin.

We took a family vote, and all five of us wanted to stay another year. Unfortunately, many of our Adaptation friends were leaving. In fact, it seemed like half the class was not coming back. We were sad to see so many of our friends go. We had become very close, due to the situation—all of us being new and knowing no one else. We had spent a lot of time together, from museum trips to potlucks, to hikes, dinners, and coffees. Strong friendships happened quickly, but then, the year was over in a blink. We understood why the French kids were hesitant to befriend the Adaptation kids, as many were "short timers." It wasn't fun to make friends who would leave so soon.

Dave discussed the plan to stay in Paris for another year with his company, and they said okay, but he'd have to go back to Santa Barbara to work a lot during the next year, much more than he'd gone this year. I wasn't going to think about it. We were staying! I was so happy.

May 7

Our first year is nearing its end, and we still haven't done several important things, which are easy day trips from Paris. Versailles is one of those things I have purposely avoided, but Matthew explained to me that his teacher said we HAVE to go. He learned a lot about the Sun King, Louis XIV, and he wants to see his castle.

The Palace of Versailles is huge and was built in the classic Baroque style. Famous garden designer, André Le Notre, created the meticulously manicured gardens. In the summer, the Palace hosts evening, hydraulic, fountain shows in the gardens, which are popular with tourists and Parisians. Versailles' size is daunting. It's one of the most visited sights in France and always crowded with tourists, which is why I'd been avoiding it, but the time had come. We readied ourselves for a big day trip to Versailles.

It was about a forty-minute train ride, €6 per person, and then a ten-minute walk to the Palace. I groaned when I caught sight of the long, serpentine line of people waiting to get in. It was glaringly hot, and we weren't prepared. We were never without sunblock and sunglasses in the past, but we were completely out of the habit. I asked a guard how long the wait would be, and he said about an hour *(grumble, grumble)*. "The lines were shorter for the Tour of the Gardens," he said. I looked optimistically at Matthew… "Garden tour??"… No go… he wanted to see the Palace. Luckily, the kids all had their iPods and Nintendos. Dave and I got friendly with some other tourists in the line.

At last! We were in, sweaty and sunburned. We moved like sheep from room to room. That's what it feels like to me in places like this, "Baaaa, baaaa." The rooms weren't all that interesting except for the Hall of Mirrors, the biggest room in the Palace that overlooks the gardens, and the king's tiny bed, which looked like a toddler bed. Apparently, he was a very small person. All of a sudden, I looked around and didn't see Katherine, again! (I know, what happened to the plan we made to always hold hands?!) I panicked, and went over to the guard and told him our six-year-old daughter was missing. He radioed the other guards. Dave grabbed Julia and Matthew, and they pushed ahead through the crowds. I went back in the direction we'd come from, against the traffic. Finally, I saw Katherine up on the shoulders of a guard coming towards me. Tears in my eyes and in hers—we hugged. Katherine told me she had stopped to look at a painting in a room, and when she looked away, we were gone. We must have kept walking along with the crowd, not realizing she wasn't with us.

Time for some fresh air! "Let's go outside," I said to Dave and the kids. I think I felt the way Marie Antoinette did when she created the Hamlet, outside of the castle. I needed to get out of there.

Marie Antoinette was the only queen who lived at Versailles who was a designer. Her husband, King Louis XVI, gave her a private area to develop as she wished. The Hamlet, as it is called, is the little village she designed, comprised of a mill and twelve cottages—nine of which are still standing—encircled by vegetable and flower gardens, and all arranged around a little lake. In her day, no one could enter the Hamlet without her invitation. She imposed her own personal taste on the Hamlet. It was funky, peaceful, and very much a surprise compared to the rest of the formal surroundings. The kids learned that Marie Antoinette was a strong woman and a free thinker, which at the time was unheard of. Unfortunately, it got her killed, but she stood for what she believed in.

This was the kind of thing that living in Europe made me appreciate. History was made real. After we saw the Hamlet, I knew I had to go on a tour of the Conciergerie next, the Paris jail that was Marie Antoinette's last home, and the last home of many prisoners after the French Revolution. It was, of course, also where she was beheaded. As luck had it, a tour of the Conciergerie was offered on the school website soon thereafter, and Dave and I took advantage of it when the kids were in school. We'd walked by it many times on the Ile-de-la-Cité, but we had never been inside. Apparently, it's one of the finest examples of gothic, secular architecture in Europe. It's very touristy inside though, designed for tourists to follow a story line. All the rooms are reconstructed with stuffed dummies as actors. It was kind of corny, and a bit morbid, but worth a few giggles. There was a dummy in the Clerk's office, where prisoners names were registered, a dummy in the Concierge's office, who was in charge of the prisoners, and even more gruesome, there was hair in a basket in the Grooming Room, where condemned prisoners were stripped of their personal belongings and had to get their hair cut off before they went to the guillotine (so it wouldn't be in the way). They even had to tip the hairdresser on the way out (as was and still is customary). We saw Marie Antoinette's Chapel, which was built on the exact spot where her prison cell stood, and a reconstruction of her cell. We even saw the guillotine where she and around 2,600 others were executed.

May 15

A day trip to Monet's Garden, called Giverny, was on the school blog today. It's eighty kilometers (around fifty miles) outside of Paris. It was there, that Claude Monet lived and got his inspiration for his paintings. I talked to a couple friends from Conversation Group, who also wanted to go. Lucy offered to drive, so we didn't have to take the train. Any time I get a ride in a car it feels like such a luxury these days. We had a lovely, relaxing drive out of Paris. Lucy knew the way, so the rest of us got to sit and enjoy the scenery. It was such a pleasure not to have to look up directions for once.

There were miles of open fields and farm animals next to Giverny. It was so close to Paris, yet so rural. I don't know what I was expecting, but it was surreal. We were IN the paintings that I had seen on so many museum walls. The gardens were gorgeous with pastel-colored flowers everywhere. The pond was full of the famous water lilies, and there was even a gardener with a stick in the middle of the pond, pushing the water lilies around, just like the subject in so many of Monet's paintings. The famous, bright green, Japanese bridge was there, edged with weeping willows and adorned with wisteria. My only regret was that my kids did not get to go, but that will be on the list for the future.

We had to figure out where we were going to live for the next year. Dave asked the owner if we could keep renting our current apartment, and she said we could, but she needed it in September and October for friends whom she'd promised. Okay, not a no—just another speed bump. We'd have to find somewhere else to live for two months, but we could rent it for the rest of the year.

I started researching short-term rentals. Then I thought of an idea: Maybe our neighbor downstairs would consider letting us stay with her during that time. She was a cousin of the owner of our apartment (and the mother-in-law of our friend who got us the apartment). (In fact the whole building was family-owned for many generations, which is typical in old Parisian apartment buildings.) The apartment below us was laid out almost exactly like ours, just one floor down. It was also vacant most of the time, because she left it available for her kids and their families when they came to Paris.

I got up my courage a few days later and called her. She said she didn't think her kids had any plans to come during that time, so it should be fine. Yes! What a relief! We were going home to Santa Barbara for the summer, but we'd only have to move our things down one floor, rather than packing everything up and putting it all in the *cave* (basement). That would've been a much bigger hassle. I offered to pay her the same amount for rent as we were paying upstairs, and she said that would be fine. I was so proud of myself for having the courage to ask. Dave wasn't the only one who could get things done around here!

June 2008

The kids all had End-of-Year shows called *Les Spectacles*. They were held in gorgeous Parisian theaters, and all the school families were invited. We had no idea what we were in for. I joined a group of other Adaptation moms to make the costumes for Matthew's class play. None of us had any experience making costumes, and we were given very little guidance from the teacher. All we were told was that the characters were farm animals.

We wandered the steep, narrow, cobbled streets of Montmartre searching for animal costume-making attire, and there amidst the trinket shops and tee shirt stores, we found whimsical accessory stores. We bought yellow feathers for the ducks and fake fur for the leopards and tigers. We bought buttons and yarn for eyes and whiskers, as well as colored construction paper. Then we met at Emma's (my Canadian friend from Conversation Group) to make the masks. Formality was thrown by the wayside. It was hilarious. First, one woman tried on a pig mask and made pig sounds, and things got carried away from there. No wine was involved, but way too much coffee. We got to know each other very well that day... yet another great bonding experience with new friends in Paris.

Watching the end-of-year shows, we realized how much our children had changed. First we saw Matthew's *Spectacle*, which was all in French. We could not tell the native French speakers from the Adaptation kids who had just learned French that year. Julia's show was *Alice in Wonderland*, also in French, and the same experience. They all spoke so quickly. Dave and I were in awe. Our children could speak French!

Katherine's show was the most remarkable. There were two shows: one in English and one in French, and it turned out that Katherine was the star of both of them. We had no idea. She hadn't told us anything about it, and she never practiced at home. We sat in the first row of the theater, because those seats were the only spots left when we arrived. There were at least four hundred people in the audience.

Our jaws dropped! We stared at each other in genuine disbelief when Katherine, our shy child, walked up to the front of the stage with a pink baseball hat on, flipped it around backwards, grabbed a microphone, and started rapping the *Bow Wow Yippie Yo Yay* song while the rest of her class danced hip hop in the background. WHAT?? WHO? HUH?? "Is that Katherine?!!"

Then, Katherine and her kindergarten class performed seven different dances, including the Tectonic, a frenetic street dance to electro-house music, which was a very popular dance at that time in Paris. Imagine a bunch of five- and six-year-olds all doing the same fast-paced arm movements, faster and faster, while they shuffled across the stage laughing. It was the cutest thing we had ever seen.

After that, Katherine and a boy in her class—a cool boy who wore a leather jacket and rode to school in on the back of his Dad's motorcycle—came out and did the Tango alone on the stage. At the end of the dance, the boy dipped her, almost off the end of the stage, and she looked out, upside down at us and smiled. We were in shock. The audience went wild! In the English part of the show, Katherine played the main character, Humpty Dumpty, and did a dramatic fall off the wall. Who was this child? She was not the child we came to Paris with. We were blown away.

June 6

Today, when I stepped my American tennis shoes into Roland Garros (the French Open) for the first time, one of my life-long dreams was fulfilled. Happy does not adequately describe the feeling I had. Opening Day at the French Open: four matches, great seats, and great tennis in the glorious sunshine. It was unreal. I spent the entire day basking in tennis glee! Then, something else exciting happened. While Dave, Maria

*and I were waiting to get in, Julia and Cristina ran
into some girlfriends from school (what else is new?),
who invited them to sit in their seats because they were
leaving. We told them that was fine with us. We got
up to our "nose-bleed section," near the top of the
stadium, and looked down. Two girls were waving at
us from down on the court. "Who is that?" we
wondered. It was Julia and Cristina in the front row,
in a box seat with flowers—lucky girls!*

It was a great match too! Mathilde Johannsen, the French player, was the crowd favorite, and she was playing American, Serena Williams. Serena ended up losing in the third set, but what a memory that day was: At the end of the match, Julia and Cristina rushed to the end of the court with all the French kids to try to get autographs from the players. Since Serena had lost the match, she was walking, head-down, toward the exit. Julia begged in English, "Serena, pretty please with a cherry on top?" Serena lifted up her head when she heard the English and looked at Julia and said, "Oh, okay" and signed her program. Then, ALL the French kids tried saying the same thing: *"Pretty, pretty please, Serena... with a cherry on top?"* with their strong French accents. It was hilarious.

The kids were completely smitten with their new life in Paris. Julia wrote a blog post called "Kids know how to have fun in Paris" because in one week she'd gotten an invitation to laser tag, a sleepover with twenty girls, a *boum* (dance party/boat cruise on the Seine), and a birthday dinner party at an expensive French restaurant.

Matthew went on his *Classe Verte* (Green Trip) for a week to a village called Angers in western France, about two hours on the TGV, plus one and a half hours on a bus. His class stayed in an Abbey, which he said was like a mini castle. The boys slept in one room and the girls in another. They also had a *boum*, which included a dance contest, because all kids (even boys) love to dance in Paris, he told us.

155

When Matthew's class got back, all the parents were invited to their classroom to watch a video of the trip. Then, the kids performed a dance they had learned to a song that went *"Hands up, baby hands up, give me your heart baby, give me your heart baby."* The girls made pulling gestures to their hearts as they looked into the boys' eyes, and then the boys crossed their arms over their hearts. Dave and I almost died. We could not imagine American kids EVER doing that.

June 12 (a rainy day in Paris)

It's been sunny and hot for at least a week, but today it's raining. It's very apropos, because in the last few days a lot of our friends have started packing to go home, and the mood is very melancholy. The tears are flowing.

June 18

I had my last Conversation Group meeting today. It was SO sad. Emma sang a song for us, which brought our whole group to tears. This was such a special group, and I will miss them so much.

Then, the school year really ended. We had to say goodbye to many of our closest Adaptation friends, who were leaving Paris to go back home. Happily, I found something to occupy myself with: the yearly, summer carnival was being erected in the Tuileries near the Louvre. I actually watched the giant Ferris wheel being put up, piece by piece, as I was there on my walks most every day. The prices for rides and games were a little steep, but we decided it was a great way to end our first year in Paris. We walked over with the kids after dinner one night for a late evening of summer fun. We sat together on the Ferris wheel, looking out over what now felt like "our" Paris. Everyone got minor injuries when they went on a more daring ride, the Rolling Fun House. It was basically a giant, concrete pipe that turned round and round. What was the designer thinking? But as

156

I already explained, it's "play at your own risk" in France. Of course, we all ate the requisite, tasty, and fattening snack foods that are an important part of the carnival experience—here in Paris it was *barbarpapa* (cotton candy), *beignets* (the French equivalent of funnel cakes), and caramel apples.

A big group of Adaptation families organized a Goodbye Boat Ride on the river, and we danced the night away to every kind of music: French, Spanish, Iranian, and even Egyptian music for our Egyptian friends. We had Goodbye Picnics at the Champs de Mars, and we had a Champagne Farewell on the Pont Neuf, the oldest bridge in Paris, from sunset until dark. All the kids sat, shoulder-to-shoulder, feet dangling over the edge of the Seine, while the stars flickered and reflected off the water. We reminisced about all the fun times we'd had together over the year, and we toasted to our year in Paris.

July/August 2008

Since we were flying through London on the way back to Santa Barbara, we thought, *why not stay a couple of days and see London?* Dave had been there, but the rest of us hadn't. We crossed the Chunnel, or as it is more formally named, the Channel Tunnel, on the high-speed train that goes under the ocean from Paris to London. The kids were intrigued. Would we feel a change in pressure? Would our ears pop? Turned out it wasn't nearly as cool as we thought it would be. We didn't feel anything. It just went totally dark when we entered the tunnel, and that was that. No whale or shark sightings—just a long, dark tunnel. We had to use our imaginations.

Then, there was British Customs and Passport Control upon arrival, and let me tell you, those Brits really know how to make people squirm. While waiting our turn, I looked up ahead at the Passport Control Officers. Who looked the nicest? I knew which one looked the meanest, AND sure enough, he was the one who waved us over. *Great!* I thought. I hid behind Dave and handed him our passports. Why do these people scare me so much? They never smile. The Passport Control Officer was silent for what seemed like an eternity, staring at his computer, then at our passports, then back at the computer, typing, typing, typing...

Finally he asked Dave: "Why were you in London last month?"

"I went for a meeting," Dave said.

(pause, long look at us)

"Are you working in London?"

(mean stare)

"No, it was a social meeting," Dave said.

(long pause, felt like at least a minute passed)

"Social meeting... what do you mean?"

"I met with a friend," Dave said.

(pause, typing, pause, slowly looking at each of us, one by one)

"Which one is Julia?" he asked.

"Right here," Dave said. He pulled Julia up next to him.

(short look, pause)

"Ok, go ahead," he said.

Geez, why the third degree? I guess I was holding my breath, because when I exhaled, it felt like my breath released all the resistance in my body. Those kinds of experiences are exhausting.

Outside, the fresh air made me feel better. We jumped on a Big Bus Tour: the red, double-decker buses that show you all of London in one day. You can hop on and off as often as you like, and our guide was very funny. I started to feel better.

We went to Buckingham Palace to see the Queen, but she was at her big Garden Party, and we weren't invited. Julia even had a hat—but no luck. We heard they serve 20,000 cups of tea and 20,000 sandwiches at these events to around 8,000 lucky invitees. We walked through Green Park, which was gorgeous, following women wearing fancy hats and men with top hats and canes, who had all just left the Queen's Garden Party. It was surprising to see that people really dressed like that! Then, we hopped back on the Big Bus.

Next we hopped off at the Tower Pier, next to the Tower of London, to take a boat ride on the Thames, because we heard you should really see that part of London from the water. First, we took a short tour of the Tower of London and showed the kids the crown jewels. The boat ride was just okay because the overpowering exhaust smell tarnished the experience.

We got back on the bus and saw St. Paul's Cathedral, the Houses of Parliament, and Big Ben, the famous clock tower. Then, we got off at the London Eye, the giant Ferris wheel, and took a "flight," as they called it (a very slow flight), up above London. One rotation takes thirty minutes, and that is what we got with our very expensive tickets… one rotation. Each capsule holds twenty-five people, and the whole wheel can transport eight hundred people at a time. It's huge. Boy does that earn London some revenue! We found a restaurant near our hotel for dinner and had the best fish and chips we'd ever tasted. Our first day's experiences in London were enjoyable, educational, and delicious.

When we woke up the next day, it was gray and raining, so we decided to visit the Tate Modern. This museum didn't make a big impression on any of us, but it was free and dry. We didn't have much time anyway, because our flight left for America in the early afternoon, so we just did an underwhelming, quick tour. Then, we headed to the airport to fly back to Santa Barbara to spend the summer with our families and friends.

July 7

We're back in the good old US of A! The flight was easy. Nothing dramatic happened (thank goodness), and now we're in Los Angeles where Dana, the driver we hired to pick us up in our van, is hopefully waiting outside for us. I'm looking around, and everyone looks SO American—short shorts and tee shirts, running shoes, and workout wear… It looks so WEIRD!

Later

We're back in Santa Barbara now. We took Highway 1 through Malibu along the ocean, which was gorgeous. The sun was shining and sparkling on the water. We're all excited to be back. We got to Grandma's house, where we're staying, dropped off our bags, and raced down to the beach. The kids couldn't wait to find their friends at Lifeguard Camp.

Julia's friends barely recognized her with her dark hair and white skin. She does look very different. We all do. We're all skinny and pale, all the blonde highlights long-gone from our hair. The cleaning lady was at the house, and she asked me if I was okay. I think she thought I was seriously ill.

July 8

We went with trepidation to check on our house. I had heard horror stories from two different Adaptation friends who came back to their houses and found them completely trashed by their renters. We didn't bring the kids. We could drive them by the house later, but the renters probably wouldn't appreciate the kids running into their old rooms, etc. I didn't feel nostalgic when we drove up, which I thought was interesting. One of the girls let us in. The house looked great. Everything was clean and perfect, better than we left it! The girls said that they wanted to stay another year if possible. Yes! That's just too easy!

Over the next few weeks, every single one of our relatives and many of our out-of-town friends came to visit us. In fact, there were only a few days during the whole summer that we didn't have houseguests, which was fun, but also tiring. We went on our annual, group camping trip, and we celebrated the weeklong Fiesta/Old Spanish Days with our friends – traditions that we all hold dear. The kids had play dates, tennis camps, surf camps, and art camps. Julia had a Paris-themed beach party for her twelfth birthday in July. We had a "Build the Eiffel Tower" sand castle contest, and she told her friends all about her life in Paris.

We all visited the dentist, and we checked in with the orthodontist. He said Julia could wait another year to start braces. That was a relief. We really wanted to wait until we were back in Santa Barbara permanently before she started braces. We simply weren't that confident about the French dental care. The one time Dave took Katherine to see a dentist in Paris, because she was complaining of a toothache, he told them that her teeth were perfect, and he couldn't do anything for her. When we got back to Santa Barbara, it turned out she had three cavities!

We had our annual physicals. We were all fine, just thin and pale. I had lost fifteen pounds! I guess all that walking made up for the cheese and pastries.

August 16

Dave and I worried that the kids wouldn't want to go back to Paris after being in Santa Barbara all summer, but in fact, they're excited to go back. I'm surprised! Why is life in Paris so enjoyable? And why does life seem so much calmer there than here? For me, it feels so rushed here all the time. I'm sure part of it is the ease of public transportation. I don't have to drive the kids everywhere in Paris. The longer school days definitely help. Those extra hours make a big difference. Maybe it's apartment living? There's a lot less to take care of. Also, there's the weather: we're forced to slow down and stay inside half the year because it's too cold to go out. Well, I'm just glad we're going back for another year! I can't imagine not going back. In fact, I can't wait!

We headed back to Paris via planes, trains and automobiles, but not in that order. The automobile part went smoothly. Dana drove us back to LAX in our minivan, with lots of time to spare. We even stopped at a coffee shop along the way. The airplane part of the trip went easily also—not the most relaxing flight—more like a roller coaster at Magic Mountain, but the turbulence put Katherine right to sleep, and she slept for a good eight hours. We did a marathon of family movies on board, and we had some surprisingly good airplane food. Air France still serves champagne as an aperitif, wine with dinner, cheese, desserts, and great kids' meals, unlike most other airlines, that have gone down to "bare bones" offerings.

162

Finally, came the train... and that's when things stopped going so well. We arrived in London and took a regional train to the Eurostar Station, from which we were going to take the Chunnel from London to Paris. "This is going too easily," Dave said, when we got off the train. (Shouldn't have said that, right?) A moment later, Dave said, "Doesn't it feel like we're missing a bag?" I looked at the bags and counted fourteen.

"We ARE! Oh *#%@!"

The big, blue bag (MY bag) was missing—ALL of my clothes! This was not funny. I started to hyperventilate. "Where did we leave it?" I asked Dave.

"It must be back at the Tube Station," Dave said. "I'll go back to look for it, but you'll have to take the kids by yourself. I had no choice. I had to let him go back. I was going to go through Customs and Passport Control by myself (not my favorite... It always seemed like they were trying to bust me for something) and somehow transport fourteen bags and three kids alone. I took a deep breath and said, "Okay, kids, let's go!

"Here are our tickets." (I showed him the train tickets.)

"No, I don't need to see those," he said.

"Oh okay, okay, right! Here's Katherine's passport, Katherine, Katherine! Here's Katherine. Matthew, Matthew, this is Matthew. Here's his passport... Here he is!" I rambled quickly and nervously until he was so exhausted with me, he didn't want to hear any more.

"Just go," he said.

When we got to our train, I realized we had to get all fourteen bags up the stairs and onto the train, without Dave's help, and they were very big and heavy. The big ones were seventy pounds each. (I know because we filled them to the maximum allowed weight!) There were no porters to help us, and no one else offered. I put Katherine up onto the train. Then I got on, and I told Matthew and Julia to try to hand the bags up to me. They couldn't do it. They were too heavy. I told Julia to get on the train, and Matthew and I tried handing them up to her. That worked. There wasn't enough room in the storage rack for our fourteen bags, so I had to take a few to another storage area. Luckily, there was room in the area at the other end of our car, but what a nightmare.

We sat down in our seats and looked at each other. No one was smiling. It was weird to be without Dave. We all hoped he would make it back to the train before it left, but as we sat there, I went through the timing in my head, and I knew he wasn't going to make it. The doors closed. We all looked down the *quai* (walkway) one last time, hoping to see Dave running towards the train, but he wasn't there.

The kids and I made it to Paris just fine. Once we arrived, a nice French guy named Frederik and his girlfriend Kristina who had befriended us on the train, offered to help me by pulling a couple of our bags to the Métro station. Then, once we got there, they said they'd go all the way to our apartment with us. (And people think Parisians aren't nice! They're SO nice!) Dave arrived at the apartment only a half hour after us— WITH the big blue bag. Yes, he found it! I was so happy to see him and my bag, safe and sound, back at our new, cozy apartment, one floor down in Paris.

Isabelle, the concierge, was surprised to see us return. It felt good to be welcomed back, just as though we belonged there. She handed us a stack of mail she had held for us over the summer. Wait, what was this?! On top was a letter from UCPA, the French camp Matthew and Katherine were about to go to, but it was addressed to Julia. I ripped it open and tried to read the French.

"What?" I handed the letter to Dave. Does it say Julia is registered for camp, and supposed to leave tomorrow morning?

Dave read it and confirmed: "Yep, someone cancelled and Julia is in."

The last thing we had heard before we left for summer was that Julia's camp was full. We had everything prepared for Matthew and Katherine's camps, because we knew they were leaving the next morning. We had packed their duffels in Santa Barbara before we left. But we didn't have anything packed for Julia, and now she too was supposed to leave bright and early, at

6:00 a.m. the next morning. Why was our life always like this? Once again, it was Sunday, and all the stores were closed. We raced to get a bag packed for her with all the items we could find for a week at sleep-away camp, and then we all tried to get some sleep.

In the middle of the night, Dave awoke to find jet-lagged, bleary-eyed, zombie children roaming the apartment. They had woken up after two hours of sleep, and since we had borrowed Matthew's watch as our third backup alarm clock (to make sure we awoke to take Julia to the train), they had no idea what time it was. He sent them back to sleep, but it didn't work. None of them could sleep.

Dave had been tossing and turning for two hours anyway, so he got up and cooked a 4:00 a.m. breakfast for the kids. They watched a Harry Potter movie for an hour, and I slept through it all. Then, Dave and Julia left for the train station. What a kid: massive jet lag, onto a train with a bunch of hormonal, pre-teen strangers, who spoke only French. But lo and behold, she reported six hours later, upon arrival in Montevalet (outside Bordeaux), "Everything's fine." *Check.* "Made some friends." *Check.* "They're German, but they speak great French." *Okay, whatever works!*

Dave and I both went to take Matt and Kate to their train in the afternoon. It was kind of scary sending them off to French Camp by themselves, but we had to pretend it was no big deal.

We told them, "It's gonna be great."

Dave said, "Boy, they're brave."

August 22

"WHAT was I thinking when I agreed to this" is more like it!! I can't believe we are sending our nine- and six-year-olds off to French camp by themselves— jet-lagged and alone. At least Matthew and Katherine's camps are in the same place in Normandy. Matthew, being the best older brother ever, is going to

165

look out for Katherine on the train, and then check on her at camp (if he can). He has a phone card to call us, as they requested, but Katherine doesn't. I guess she's too young for that.

These camps, called UCPA, are very popular in France and came highly recommended by my friends. I had checked them out thoroughly, I thought, but now that we were actually sending them off, I was second-guessing myself. Our plan was that they'd 'get their French back' before school started, and the camps looked as though they'd be really fun. In the end, I'm not sure it was worth all the worrying I did about Katherine. Matthew was able to watch over her pretty well, and he called with updates about how she was doing. One time he even went over to Katherine's camp and brought her to the phone, so we could talk to her. But then, one day he called and said, "I saved Katherine's life today."

"What?"

"Yeah, she would have drowned if I wasn't there."

Dave and I stared at each other in disbelief. Our nine-year-old saved our six-year-old's life? How could this be true?

"What are you talking about, Matthew?"

"Well, they were in the lake in a boat, and they were giving them a swimming test to see if they could swim from the boat back to the shore. She had a life jacket on, but it was too big, and she couldn't swim with it. It was going over her head. I saw her because we were swimming in the lake too, and I went over and helped her to the shore."

Dave said, "Put the counselor on the phone!" But there wasn't anyone around. Matthew said he'd go find someone and have him or her call us back. When they called back awhile later, the director did not speak a word of English, so Dave tried to get the real story, but it was hard to understand him. The director didn't see our concern. Katherine had a life jacket on, so how could there be any danger? Maybe he was right, but according to Matthew, she was struggling in it. We never got a clear answer on this. Julia never called after the first day, so we figured that no news was good news… but after the scary conversation with Matthew, we were a bit uneasy.

Dave and I unpacked and got settled into our new, temporary apartment, down one floor from the other one. It was a great apartment, almost exactly the same as the one upstairs, but some things were even better: There was a comfortable couch, a bigger television, and our bedroom wasn't right next to the kids' bedroom, like in the other apartment, so we had a lot more privacy. It was great for us to have some time together alone. We really needed it. We celebrated our fourteenth anniversary, and it all seemed surreal to be back in Paris. Everything was familiar, not new and exciting, but Paris was more beautiful than I remembered.

August 24

Just thinking about our summer in Santa Barbara. It was hectic, but fun, and it felt like home. Once again the incessant driving engulfed most of my time, but life in Santa Barbara is good. I can't deny it. I exercised and felt healthy again. I think I looked deathly ill when I first got back. I was so pale! In Santa Barbara, we took many fun, family hikes, and spent many days at the beach. We also loved all the BBQs at the tennis club.

Paris is all about culture, art, and challenges, and satisfying my curiosity for learning and experiencing new things. It is different in every way, just like I thought it would be. I guess the best way to look at it is: both cities offer their own rewards, and we're lucky to have this opportunity to experience them both.

August 25

The New Parent Adaptation Picnic is coming up this weekend. Clare is in charge and has asked me to come

help by meeting new parents and talking to them. Me?
She thinks I'm an experienced Adaptation parent?
Wow! I still feel pretty clueless, but I guess I know a
lot more than the new people! I've even agreed to be the
Conversation Group Coordinator and a Parent
Partner for a new family!

Year Two

Julia 12-13 years old

Matthew 9 ½ -10 ½ years old

Katherine 6 ½ -7 ½ years old

September 2008

For the kids, their arrival back in the French-speaking world brought an exciting realization: that they really could speak French. They didn't believe it until then. It was like an awakening of their senses, when the background noise was no longer background noise. Standing on the Métro, on our way back to the apartment, Matthew had a look of amazement on his face when he said to me, "Mom, I understand everything people are saying around me. When we got off the plane last year it sounded like *blah, blah, blah, blah,* but now I understand everything!" In Santa Barbara during the summer, many people had asked them if they could speak French, and they never gave a confident "yes" (like I wanted them to, proud Mama that I was). They'd answer, "a little" but they were uncertain about it. It wasn't until they were back in Paris and heard French being spoken that their disbelief was peeled away.

September 2

Well, Day One of School Year Two is over. Matt was the only pensive one this morning. Katherine was totally relaxed, and Julia was excited. Their friends were surprised to see them. I guess they just expected that they wouldn't come back. Our kids realized how many friends they have in Paris. At school, they noticed how French everything was. Being back in Santa Barbara made the differences more obvious to them. They had forgotten how strict life was here.

"The day is so long," Katherine said. "We don't get chances anymore."

Apparently, in *Grande Section* (kindergarten), when they were scolded, they'd get another chance before they were really in trouble. Her new teacher for first grade said this was no longer the case… *Yikes! What did that mean?*

"My teacher screams at us all the time," Julia said.

"My teacher grabs us and moves us where she wants us," Katherine said.

"At lunch, they are constantly telling us to push in our chairs… closer… closer… and to sit up straight, sit correctly, use our fork and knife, and no touching the food with our hands. And we have to eat everything we take," Matthew said.

Zeros were normal grades for their *dictées* (dictations). Sometimes they even got negative grades, like negative ten or twenty. There was no "sugar coating" to keep their self-esteem up. Nope, the French don't believe in it. The best they were ever told was "*pas mal*" (not bad). But Day One of Year Two was definitely easier than Day One of the first year. They all knew where to go, how to get there, and how long it would take. We knew (mostly) what the school supplies were. We were confident that the kids were prepared. And this is a big one: They all could speak French, and they were no longer shy about it. Katherine came out of her first day of school with a huge smile on her face saying, "I understood every single word my teacher said!"

Matthew said, "I miss Adaptation," but he was smiling and said he had two of his best friends in his class. And Julia… well, as we were walking up the street towards school, she saw her friends huddled in a big group, and they all screamed, "JULIAAA!!!" Then they all ran up and hugged her. So life could not have been better at that moment. Then, they all checked out each other's new bags. Dave reenacted it perfectly for the parents at the café afterward, which was hilarious. "*Ohhh, j'adooore ton sac!!*" (Ohhh, I looove your bag!)

A friend had told me before we moved to Paris, "Your kids are going to be THIS BIG when you get back!" (She had her arms spread straight out like THIS BIG—and she didn't mean taller or fatter.) We weren't coming back just yet, but I could already see how much they'd all "grown." It was their minds that had expanded, stretched, and bloomed.

Now that they could speak French, there was so much more we could do in Paris. All the things that weren't desirable the first year were now viable. For example, there were many small museums that weren't on our first-year radar: the Museum of Magic, for example. It sounded like a great museum for kids, but it was all in French with no translations. When we went the second year, we sat in the theater and watched a French magic show. My kids participated, laughed, and understood everything. I didn't grasp most of it, but I didn't care because it was so gratifying to watch the kids understand it all. We also went back to the Science Museum, which had been a terrible experience the first time. The second time, it was fabulous.

The kids' French was becoming second nature to them. Katherine told me that she and her best friend Colette sometimes got tired of speaking English and using the same words all the time, so they'd just switch to French in the middle of a sentence. She said sometimes it even happened in the middle of a word. Remarkable! She'd come so far!

September 12

Dave is out of town, so Matthew called Pizza Hut for me tonight. Yes, they have Pizza Hut in Paris, but that doesn't mean Americans work there. They don't. Nor does it mean that the people who work there speak any English, especially on orders taken over the phone. In fact, they hung up on me, mid-order, because I was too slow trying to figure out how to answer: "Sur place ou à emporter?" (For here or to go?) Matthew used a strong, French accent when he said American words like "Pepperoni Lovers" and "Hawaiian," because he said that was the only way they'd understand. It was TOO cute!

One day after school, Julia walked in on my new Conversation Group that I was hosting. Some women from my prior year's group were in it, as well as several new women. Lucy started talking to Julia in French. When Julia left, Lucy told

175

everyone, "She has a perfect accent." Then Wendy, a new American Mom said, "Wow! Are my kids going to speak that well by next year?" I was so proud.

That didn't mean there weren't any problems, however. For example, Julia's math class (in French) was getting harder. Dave was gone a lot, and I couldn't help her at all. One night Dave was on a video call with Julia, trying to help her with her geometry homework. Julia tried to explain the problem to him in English, but then she gave up, and switched to French. She didn't know the geometry words in English. Dave didn't know the words in French.

As an expat in a foreign country, you regularly think, "Thank goodness for modern technology!" With online translation programs and quick online searches, as well as video calls, everything eventually gets figured out, but it is still quite challenging. We definitely needed to find a math tutor who spoke French. Once again, no problem, thanks to the tutor and babysitter list provided by the awesome Parent Group from the school. In stepped Philip, a cute, red-haired *Première* student (a junior in American high school), who Julia got along with fabulously. They met at the park after school to do homework. He helped her with math, and she helped him with his poetry memorizations, and all was well.

September 16

I just heard Matthew and Katherine in their room speaking French to each other while they were playing. I snuck down the hallway to listen. I couldn't help but eavesdrop. It seemed like they were just kidding around at first, but it's become normal for them to speak French to each other. Trop cool!!! (SO COOL!)

On the other hand, the kids also used French as a way to annoy me: When I asked Julia a question that she didn't want to answer, she'd answer in French, speaking really fast. Her "kid French" had a lot of slang in it, so it was hard to decipher. Julia also spoke French to her friends on Skype when she didn't want

176

me to know what she was saying. She'd speak French "under her breath" when she wanted to say something rude to me. But Kate or Matt would usually tell me what she said. *(Haha!)*

September 17

Yeah, I was just thinking how much less intimidated I am now with... I was going to say, "shopping in Paris"... but actually, it's more than shopping; it's basically going out to run errands in general. It's gotten easier, but I still have to pump myself up sometimes.

Of course, I know this is taking me longer than most people. Dave was always around last year and always willing to help me. That made it easy for me to avoid doing any of the difficult things. Now that he's gone so much, I have to handle things myself. Yes, it's exhilarating for sure, especially when I succeed with even small things, but when I fail, I feel like my confidence gets drained out of my body. It's easier to just stay in my safe, English-speaking home, and wait for my mini-translators to accompany me on errands.

I KNOW, I KNOW! WHY the heck have I not spent more time in French classes? The truth is, I didn't want to. I still don't. I mean, if we were moving here permanently, I'd do it, but as it is, we're leaving after this year, and I do get along pretty well now. In fact, I think I followed 80% of the discussion in the monthly Parent Meeting this morning—and YES, It was all in FRENCH!

SOOOO, I'd rather go to a potluck (like today), or a museum tour, or a walk through the Bon Marché with a French friend to practice French, than sit in a

*classroom while my short time left in Paris tick, tick,
ticks away!*

September 18

*Today, I succeeded in buying Matthew a piece of
construction paper—yes, just a piece of construction
paper, but anything that I'm able to do reassures me. I
knew of a store that carried the paper. I knew how to
get there. I knew the paper was upstairs in the back
room. I was able to understand the guy when he said
the price—in French, and I paid with cash,
INCLUDING counting out the change. (Usually I
just hand over my card because it's easier.) Little
successes are encouraging. They refresh my confidence.*

*You know, I never thought of myself as insecure before
I moved to Paris, but it sure seems like I don't do
things because I'm scared of the results. Truth is,
everything is harder to do in Paris. It just is. I do
realize that being fluent in French would definitely
enhance my quality of life here, but ugh… whatever!*

On another day, I shopped for food. No, not at the
outdoor market, just at the Franprix down the street. The
difference was that I now knew where everything was, and what
everything was, and how to ask for anything I didn't know the
whereabouts of. Big change from last year! For example, I
couldn't find the baguettes, but I knew how to ask for them in
French. I was evolving from a befuddled, first-time expat into a
near-local *Parisienne*! (Not quite, as you'll soon see…)

When I got home, I was proud of myself for
remembering the key for our broken door (the code was not
working), so I wasn't locked out again. Then, the elevator
worked (it had been broken for a week), which made me very
happy, because I thought I was going to have to trek up the
stairs again with my heavy bag of groceries. BUT, not everything

went this perfectly. When I got inside the apartment, there was a letter from the bank that had been slipped under the door.

September 19

Uh-oh! I just opened a letter from our bank... I'm pretty sure it says I have to write them back a letter (by TODAY) saying why we bounced a check last week. WHAT? Like hand-write them a letter? The letter arrived TODAY and they want it by TODAY (in French, of course), and if delayed, there will be consequences. I'm not sure what that means... Crap! Well, I can't do it. Dave's in Santa Barbara (nine hours behind us here, and he's currently sleeping), and writing them a letter in French would be impossible for me. Ha, I'll just tell them it's impossible... a taste of their own medicine! Okay, I'm off to the potluck!

Even such things as a trip to the post office to buy stamps and mail letters and packages may sound ridiculously easy and silly to anyone who has not lived in Paris, but as I've said, nothing is ever easy in Paris. Post office lines always take forever, no matter where you live, and impatience brings out the worst in people. Parisian post office workers were not the most tolerant or understanding people either. In line, I'd get nervous, trying to remember what I needed to say, and when I got to the front of the line, I'd sometimes panic because I didn't know the vocabulary related to shipping, etc., and if they asked me any questions, I was definitely in trouble.

One day, I succeeded in buying the right kind of stamps for all the different destinations I was mailing letters to, after discussing it (in French) with the post office worker. (Victory!) Then, I went to put the letters in the mailbox. Shouldn't be that difficult, right? Wrong! There were four different boxes for mail—each with a different label. They said: *"Paris, Banlieu, Étranger, and DOM."* Of course, I knew what the one marked *"Paris"* was for. Easy! But I needed to mail one of the letters to my cousins in Provence, and one to the U.S. I was sure that the one for the U.S. went in the box marked "*Étranger*," and pretty sure that the letter to Provence went in the one labeled "*Banlieu*," so I dropped it in. The fourth box was labeled "*DOM*"—call me clueless, but I didn't have any idea what that meant! I had already dropped all the letters in boxes, so *voila*, it didn't matter, and I was energized. Astounding that such happiness and confidence can be gained by just mailing a few letters, right?!

(Side note: I recently learned that the Provence letter should've gone in the "DOM" box, not "Banlieu," so that letter probably never made it to my cousins! Oh well, at the time, I was totally self-assured.)

Another bonus that made our second year better than the first was that two of my Santa Barbara friends joined us in France for the year. One of my friends had decided to come to Paris to try to save her failing marriage. She brought her two younger children, who were friends of Matthew and Katherine. She rented an apartment near ours, so close that the kids could ride their scooters back and forth for play dates. Then, a second Santa Barbara friend and I were talking on Skype one night. I suggested to her, quite earnestly, that she and her family should join us in Paris for the year. I knew she wanted to spend a year in France, but she didn't think her husband would go for it. They had already spent some time abroad a few years earlier and had a great experience, but she doubted he'd want to do it again. (Their experience was actually part of our impetus to take our kids abroad.) Her husband could do his job from afar, so that wasn't a problem. She decided to go for it and ask him. He loved the idea, so they came too.

We tried to find them an apartment in Paris, but they decided instead to rent a big country house in a town outside of Paris, just on the edge of the forest of Fontainebleau. There was another bilingual school that their kids could attend there. They could bring their dog and cat and have houseguests. Harper and Mike and their two girls, Anabelle and Sabrina, called themselves the "country mice" and we were the "city mice." It was only forty minutes from our door to theirs. The house in Moret-sur-Loing turned out to be a good decision for them, and they were very happy there. We loved it too, when we visited. We got to experience the French country life with them, and of course, they came to Paris many times.

September 20

Today we took our first trip out to see Harper and Mike's charming country house. What a fun day! I'm so thrilled they came to France!

The country mice took us on a tour of Moret (short for Moret-sur-Loing). There were nine of us; so we had to take two car trips, but their house was only five minutes away. We drove in through two impressive gateways, and Mike pointed out a dungeon from the 12th century. The old walls and towers served as protection for the Kingdom of France from the supporters of the Duke of Burgundy. I don't think any of us could quite grasp how old the town is... we're talking Middle Ages! The town museum had gorgeous Impressionist-style paintings, mostly by Alfred Sisley, who was one of the French Impressionism masters. He painted more than four hundred scenes of Moret-sur-Loing, its river landscapes, and its surroundings. The river Loing, which eventually empties into the Seine, was right behind their house. The house came with a bright red canoe, almost too picture perfect to float along in the river. We all took turns paddling to the turnstile at the end and back, with the quacking ducks and geese paddling along next to us. The kids played croquet, and we sat in lawn chairs, glasses of good French chablis in hand. The idyllic scene was not lost on us. We all soaked it in.

September 22

I'm noticing funny little things such as the "merci" whisper by each person as the door to exit to the Métro is held for them. Then, there's the Parisian "quick inhale" in conversation, which means "Oh!" (They do this ALL the time) and the way they say "Oui" like "Ouisch." And now I'm finding myself doing these things!

October 2008

When you're a tourist, you run around with a guidebook, trying to see all the major monuments. But you're in too much of a hurry to notice the small things. It's only after you've done all the famous things and you have time to spare (and be bored), that you really start to see the real city. There were things about Paris that made it special, and I was starting to figure that out.

October 3

Why do I love this place so much?

Some of the reasons:

It's a quiet city.

The buildings are charming and historic. I love looking up at the balconies and seeing the different designs of metalwork, and I especially love the bright bursts of colored flowers in the flower boxes against the pale colored buildings.

People are stylish and always try to look their best. They're also very polite.

The food is delicious, even in the grocery stores.

Some things are still so basic here: such as the French belief that "life is for enjoying."

They are intensely faithful to food, family, and traditions. For example: extended family meals— especially Sunday lunches—are a time-honored custom.

They drink wine with lunch.

Making kids into "gourmands" is an important society norm, beginning at birth.

Public transportation is great (usually).

Paris is a walking city, and I've embraced this. Today, for example, as I walked along the edge of the Seine, my mind drifted away from my day-to-day trivialities. As I looked from the uneven cobblestones to the slow moving ripples in the river, to the puffy, white clouds in the sky, it felt like I was in a painting. These solitary walks are mesmerizing and calming.

I also love to wander through the parks and look at the sculptures—some modern, some mythical. The statues of Greek Gods in the Tuileries take me back to the stories I learned as a child, and modern sculptures, such as "The Reclining Figure" by Henry Moore, an abstraction of the human form, fascinate me. "The Kiss" by Auguste Rodin, in front of the Orangerie Museum, where the lovers' lips are close but not touching, is one of my favorites.

I agreed wholeheartedly with my friend Farah's words describing her reason for moving to Paris after living in Atlanta for nineteen years: "In Atlanta, my life was comfortable, like a comfy pair of slippers. Life there was lived in the car. You drove the kids to school; you picked them up from school—not even getting out of the car at the school gates. You became a taxi driver. That life can drain your energy. In Paris, you walk. And by walking you have experiences; you discover hidden treasures on every street." That's it—walking! That's a huge part of why people love Paris.

And Paris is art—not just the paintings and sculptures. Everything is raised to an art form and done with precision and style. Art is an integral part of French society, starting with exposure for the children from a very early age. Museum tours and art classes in an *atelier d'art* (art workshop) below the Louvre were just some of Katherine's kindergarten experiences. And Paris is history. It can be felt in the old cobblestone streets and in the buildings. "Paris is all the world in one place," my friend once said.

Falling in love with a city is not because of the tourist attractions. It's not the monuments that people love when they say they love Paris. It's the feeling you get when you walk down the street, and you feel immersed in the culture. There's a rhythm to life in Paris. Each season has different foods in the cafés and seasonal fruits and vegetables in the markets. We learned to anticipate what would come with each season. In the fall, there were steaming *moules* (mussels from Normandy and Brittany), bathed in shallots and butter. In the winter, came "comfort foods" like *cassoulet* (a French stew) and soups, oysters, and shiny, orange tangerines in perfect rows in the fruit stands. In the spring, there were loads of tourists around, the parks got crowded, and people were outside picnicking everywhere. There were the bi-yearly *Soldes*, one big sale in the summer and one in the winter - when all Parisians went out, in force, to shop. (And now I did as well.) People always kissed on both cheeks (*le bisou*). Even kids (older ones) gave each other *les bises* (kisses on cheeks). Everyone got daily, fresh baguettes from their local bakery, usually twice a day (and they're baked twice a day). *(The anti-bread/anti-carb/anti-gluten diet, popular in the U.S., is not as popular in Paris.)* There's a pharmacy on every corner—with helpful, knowledgeable pharmacists who are all trained in first aid, homeopathy, and nutrition, and you know your local storekeepers. We were starting to feel like we were "in the know," and with that came a sense of security and of belonging. Paris was truly beginning to feel like home.

October 6

> *Oh! I found out why each day's lunch is posted outside the primary schools, like Katherine's. It's because it enables French citizens (who walk by) to make sure*

the standards of eating habits of the next generation of Parisians is being upheld. Wow!

October 11

Today, Dave and I went on a tour of the Musée Jacquemart-André in the eighth arrondissement. Since it was refurbished five years ago, it has been the talk of the international art world (apparently). We went with thirty parents from the school and an English-speaking guide (who reminded me a bit of Natasha from Bullwinkle). Afterwards, we had lunch with the group in the popular museum café/tea room. It was so much fun. I love talking about art exhibits and getting to know new people.

October 13

Today, we went out of town with some friends and their kids, to pick fruit, vegetables, and flowers at a farm called La Ferme de Viltain. Even though we should've been unpacking and getting our apartment organized (we moved yesterday), we couldn't pass up the offer of a convertible ride in this gorgeous weather.

On the way back, we stopped at a charming restaurant our friends liked, called Robin de Bois (Robin Hood), and had a delicious lunch outside on the sunny terrace. Their specialty was sliced meat that we cooked ourselves on a little stove in the middle of the table. The kids sat at their own table and had their own stove to cook their meat on. "It was the most entertaining lunch ever," our kids said.

Despite all that I've said, some things about Paris were getting to me again. After being back in casual, easy-going Santa

Barbara, I'd returned to the formal, always perfect-looking, French people. Even their scarves looked as though they'd taken an hour to perfect every last fold. How did they manage to look so put-together ALL the time, cook delicious, healthy meals, and speed walk in three-inch heels? Everything seemed so effortless for them.

I learned in Conversation Group that the word "comfort" was not in the French vocabulary, or even translatable into French. No joke! We Americans love comfort. We love our big, comfy, down-filled couches and our Ugg boots, our workout wear and running shoes, and we'll wear them all day. The French prefer words like "chic" and "sexy" to the word "comfortable." French style is not about comfort. They don't really even understand why it's so desirable for Americans. Chic is a way of life. French men are not scared to say these words either. They not only say them, they too try to be sexy and chic, as well.

"Comfort? What is that?" a French, male friend asked me once, quite earnestly.

"You know, forget the shave for once, and don't style your hair—(Gasp!) Try a good old tee shirt and unpressed pants—(Another gasp!) Maybe a pair of flip-flops—" Nope. Never going to happen!

But back to the women: Another exasperating thing is their emphasis on lingerie. French women do not just look good on the outside; they look good underneath their clothes too! I guess I've always been a low maintenance girl, but my faded cotton panties and functional, comfortable bras will never cut it in Paris. I was surrounded with billboards and advertisements telling me how inadequate my undergarments were. I couldn't avoid them.

French girls are taught at an early age to always wear their lacy best, not just on special occasions. They spend tons of money on their undergarments. Bras and panties need to match. Sleepwear does not mean an oversized tee shirt. In conversations about this subject with French friends, I learned that beautiful undergarments are not worn for one's lover, but for oneself. (I mean the other is also true, but they believe that it is a pleasure all women deserve—wearing pretty things close to their body.) So I went shopping—and had a lot of fun—buying some pretty, new ensembles. Dave wasn't too upset with "the new me," either.

It also irritated me how effortlessly my French friends cooked. Gastronomy is serious business, even in one's home kitchen. Eating (and drinking wine) is such an important part of their culture that cooking good food is not a choice. But somehow, they don't spend all day in the kitchen. Most French women work outside the home, and then prepare fabulous meals in thirty minutes flat. There are rules one must follow: One does not eat standing up. One does not eat "on the go." The French stop everything to eat, and they eat properly. While I could appreciate this to some extent, I was really craving a "double-double" from an In-n-Out Burger drive-through!

October 14

I just found out about a HUGE Paris secret today: Picard is a frozen food grocery store! I've walked by these stores many times, but I never thought to go in. I thought "Picard, Les Surgeles," sounded like "surgery." I thought it was some kind of medical supply store. The rows of white freezers and staff walking around in white lab coats actually scared me. I didn't really want to know what was in those iceboxes! No, there was nothing inviting or obvious about it. But Dave figured it out. He went in to investigate and came home to tell me. Picard's frozen food is apparently so high quality that even chefs at famous cooking schools buy their pastry crusts there, and Parisians serve Picard food at their fancy dinner parties (although they would never admit that). Haha! Salmon in puff pastry (it's even shaped like a fish) was on our table tonight! Yep, I just defrosted it and voila, dinner was a work of art! Now I know the shortcut

*those Parisian women all know! Dinners in Paris are
going to be so much easier from now on!*

Everyone always wonders: "How do French women stay
so thin while eating so much dessert and cheese and bread and
wine?" Well, I've got the answer. They do eat those things, but
they eat like small birds or rabbits. If they eat cheese, it's a little
piece of cheese, on a little piece of bread. They drink a lot of tiny
little coffees, and they eat a lot of leaves. When I say leaves, I am
talking about lettuce—a very important part of the Parisian
woman's diet. The different kinds of leaves are many. The
lettuces in the produce stands and even most grocery stores are
beautiful. Leaves will not make a person fat no matter how many
she eats. Furthermore, chocolate is considered healthy. The
French truly believe in the powerful, positive effects of
chocolate—but only a very little piece of chocolate each day...
that is ALL one needs. And, as I've already said, French women
do not snack, and they walk a lot, and they do a lot of stairs (in
their high heels)!

October 15

*Brainstorm! I finally now know that my clothes dryer
does NOT have a setting for dry. Honestly, I couldn't
figure it out. It was a conundrum. I tried every setting
many times, but NEVER ever did things come out
completely dry, and now I know why. Since we've been
sharing the laundry room downstairs with the owner, I
asked her about it, and she looked puzzled and said,
"Why would you want your clothes dry? Then you
can't press them... "*

"OH!!!" I finally get it!!!

The obsession with *pressing* (ironing) is so important to
Parisians that I would say that it's part of their culture (and
therefore my culture shock). There should be a warning sign
when you arrive in Paris that says: "If you don't like ironing, you

188

cannot live here." They iron everything, even their underwear. I'm not kidding. I promise. Granted, I come from a place where many people don't even own an iron—and they're proud of that fact. (My French friends just gasped.) But, honestly, if you went around Paris in wrinkled clothes, you'd look like a slob, and you'd feel very self-conscious.

And I still couldn't understand how they all kept their clothes so clean, pill, and lint free? I swear I rarely saw a spec of lint or a wrinkle on anyone. I was becoming quite obsessed with the French ideal of perfection. It was truly phenomenal how they kept their clothes brand-new looking all the time. Being the curious and investigative person that I am, I had to figure it out. And I DID—at least somewhat, but it was a start! There WAS a special tool that Parisians use, and non-Parisians don't know about. No, it's not the tape wheel, although those are more than plentiful in French homes, there's another tool—a pilling remover—which has one side for cashmere and one side for "less sensitive" wool (as they call it). This cheap, little, plastic tool is sold in dry cleaning shops. It only costs around €6, but it works astonishingly well.

At my Conversation Group meeting we discussed the "best macarons in Paris," a popular topic here. (Just to clarify: macarons are not the same thing as macaroons. It's not an alternative spelling. They're both cookies, but the similarities end there. Macarons are the multi-colored, meringue-based, sandwich cookies, and macaroons are the dense, coconut cookies, which in France are called *congolais*.) I had been wondering about that for a long time.

The two places my group argued were the best were Ladurée and Pierre Hermé. So after a fantastic school tour of the Opera Garnier, my friends Maria, Farah and I went to try the macarons at Ladurée—the original store on rue Royale. Farah could not believe I hadn't been there yet. The line for lunch was long, but it was worth the wait. We all ordered the club sandwiches with four French fries (really, that's all they gave us, but they were four, large French fries), and afterward we waited in line to buy macarons (in the most gorgeous boxes I've ever seen). I picked caramel, rose, coffee, raspberry, lemon, and chocolate, and took them home for Dave and the kids to try.

I never really liked macarons before. I thought they were too sweet. But after trying them at Ladurée, I'm now a believer. This was the equivalent to the over-the-top experience I had with Dave at my birthday lunch, where the appetizer was €38 and I said, "Really, how good can it be? It can't be worth it." But it was, and so were the macarons! They were delicious. But I still planned to try them at Pierre Hermé to compare.

People say travel broadens your horizons, but travel usually means a short stay. Travel gives you glimpses of other cultures and environments, but it takes time to have real discovery. That was why we decided to stay in France for our vacations the second year, instead of traveling to other countries. We wanted to gain as much understanding of the French culture as we could. So, when our Santa Barbara friends (the country mice) asked us if we'd like to join them on a trip to Normandy, Brittany, and the Mont St. Michel, all in northwestern France for Touissant (the first of the school vacations), that was exactly what we did! And, lucky for us, they had already planned the whole trip, so all we had to do was join them. We were super-excited to travel with them, and since Mike is a history buff, we knew it'd be great to be with them in these areas where there was so much American history.

October 26

We're at our first stop in Normandy at the Château de Vouilly, a charming Château used by the press in World War II. We met up with the country mice here and got to watch eighty cows get milked at super-speed right after we arrived. After that, we found our rooms (upstairs at opposite ends of the hallway).

4:00 p.m.

I'm in our room now. Strangers are staring at me from portraits on the walls as I write this. There are a few

cats running around, several old urns (I hope there's
nothing in them… yikes), and some big windows,
looking out over grassy fields that go on forever. I've
never stayed anywhere like this before. The owners are
very friendly and they like to share stories with us (in
French, so I only understand a little, but everyone else
understands).

11:22 p.m.

We all went out to dinner tonight and had the best
French onion soup EVER, and our first taste of
Calvados, the apple liqueur that Normandy is famous
for. After that, we walked through the town, went
Calvados tasting (the adults), and bought some to take
home. We're back at the Château now, and I just put
the kids to bed. Dave, Mike and Harper are siting
down in the living room sipping Calvados and
discussing plans for tomorrow. I wish I could join
them, but I'm too tired. I'm going to sleep.

When we woke up the next morning, we dressed and
headed down to the communal dining area. All the guests sat
together in a big room, which was the pressroom in World War
II. There was memorabilia on the walls, old typewriters and
newspapers—real copies from the war. The owner showed us a
real World War II Jeep that he had in the garage.

After breakfast and checking out the gorgeous Château
grounds, including a real moat, which the kids loved, we headed
over to see the D-day Beaches and the American Cemetery. The
weather was cold, but sunny and clear. We stopped first at Point
du Hoc, a cliff top location by Omaha Beach, which was a point
of attack by the United States army rangers in the war, Mike told
us. The kids found the bomb holes, bunkers, and arsenals a fun
playground, but the scene was an intense reminder of the war—
well preserved and real.

Next we went to the American Cemetery and the Musée du Débarquement. We took everyone on a somber walk through the hundreds of crosses and stars that lined the cemetery. The kids asked many history questions, which thankfully Mike was able to answer. We walked down the cliff from the cemetery to Omaha Beach, the location of the worst battle of D-Day. It was bittersweet because it was such a lovely beach, but all we could think of was the boats coming in, and the battle that ensued there. We kept imagining the soldiers, hiding in the bunkers, with guns aimed at the men coming off the boats, headed for the shore. It must have been terrifying. Being there made it seem so real. When a rainbow peeked out, the light between the clouds made the whole scene seem ethereal. After Omaha Beach, we went to Arromanches to see the remains of one of the British harbors used as a landing spot for D-Day.

Then, we headed up to Bayeux, a city about twenty minutes inland, to see the Bayeux tapestry. Julia had studied it in school, so she was excited to see the real thing. The Bayeux tapestry, a two hundred and thirty foot long embroidered cloth, describes the events leading up to the 1066 Norman invasion of England, as well as the invasion itself. The main characters were William the Conqueror, who led the Normans, and Harold Godwinson, the recently crowned King of England, who led the English.

The tapestry showed the monastery of Mont St-Michel (which was a destination on our agenda), and Haley's Comet, which people in the Middle Ages were sure was a warning of impending doom. With child-friendly and adult-friendly English audio guides in hand, we all enjoyed the story and learning about this part of European history.

To lighten the history lesson, we stopped at a caramel factory to buy some delicious, salted caramel candies. And for our last stop, on our way out of Normandy, we spent some time at a dairy processing plant, where the kids got to see how cheese and butter are made. We all found it very interesting!

We said *au revoir* to our kind hosts at the Château de Vouilly, and headed further west to St. Malo in Brittany. St. Malo is a tiny port city with a six-meter wide wall around it. It felt really old. We had booked different hotels than the country mice, so we each went to check in and planned to meet up later. Needless to say, the first thing our kids wanted to do was to check out the wall surrounding the city. It was freezing cold, but that wasn't going to stop them, which meant us too! We walked around the perimeter at the top of the high wall, where we could see the crashing waves and a fortress out in the sea. Dave explained that it must be low tide because the rocky causeway to the fortress was showing. When the kids heard that, they begged to go out and see it. The wind was blowing, and it was really, really cold, but again, we couldn't let that stop us from adventuring. Dave carried Katherine on his shoulders, while Matt and Julia rock climbed and explored the tide pools along the way.

When we got back, we met up with the country mice and we all went to the museum of St. Malo. There we learned about the notorious French corsairs and pirates. What a surprise it was to hear that Harper was actually a descendent of the most famous pirate of St. Malo. She had never told us this! We took some pictures of her daughters next to their great, great, great relatives, admiring the family resemblance and familial smirk. When we told people she was related to him, we got free things everywhere.

After two days exploring St. Malo, we headed to our last stop, the Abby of Mont-Saint Michel. The Mont-Saint Michel is a marvel of medieval architecture, originally built in the eighth century. It's a small island, half a mile out in the ocean, also connected by a causeway, which is covered and inaccessible at high tide. Luckily, we arrived during low tide! It was getting dark when we arrived, which made the Mont very spooky-looking. Spending Halloween there was going to be quite a dramatic experience.

October 31

We had a fun Halloween celebration tonight. We met up in Harper and Mike's hotel room, and Harper tied a scarf around her head like a fortune-teller, rubbed the "magic pumpkin," and told the kids what it foretold about their futures. The "magic pumpkin" was actually a huge, heavy pumpkin we bought at an outdoor market earlier today, and took turns carrying up the many stairs to the hotel.

Halloween *à la française:* Mike told scary ghost stories, found on the Internet, in the dark of the hotel room, with only the spooky glow of the computer. *(Oooh!)* Then the kids searched for Halloween candy we'd hidden in the small cemetery, just outside our hotel rooms. Surprisingly, the kids weren't at all frightened walking through the cemetery, but I thought it was creepy. Then we enjoyed some of the special, fifty-year-old Calvados that Mike and Harper had bought in Normandy. It was delicious! (Aged Calvados is definitely better than the stuff we bought!) Altogether, it was a spirited, fun, and delicious night we'll all remember forever.

November 2008

The night after we got back from our trip, Katherine got really sick. (It's no wonder being out in that weather.) Dave was back in Santa Barbara again, so I was on my own. It was unbelievably cold in Paris, and I could not imagine how I was going to get Katherine to the doctor's office. Her fever was so high that she was hysterical, screaming out in pain. I had never seen her like that before, nor any of my kids for that matter. I didn't know what to do. I started to panic. I called my downstairs neighbor, who said she would call *SOS Medecin* for me, which is the equivalent of calling 911 for a doctor.

A nice, female, Indian doctor arrived at my apartment within thirty minutes. My neighbor came up to make sure I understood everything, because the doctor might not speak English (yes, another sweet, helpful Parisian). The doctor said that Katherine had tonsillitis, sinusitis, and an ear infection, all at the same time. No wonder she was screaming.

She had medications in her bag, which she was not supposed to give Katherine apparently, but she felt so bad for her, that she decided to bend the rules. (Once again, rules are subjective.) She also prescribed five other medications that I needed to get from the pharmacy. *Yikes,* I thought, *how much is that going to cost?* There was a steroid, an antibiotic, aspirin, acetaminophen, and one other thing I can't remember. The French have different ways of treating illnesses than we do. We use a lot of ibuprofen, but they don't believe in it. My sweet neighbor offered to go to the pharmacy for me in the morning, for which I was very grateful. She picked up the prescriptions, all five of which cost only €15. That wasn't the copay—that was the total cost. The doctor's house call was only €100. Wow! We were really enjoying the benefits of the French health care system.

November 5

*Katherine woke up feeling better. Thank goodness—
just in time for her birthday party this weekend. We've
planned a "boum" (a dance party), since last year our
apartment was too small for almost any party, let
alone a dance party! Plus, Katherine had only two
friends at this time last year. Now, she has lots of
friends, and our apartment is definitely big enough for
a party. Julia and Matt told her all about "boums."
They're very popular with kids in Paris. They
LOVE to dance. Dave brought a disco ball and
strobe lights back from the U.S., which we set up in
the living room, and we've asked all the kids to dress
up in disco attire or "rigolo" (in a silly costume).*

Katherine's dance party was a huge success. Some of the
kids only spoke French, so Katherine had to do some translating
for me, but it was easy for her. It surprised us that Katherine had
non-English-speaking friends! One boy (the one she danced the
Tango with at the end-of-year show) walked into the party with a
big black wig on his head. What a ham! He was so adorable. I
welcomed the French parents at the door and tried to invite
them in, but none dared. That's not normally done in Paris.
Parents drop their kids at the door for parties.

The kids danced and played games. Katherine taught her
friends two American dances, the Macarena and the Hokey
Pokey. If you know those dances, I needn't add that everyone
caught on to the catchy choruses, laughed, and wiggled, and had
a great time.

Her big gift from us was a shiny red bike. Formerly, it
was Matthew's old bike, but Dave painted it while he was in
Santa Barbara and brought it back in a suitcase! Yep, he took the
bike apart, and put it back together to fit it in the suitcase—
another MacGyver maneuver.

November 8

We've lived in Paris for a total of thirteen months and I can finally say that the "Paris Intimidation Factor" is finally diminishing. I'm feeling a lot more confident. Somehow, the words are coming out of my mouth in French, without having to translate them in my head beforehand. That's NOT to say I still don't have experiences that set me back. Everything can be intimidating if I let it, but I'm not afraid to try now.

November 9

I have to go to Julia's parent/teacher conferences alone tonight. Dave won't be back in time. Each meeting is five minutes long (seriously)! So… if I can find each classroom (it's a big school, and I've never been to any of her classrooms before), and I'm on time, and the teacher is on schedule… then we'll get five whole minutes together (most likely in French). I know some of them don't speak English, but if there's a problem, I'm sure they'll find a way to make me understand. I don't have any major issues to bring up, so I'm not that worried.

First I met with Julia's math teacher, then her French teacher, and then her history/geography teacher. By the time I got to the English meeting, I was running late. This was due to the teachers running late and additionally, I could not find the building. The English teacher said I was out of luck because I was late.

"It's not my fault," I said, realizing I sounded like a typical middle school student. I waited a little while by the door, and she squeezed me in when someone else arrived late. (Understand that this was all very stressful, with everyone waiting and watching the meetings from the doorways, anticipating their five-minute time slot, and not knowing if they

197

should skip it and run to the next one, etc.) In the end, however, I found all of Julia's teachers very nice, optimistic, and quite motivational. We were able to understand each other pretty well. (Also, when I attempted to speak French, they typically resorted to English, realizing that their English was always better than my French.) They really seemed to care about Julia. I was happy with the education she was getting in Paris... and who would've thought I could get all that out of five-minute conferences?

November 15

Today I went on a tour of the fabulous Musée Carnavalet, the Museum of the History of Paris. Our group had a very knowledgeable, English-speaking guide, and it was super (my new favorite "Franglish" word). This large museum is in the Marais (the 4th arrondissement of Paris). It has a vast collection of art and historical objects from the prehistoric era to modern times, and it really gave me a feeling for how Paris evolved.

My favorite display was a model of the Île de la Cité, the bigger of the two natural islands that sits in the middle of the Seine. It showed the Île de la Cité as it was in the 16th century and how the sayings "rive droite" and "rive gauche" (right bank and left bank) came about. The guide said to pretend the island is a boat and you are standing on the front facing forward (like Kate Winslet did in the movie Titanic). When you do that, the left side of the boat is the "rive gauche" and the right side is the "rive droite"—much easier than north, south, east and west, at least for me!

Dave got back from the U.S. late that evening, after the conferences. The next day we woke up to the most beautiful light, softly illuminating the apartment building across the street, bright blue skies with fake-looking, puffy clouds, and the street cleaners busily cleaning. It was Saturday in Paris. Julia headed out to the bakery across the street to get a (hopefully still hot) *baguette tradition*—the thicker crusted, chewier type of baguette, which is our favorite, and a loaf of bread for toast.

She asked me, "How do you say 'sliced' again?"

"*Pan tranche*," I said, and she was out the door.

Breakfast, homework, and a walk down the street for some groceries—a typical Saturday for a family in Paris. Julia was invited to breakfast with her friend Talia at Angelina's, probably the most famous breakfast place in Paris. Talia's mom offered to take them to the Champs Elysées to cruise around for a couple of hours after breakfast. I walked her to Angelina's on rue de Rivoli, just across the Tuileries, a ten-minute walk from our apartment. We crossed the river, avoiding the local beggar who hung out on the Pont de Solferino, stopped to listen to some music by the sax player who played at the river entrance to the Tuileries, dropped a couple of coins in his can, and then crossed through the traffic of people walking toward the Louvre. We were a little early, so we window-shopped for ten minutes on the rue de Rivoli, checking out the trinkets and tee shirts in the souvenir shops. I made a mental note to come back there for stocking stuffers for the kids. Julia's friend arrived and we all gave our now well-established ritual of *les bises* (kisses on both cheeks). After that, I headed back home.

Next stop: taking Katherine to her friend's birthday party. Katherine put on her *déguise* (costume), which was required according to the invitation (and a common request for younger children's birthday parties). Matthew was going to have a friend sleep over, so he was trying to finish his studying. I helped Katherine practice memorizing her weekly French poem, a twenty-line poem/song called "*Maison Citrouille*" (Pumpkin House), where she had to stomp, clap, and snap her fingers, and *clack, clack, clack* (snap, snap, snap) for the chorus.

Finally, I took Katherine to her party at an apartment behind the Hôtel des Invalides, a complex of buildings all relating to the military history of France. *(Side note: Last weekend she went to a birthday party at the Musée des Arts Decoratifs in the left*

199

wing of the Louvre. Not bad, eh? Better than Chuck E. Cheese for a six year old's birthday party!) Meanwhile, Dave and Matthew waited for Matt's friend to get dropped off. When he arrived, they packed the rolling, shopping bag up with all the rollerblades (they were too heavy to carry, and it was too hard to rollerblade on cobblestones), and they walked over to the concrete area near Les Invalides to play hockey. Unfortunately, Matthew's friend fell within the first ten minutes and had to be picked up by his mother, my friend Emma. (Later, we found out the poor guy broke his arm that day—on our watch. Ugh!)

After dropping off Katherine, I went looking for napkins with "designs" on them (an obscure, six-year-old description), which she had just informed me she needed for school on Monday. (Thanks for the notice!) And why, I wondered, did there need to be "designs" on them? What kind of "designs"? Nothing, including Monoprix, which is like the French version of Target, would be open on Sunday, so I needed to find them before the stores closed. It was getting dark and it was drizzling. Luckily, I found some napkins with teacups on them, close by, in a little bookshop on rue St. Dominique. I hoped that would work! Then I texted Julia, "Are you still on the Champs or back at Talia's?"

"Still at the Champs. We're watching a James Bond movie... met up with some boys from school—" *How fun to be a twelve year old girl living in Paris,* I thought.

A chic brown coat and tall boots in a window display caught my eye. The weather had just gotten cold and last year's clothes were pretty worn-looking. They'd definitely gotten a lot of use last winter! So, while I waited to pick Julia up, I explored the new styles of the season. When Julia's movie ended, she texted me, and I went to pick her up by the Gaumont movie theater on the Champs Elysées. It was dark and cold and the girls were sitting in a café having *thé au lait* (tea with milk). *How grown up they looked!* Then Julia and I walked down the stairs to the Métro and went home.

Meanwhile, Dave and Matthew picked up Katherine from her friend's birthday party, and we all met back at home for some good old American cheeseburgers and French fries. Julia and Dave made a strong and determined effort to finish *The Hunchback of Notre Dame* (in French), while Kate, Matt & Max (Matthew's friend), watched *Camp Rock,* an American video that Katherine had received from her grandparents. That was a typical Saturday in Paris for us.

Then, it was Thanksgiving time again. We did not want to reenact the Paris Hard Rock Café fiasco from the prior year. So instead, we decided to celebrate with our dear French friends, Valerie and Jean Pierre, and their children. Jean Pierre was Dave's friend from childhood. He was the one Dave did an exchange with when he was fifteen. Jean Pierre came to Santa Barbara, and Dave went to Paris. Jean Pierre and Valerie even had an oven that was big enough to cook a turkey in, which was unusual for a Paris apartment. But, when I found out there was a store called Thanksgiving in Paris where we could order a pre-cooked, pre-stuffed turkey, we decided to do that instead. *(Side note: There are so many Americans in Paris that there's actually enough demand for this store.)* There was also another store I knew about, called The Real McCoy, which imported many of the other American items necessary for a traditional Thanksgiving dinner, but they charged "a wing and a leg" for them. (That's another one of Dave's jokes). Luckily, Dave had brought back most of the things we needed for our feast on his last trip home: two boxes of stuffing, sweet potatoes, marshmallows, canned pumpkin, evaporated milk, and fried onions for the string bean casserole.

November 27

Thanksgiving was a huge success! We cooked everything at Valerie and Jean Pierre's apartment. Valerie picked up the turkey from Thanksgiving in Paris, and we all enjoyed the dinner together. It's funny how some things were lost in translation though— stuffing, for example: Jean Pierre, Valerie and their kids weren't too sure about the stuffing. They just couldn't understand the concept of it… chopped up soggy bread? (I guess when you put it that way, it does sound a bit weird!) Also, they had never tasted pumpkin pie before, but that they liked. It's always great to see them and reminisce about old times. For us, Thanksgiving in America was always a warm, wonderful time, but I have to say this French Thanksgiving felt just as wonderful, despite the fact that our "real" family was an ocean away.

December 2008

December 6

Took the kids to the Île de la Cité to visit Notre Dame Cathedral today. We went up a very narrow, winding staircase (three hundred eighty-six steps to the bell tower, the kids counted), to see the gargoyles up close—what scary-looking creatures! After that, we went to the nearby Cathedral of Sainte Chapelle. We bought a coloring book filled with pictures of the cathedral's stained glass windows. When the kids found the window with the corresponding design in the book, they colored it in with the same colors. It made the tour a lot more engaging for them.

December 11

I need to plan Matthew's birthday party. It's tough having a birthday ten days after Christmas. Everyone's usually away on vacation, so, we're doing it the weekend after instead. What can I do with a bunch of ten-year-old boys in the winter? I know I DON'T want them running around inside our apartment. Matt suggested bowling, ice-skating, laser tag, or paint ball. Hmmm…

December 15

I went on a tour at the Grand Palais today called "Picasso and the Grand Masters." I had never been inside the Grand Palais before, nor did I know that there were temporary exhibits there. Anyway, it was

*fabulous and worth fighting the crowds. There were
over two hundred works from the most prestigious
public and private collections in the world. Apparently,
a bomb scare sent everyone out of the Grand Palais
earlier today. (I saw them, freezing, without their coats
in the Métro station, and I couldn't figure out what
was going on.) But fortunately, there was no bomb,
and we were able to go on the tour!*

December 20

*I'm still learning more lessons (some, the hard way),
such as: do not bring flowers as a hostess gift, because
flowers can mean specific things to a French person.
Tonight, I was so proud to present my French friend
Marie with some gorgeously wrapped snapdragons at
her Christmas party. Later, I found out that
snapdragons mean I'm full of desire. No wonder she
had such a weird look on her face when she received
them! Oh my gosh!*

More about hostess gifts: we learned that chocolate is the
best choice—and the fancier, the better. Fancy teas are also a
great gift. One should not normally bring wine, unless you're
asked to. The host and hostess like to pick the wine for their
party, and the wines are usually specific to each course that will
be served. If you bring wine, they might feel obliged to serve it,
and it might not go with their meal.

Then, at my Conversation Group last week, I learned
that it isn't polite to pour your own wine at someone else's
home. It's the host's responsibility to make sure his guests are
amply supplied with wine. If he doesn't notice, you have to wait!
(Again, that WAITING thing!)

December 23

*At Conversation Group today I was really not happy
to hear that women who pour their own wine are
usually considered alcoholics in Paris. And now I'm
remembering our lunch at Valerie and Jean Pierre's
house, when I asked Valerie if she wanted more wine
(our glasses were empty and the wine bottle was right
next to me), and she kind of giggled. Ah geez!!!*

We've been learning other lessons too—such as not
piling up food on your plate—because if you don't finish
everything, you will offend your host. Then, there's "French
timing." If you're not at least ten minutes late to a party, you will
be too early. I once came early to a Conversation Group meeting
at a French friend's house. I think I was ten minutes early. I
thought we'd become close enough that I could help her set up,
make coffee, etc. When her teenage daughter answered the door
and said her Mom was still sleeping, I wanted to crawl into a
hole. I offered to come back, but she wouldn't let me leave. She
woke her mom, who said she had to get up anyway, so no
worries, but she wasn't expecting anyone so "early." *(Ugh again!)*

We spent our second Christmas at home in our beautiful
Paris apartment. We knew the French traditions by then, and we
were all feeling melancholy that this would be our last Christmas
in Paris. We went ice-skating at Montparnasse, and again at the
Hotel de Ville outdoor rink. We drank lots of hot tea, steeped in
Dave's stylish, black iron teapot that I bought him at Mariages
Frères, a famous teahouse in Paris. We bundled up and went out
to the festive holiday markets nearby in Saint-Germain-des-Prés.
We bought another mini-tree. We were invited to dinner parties
and cocktail parties, and we felt like we belonged in Paris. It
finally felt like home.

December 27

*Christmas Eve was a very special night. We dressed
up and went with several friends to the late mass at the*

*American Cathedral. The organ music and Christmas
choir songs made me cry, which then made Julia cry. I
tried not to, but I cry easily (and so does she). It was
just so beautiful and so Christmasy!*

After Christmas, we took off for yet another trip.
Karolina, one of my best girlfriends, invited us to her vacation
home in a small town called Imperia on the Italian Riviera, just
over the border from France.

"I didn't know you had a house in Italy," I said. She had
never mentioned it. But when I told her we didn't have a trip
planned for Christmas break she said, "Well, we could always go
to our house in Italy. It's not that exciting but it's right by
Monaco. So we can go to Monte Carlo if you like, and there's
plenty of room for all of us."

"Are you kidding? Sounds awesome! Let's do it!" I said.

So we rented a big French car, a Peugeot 607—not the
best car for getting around narrow village streets, but we weren't
thinking about that when they said they'd "upgrade" us to a
bigger car. *How nice*, we thought. *A bigger car sounded good.* We had
no idea that the corkscrew village roads would be so narrow, and
the turns so sharp, that it would be WAY too serpentine for
such a big car. They were probably laughing at us—silly
Americans who love big cars!

Nicole and Gerard's house in Provence was right on our
route to Imperia, so we planned to stop for a night with them.
We hadn't seen them in a while, so we thought this was a great
opportunity. However, we soon realized that driving out of Paris
over Christmas break was not the smartest plan! Everyone
seemed to have the same idea. It was complete gridlock. And
then, as we sat idling on the freeway and the TGV sped past us
at over a hundred miles an hour, Dave and I looked at each
other despondently. What were we thinking? Why didn't we take
the train? When we got to Dijon—which was normally three
hours from Paris—we realized it had taken us five, and we didn't
think we were going to make it. We were only a third of the way
to Provence, and we couldn't arrive at Nicole and Gerard's in

the middle of the night. We seriously debated going back to Paris and skipping the whole thing, but just about then, the traffic disappeared, and Dave was able to speed. Unfortunately, we couldn't tell if we were getting speeding tickets, because there are secret cameras all along the freeway, but we didn't care at that point. We just wanted to get there. Remarkably, we made it to Nicole and Gerard's house in time for a late dinner (and another long and yummy dinner it was).

December 30

Today was the epitome of the "French country experience." After breakfast, we headed out for a hike with Nicole and Gerard. We drove to the starting point, just in front of their neighbor's house. The neighbor saw us outside and invited us in. He offered us homemade tapenades—strongly seasoned spreads that you put on slices of crusty baguette—very popular in the south of France. One was eggplant and garlic, another creamy tuna, another anchovy, olive oil and garlic, and, lastly, the pièce de résistance was his foie gras—each in its own little hand-made glass container. He kept finding more and more day-old bread, which he softened on the wood-burning stove, and the kids kept accepting. They thought it was all delicious! He also served his son's homemade peach wine. He was very proud of it because apparently, you need a special chemist's license to make fortified wine in France, and not many people have one. He was charmed by our French-speaking, American children who loved his strong French tapenades.

After lunch, we rolled ourselves out of his house and finally took our short hike along the streets of Fayence. Then, we said goodbye to Nicole and Gerard and headed to Italy, driving through Nice and Cannes, and then over the border to the Italian Riviera to the seaside town of Imperia. We saw old fountains in the crossroads and old castles along the sides of the road. We drove by small Provençal-style restaurants and boutiques, which we wanted to stop in, but we didn't have time. We were meeting Karolina and Andreas in Ventimiglia—a town on the French-Italian border, so we could follow them to their vacation house in Imperia.

When we got to Ventimiglia, Andreas joined Dave, Julia, and Katherine in our rental car, while Matthew and I went with Karolina in her Mini Cooper. Andreas and Karolina are German, and they are great drivers, but, like many Germans, they pride themselves on driving fast. The race was on between husband and wife, and Matthew and I held on for dear life.

"S#*%!" Karolina cursed when she missed the freeway onramp. She thought about backing up on the freeway, but when we looked at the road above us, there were police watching us—quite amused! Karolina sped even faster to try to make up the time. Dave said Andreas was laughing hysterically when he saw her miss the turn. He knew how furious she'd be. Luckily, we all arrived safely—almost exactly at the same time—at their cute house up in the hills overlooking the ocean where Kellen and Louie, their boys, were waiting. We all got dressed up and went out to an authentic Italian dinner in Old Town, very impressed that they all spoke Italian too—these Europeans, so multilingual!

Julia could hardly wait to get to Monte Carlo, the land of the mega rich, the next morning. We walked through the luxury stores in town while the boys salivated over the world's most exclusive cars at a car show down by the harbor. Ferraris and Lamborghinis were everywhere on the streets, and I have never seen so many mink coats in my life. It was just as I imagined it.

We picked up some sandwiches and met the boys for lunch in a park—where we were not allowed to touch anything. There were guards everywhere, and they were even stricter than in Paris. We tried to take the kids into the casino, but they weren't allowed there either. Instead, we went down to see the "super-yachts" in the marina. I was sure some were cruise ships, but they were all privately owned. They were as big as mansions.

It was quite impressive. I also noticed that there was a framed picture of the Prince of Monaco in every single building. We wondered if that's required, or if they're just emphatically loyal.

After our day in Monte Carlo, we drove back to Imperia and shopped for dinner in Old Town. The town of Imperia is not touristy at all, so we really got the feel for living in an old, Italian village. We bought some fresh pasta called *trofie*—two to three inch, thin, twisted and rolled pasta that's traditional for that area. We also bought fresh pesto and a couple of baguettes for garlic bread and took it all back to the house. That night we cooked up a great meal. We made a fire in the fireplace, talked, and relaxed into the evening, while the kids all played raucously downstairs.

The next day we hiked from their house to the terraced countryside of Imperia. We investigated an old church along the road that was built in the 1100's—things are so old there! Then, in the afternoon we headed down to the local beach. It was very charming with striped cabanas, a cute, casual, seafood restaurant, a pier, and a harbor over the breakwater. The smell of the salty sea air was just what we needed. We all breathed it in, which made us nostalgic, as the ocean is such a big part of our lives in Santa Barbara. The kids clambered around on the rocks, slid down the sand walls, and played in the sand.

New Year's Eve was the next night, and we decided it would be fun to take the kids down to the beach restaurant for dinner. It was pitch dark and pouring rain when we went out to get in the cars. It was pretty hard to see. Accidentally, we swiped the side of the rental car on the wall on the way down the driveway, not realizing how big our "upgrade" really was. It was pretty minor, so we decided not to worry about it for the night and enjoy our evening.

It was cozy and warm inside the small restaurant, with the cold, pouring rain outside. We sat at a table by a window and watched the rain outside on the beach. A man came through the restaurant, selling party favors and hats for New Year's Eve. He did several magic tricks, which delighted the kids. After an excellent fish dinner, we headed back to their house. The kids went to sleep downstairs but Dave and I stayed up with our hosts, drank Limoncello and some other new spirits we were unfamiliar with, and at midnight, we all toasted the New Year 2009.

January 2009

It's hardly surprising at this point to say that it was time for another "mis-adventure." We said goodbye to our friends and set out on our drive back to Paris. Dave pulled up to the pump at a French gas station, about an hour from the French/Italian border, to fill up the rental car. With so many distractions—like the kids arguing in the car, the scrape on the car, and our directions back to Paris, it was no wonder that Dave wasn't paying close attention to what he was doing. He was standing by the pump, the tank half-full, when he realized it.

"Oh no!" Dave said.

He looked at me, and a lump formed in my throat.

"I think I just put the wrong kind of gas in the car."

"No, you didn't," I said incredulously. It was New Year's Day. We were in the middle of nowhere. I resisted all thoughts of how to kill my husband.

"I could siphon it with my mouth if we drive over there—where no one can see me," he said. "It's totally illegal though."

Great! I thought. *Getting arrested might be fun!* "How about we call a tow truck instead?"

Dave didn't want to tell the gas station attendant what had happened—in case he decided to do the illegal "MacGyver maneuver"—but they were watching us from inside the store. Dave went in to ask whom we could call for help. They suggested a tow-truck service, which said they could come in an hour. Unfortunately, it was going to cost double since it was a holiday. *(Sigh)* They'd have to tow the car to their service station to siphon the gas out. *(Ah, geez… really?)*

So we waited. It started raining—hailing actually—so we ducked into the station store, checking out the souvenirs, and buying candy to pass the time. It seemed to take forever. When the tow truck finally arrived, the driver told us all to get into our car and ride to the service station on the flatbed of the tow truck. Now this was truly an adventure! They would never have us do that in the U.S.

We rode in our car on the flatbed of the tow truck—windows totally fogged up—to the station. The mechanic successfully got the gas out of our car, fixed everything up, and even gave us a gallon of gas to get back to the other gas station. For around €500 we were back on our way, a little worse for wear, but Dave, the guilt-ridden but eternal optimist said that "since he had paid for the American Express trip insurance, the whole bill might be paid for." (I hoped so... and luckily, it turned out it was!)

When we finally arrived back at our apartment, it looked as though a magic wand had been waved over Paris. Everything was enchanted. A white blanket of snow covered the streets and the cars. We hadn't seen snow in Paris since we'd been there. We looked down from our third floor window (we moved back upstairs before we left for vacation), and smiled at the tiny Smart cars, parked two in a single spot, and covered with snow. We looked down to the church and the snow-covered park at the end of the street. It was silent and magical. We all felt a new sense of awe looking out at our beautiful neighborhood.

January 2

For Matthew's birthday party, we've decided on bowling at the rink below the Arc de Triomphe. Of course, he wants an "American birthday cake" for his party. Oh, easy, one would think: Get a cheap box of cake mix and some pre-made frosting at the grocery store and voila! However, an American cake is only easy in America. They don't sell boxed cakes in Paris. I looked up recipes for similar types of cakes, but I couldn't be sure if they'd taste good. The measurements are not easy to convert, and even after more than a year, the different flours, sugars, baking sodas, and powders still confound me. I can never remember which is which. I'm going to head over to "The Real McCoy" and see if they carry American cake mix.

Later

Just got back and sure enough, they had good old Betty Crocker cake mix! So for around €10 for the cake mix and €16 for two jars of frosting, I can bake Matthew an American birthday cake! At the current exchange rate that's about $35. Of course, I could buy an ornate, professionally decorated, French cake for that price. But NO, Matthew wants an American cake! I snuck in some American candy while there too (for me—oops, I meant for party favors, haha). I cannot believe I just paid that much for a box of Betty Crocker cake mix and frosting! It would cost $4.00 in the states!!! Oh well.

Six boys met us at the bowling alley for the party. They bowled, laughed, and sat on each other like puppies. They didn't really care who won—it was more of a comedy show—since none of them was very good at bowling. There were only four plastic bucket seats to sit in while they waited their turn, so it was also a game of musical chairs. When one boy got up, someone else raced into his seat. (Fun, fun!)

I was a little nervous about taking all the boys on the Métro to our apartment for the cake because I didn't want to lose anyone (remember, still no cell phones). I imagined them all running to different cars, like my kids always did. Fortunately, they were all so used to taking the Métro they behaved perfectly, and it wasn't crowded at all. My Betty Crocker yellow cake with chocolate frosting and sprinkles was a big hit. None of the boys, besides Martin, had ever tasted an American cake before. They all thought it was delicious! Matthew opened his presents, and had a wonderful time.

January 8

*Sitting here remembering "the good old days" when I
was a kid... Okay, I cannot believe I just said that. I
must be delirious. What I mean is—before computers.
I remember being really bored. We played games with
real cards, game boards, and play money. My sister
and I even made up our own games. Now with
computers, email, Facebook, TV, movies on demand,
Wii, and Nintendo, it's hard for kids to get bored.
But it's happened! Even with all the electronic
crutches, we are really, really, really bored and really
sick of being inside.*

Winter in Paris definitely held its challenges for us, as we
are used to a year-round-outdoor playground in Santa Barbara.
We are a "sporty" family and Santa Barbara is a "sporty" place.
(I just love that word! Julia's friend Jasmin uses it to describe us.)
All we do in Santa Barbara is sports. In fact, many Santa
Barbarans—us included—are fanatic exercisers. We hike, we
bike, we rollerblade, we play tennis, we surf, we swim, we run,
and it's all for fun. But Parisians are not very "sporty." Most I've
met actually despise scheduled exercise. (Hey, maybe it's because
everything in life in Paris is an exercise in frustration!) Anyway,
winter in Paris definitely did not lend itself to sports. I had to get
creative and think "outside the box." I called going up and down
the stairs of our apartment "French stadiums." We went bowling
often—that's kind of like exercise, right? Mostly though, we
stayed inside. The thought of going out was not appealing. It was
just TOO cold.

It was tough—not being able to exercise. Exercise gets
rid of built-up angst and energy. Where does it go if you don't
exercise? Of course you can go to the gym with all the other
Americans, but I didn't want to do that. I could swim in the
public, indoor pools with Dave and the kids, but I didn't like
that very much either. Swimming is actually one of the few
sports that Parisians like to do, and there are a lot of public,
indoor pools. Anyone can use them, but there are strict rules to

follow (of course). *(Okay, I'm realizing where Matthew gets his in-depth, descriptive soliloquies from.)* First of all, you need a cap and goggles, and if you don't have any of these, you can buy them from vending machines at the entrance. They are required. You must enter the dressing rooms from one side, where you change out of your clothes and shoes. Then, you walk out the other side—there are doors on both sides—to drop off your shoes and clothes with an attendant, who puts them in a locker for you. In some pools, you find your own locker. You then walk through a shallow basin of highly chlorinated water to make sure your feet are really clean, before you go into the pool area. This sterile cleanliness is serious business! I'm not done yet! There are no swim trunks allowed, only Speedos. (We were kicked out of the pool the first time we went to a pool in Paris because Matthew had trunks on.) Speedos are not just the European sense of style, they are required. Some of the bathrooms are coed. (This is common, and very hard to get used to.)

For me, the swimming experience mostly consisted of standing in waist-deep, cold water watching Katherine swim and play around. I was usually freezing, but no, I wasn't allowed to wear my wet-suit shirt, which I'd expressly bought to help keep me warm. "Why not?" I asked. Just *"Non."* I tried the convincing strategy, but *"Non"* was the only response. Needless to say, swimming in the public pools was not my favorite outing, so I avoided it as much as possible, but Dave and the kids liked it.

Playing tennis in Paris was just about as difficult as swimming—that is, if you weren't a member of an elite Paris tennis club—which we weren't. My calf muscle seemed pretty well healed, so I thought I could try hitting some balls with Matthew and Dave. I wanted to start playing again. However, to play tennis on the public courts in Paris took a lot of effort. First we had to register. Once registered, we had to go online to find an available court—somewhere in Paris—and book it for one hour and one hour only. It wasn't possible to book it for longer. Next, we had to map out where the court was and how to get there. Sometimes the court was far away and not always in the best of neighborhoods. We never knew what we'd find when we got there. Sometimes the courts were clay, sometimes concrete with basketball lines crisscrossing the tennis lines. One had fake grass with sand in it. That was different! Some were made from rubber tires, such as the material used to cushion playgrounds. Next, we had to find the public employee, who never spoke a word of English, to take our €6 fee for the hour. Occasionally, we even had to kick people off the court. That was not the public employee's job, *non*, of course not. Sometimes, by the time we actually got on the court to play, we'd barely have any time left.

We did have some fun, family rollerblading sessions. These took place on weekend days when the city closed off streets and tunnels to cars. I have to admit, the rollerblading sessions were great, but in general, I just decided that exercising in Paris was overrated. I decided to exercise my mind instead... and just eat less... and take up smoking like everyone else. (*Side note: That was a joke. I did NOT do that! But it really did surprise me how much people did continue to smoke in Paris.*)

January 13

> *I'm starting to embrace the indoor lifestyle. It feels so cozy in our apartment. I close all the curtains and feel a serene sense of warmth, of family, and of home. It makes me want to be more domestic. The kids snuggle in their beds, even in the daytime, and they read non-stop. I had to FORCE them to read in Santa Barbara! They were so bored the other day that Matthew actually took out paper and started drawing! Now that's a first. Katherine made up a play and Matthew made up a song to go with it on the keyboard. Julia made a fashion collage. They're finally getting creative. It took a very long, cold winter, but it's happened—and it makes me happy. I feel like the "good old days" are back.*

I found some recipes for wintery meals like soups and

stews. It was fun when we all cooked together. David bought me a Julia Child cookbook, and I made my first *cassoulet*: the rich, slow-cooked French casserole made with meat, sausages, and beans. Dave and I made *beef bourguignon*: a deep, aromatic beef stew, with a dark silky sauce. They were both delicious. This is kind of scary, but ironing became an enjoyable activity for me. I had nothing but time and ironing was actually quite satisfying. It gave me a sense of accomplishment. Dave and I started reading the International Herald Tribune, and we both felt more tuned into the world. We ordered a subscription and it felt like such a luxury to have it delivered under our kitchen door every morning. It's such a great newspaper—short, concise, and intelligently written. We'd read and discuss, and read and discuss. It made us feel like "real" grown ups.

It was interesting how boredom led us to creativity and inspiration. Katherine and Julia made about a hundred watercolor paintings, sitting in the kitchen, while I cooked. Katherine taught herself ballet and guitar. I reminded everyone how last winter, at exactly this same time of year, we all tried writing poetry. Some of the poems were better than others. (Some were really bad, but it was a fun thing to do.) Again, we desperately needed indoor activities. Dave led us in family yoga sessions. Katherine read all the French books we had in the apartment. I had subscribed to a bi-monthly, age-appropriate book club for her, but she needed even more books. I found her trying to climb the built-in shelves in her room to get to the English books, which we had put up on the top shelves. We were strictly told to keep all English books out of her reach until second grade. The school was afraid it would confuse her. She had to learn to read and write in French first.

January 15

Our second year is more than halfway over. I'm not usually the kind of person who looks at the cup as half empty, but I can't help it! It actually feels only a quarter of the way full, with "backwash" in it. Oh

*geez, it's not that empty! We still have six months left.
We're living the dream! I just don't want it to end...*

*We have so much stuff! Look at all these books,
furniture, and French knick-knacks. What are we
going to do with it all? I need to make doctor and
dentist appointments for everyone when we get back.
Are we really going home??? I'm in denial.*

January 16

*Just received a call from a mom in Matthew's class.
She wants to know if anyone has "dibs" on our
apartment next year. OMG! WHAT? I almost
started crying. "You're sure you're leaving, right?" she
asked. I thought so, but now I'm really dwelling!
Nooo!! It's OUR apartment!*

Dave was ready to go. His decision was made. He had
traveled back and forth every three weeks during the year, and
he was tired and jet-lagged all the time. He knew his company
would not let him stay in Paris any longer, so unless a miracle
happened, we didn't have a choice. We had to deal with reality,
and the right decision was to leave. I had to accept our fate and
appreciate the time we had left. We had gotten as much out of
this experience as we could ever have hoped for. But even
though I knew that, I also knew that there was so much more
growing that could still be done.

January 19

*Harper invited me out to Moret for the weekend after
I told her how bad our cabin fever was. Dave is back
in Santa Barbara once again, and another frigid
weekend is upon us. I checked the weather in Santa
Barbara. Of course, it's a sunny 70 degrees—just like
always. That's one thing we have to look forward to.*

Dave always comes back tanner than when he left. We never allow him to talk about how nice the weather was or how many waves he caught, but I guess we should start letting him now.

Harper and Mike had a great idea: rock climbing in the forest at a place called Devil's Rocks. Cool! The kids were fired up. We packed our overnight bags and headed to the train station. They picked us up in their car and we went straight to the Fontainebleau forest.

Devil's Rocks was intense. I didn't realize we were going on the Black Diamond of rock climbing. I was trying to watch Katherine, but then I heard a hair-raising, "MOM!!!" Julia was stuck in a very precarious spot. Normally, Dave would come to the rescue in a sticky situation like this, but Mike and Harper were trying to watch their own kids, and I started to panic. Then Matthew yelled out that he, too, was stuck and couldn't climb down. What was I going to do? I was wearing fancy flats and a skirt (hardly what you'd call climbing attire), because I was planning on going on a tour of the Château of Fontainebleau after the Devil's Rocks. I was not prepared to go clambering over rocks to help them. After about fifteen minutes, Matt got himself down. He said that without the expert rock climbing lessons he received from his Uncle, he would never have been able to do it. Then Matt clambered over and helped Julia get down as well. I was hugely relieved.

Julia accompanied me to the Château de Fontainebleau, while the other kids went home to play Wii at the house. I was quite surprised when Julia said, "Yes" without any begging on my part, but she is sweet that way. We listened to English audio guides and learned a lot of interesting facts about the famous Château. For example: Fontainebleau was apparently the abode of eight centuries of French kings and queens. There was a real throne with the initial "N" in the throne room (for Napoleon I). It's the only real one left in France. Napoleon spent lavishly on Fontainebleau. He used it as a resort, and hunted in its forest. The famous, horseshoe-shaped staircase that dominates the front façade is called the Cour des Adieux. It was down that staircase that Napoleon made his way slowly, to take his final salute as he left for his exile on the Mediterranean island of Elba in 1814. Julia and I learned a lot of history on what was really just a short tour of the Château. English audio guides were definitely the way to go!

The next day, we headed back to Paris. Dave was finally back from Santa Barbara. He had bought the kids a pack of silver, metallic, *pétanque boules* (balls). *Pétanque* is perhaps the sport that is closest to French hearts. It is very similar to *bocce ball*, which is also very popular in Santa Barbara. *Bocce* is the Italian name. The French version is traditionally played on a dirt surface beneath plane trees (a type of Sycamore), with a glass of *Pastis*, an anise-flavored liqueur, in hand. In Santa Barbara, *Pastis* is exchanged for margaritas. The object of the game is to throw your balls—usually with somewhat of an arched back-spin—so that they land closer to the small object ball (called a *cochonnet* in France) than those of your opponent, or strike and drive the object ball toward your other balls, and away from those of your opponents. We took the kids down to the courts in the dirt area in front of the Hôtel des Invalides and had a great time, even without the *Pastis* or margaritas. It's hard to say who won because with five people we were constantly changing the teams around, but it was great just to be outside enjoying the (finally!) warmer weather.

The next day we went and saw the *marionettes* (puppets) on the Champs Elysées. The kids and Dave laughed their heads off. I didn't really understand most of it, but I still got a kick out of watching them understand and enjoy it so much.

Julia and I went to a fabulous Sonia Rykiel exhibit, to celebrate forty years of her clothing designs in Paris. It was at the Musée des Arts Decoratifs in the left wing of the Louvre. Julia really enjoyed it because she has dreams of being a famous fashion designer someday. The exhibit had two hundred and twenty garments, fashion shows, videos, and photos. It was like taking a walk down "fashion-memory lane," shoulder pads and all. I love that all these experiences are possible because "we" can speak French now.

January 23

The countdown is on! It's only January, but it feels like our time here is nearing its end. We planned and planned and did all we had to do to make it happen. And we DID IT! We're DOING it! But… at some point, I have to disengage and start thinking about the future. I'd like to continue to live in the moment, but the going back part is inevitable, and that takes considerable planning as well. There are decisions to make: Do we want to send our kids to an international, or a bilingual school when we get back? Where do we want to live? Back in our house or somewhere else?

Needless to say, it's difficult to make such dear friends and then leave them. Some people have moved many times in their lives, but not me! For me, this is SO hard! I keep asking myself, should we stay another year? Will two years turn into three, four, twenty? This is not unheard of. Many friends have told me that was how they got here. I know that it's even worse if we have a choice (to stay longer or to go back) because it's another tough decision. I need to accept our decision and start doing all the things I haven't done yet. BUT, if we're still not totally decided, then I'll keep procrastinating and dwelling!

February 2009

Julia and Matt have been studying hard for their upcoming "Compos" (tests) but we ALL need a break. Dave's gone again, so we're going to head out to Moret for the day. Harper and I are going to take the kids to a zip-line park. It's right in the Fontainebleau forest near their house. The kids are SO excited.

Accrobranche (zip-lining) is very popular in France. Julia tried it at her French camp and told me in all seriousness, "Mom, if you don't hook up right, you can fall and die... so, I made sure I hooked it up right." Alrighty then! After the Black Diamond rock climbing experience, why not do some precarious zip lining, right?

Harper picked us up and we drove straight to the Accrobranche Park. We got our harnesses on and listened to the instructions (all in French, which I wasn't expecting for some reason). I wasn't sure I understood everything the guide said, so I was actually a bit nervous. I thought he said something about having Katherine stop at a certain point, or was it that all the kids were to stop? Where? I had no idea! It seemed that the kids all understood the rules, but they didn't want to tell me because they wanted to go as high as they could. Harper said she understood, so we set out for the trees.

The French guides watched us on the first tree but then, remarkably, they left us on our own. Yep, no double-checking at all. Because of the "play at your own risk" mentality in France, I was more than a little nervous. About mid-way through the park, another person came to check on us, and as is typical of the French, they walked around and handed out yellow cards (warnings), and then red cards (you're kicked out), if they

222

noticed someone doing something wrong. Luckily, our group didn't get any cards.

The higher we went, the more difficult it became. We walked on tightropes, bridges, and swinging logs. We swung from ropes, and did zip lines, which we hooked ourselves into with no supervision, I might add. Even little Katherine did it, all by herself. Harper and I tried to stay with her but at some points it wasn't possible. We didn't sign anything—no waivers, no contracts, no insurance—nothing! They didn't even know our names. Thank goodness we all lived through it. And it WAS really fun. I admit it.

Back in Paris there were still some French specialties that I wanted to learn to bake before we left. One of them was the little shell-shaped Madeline cookie. While learning the process of baking them, I also learned what not to do when trying to follow a French recipe: 1. Don't ever try to guess at what words mean. 2. Don't ask your husband what words mean (even if he's better at French than you). 3. Don't wait until you've already started the recipe to look up what words mean. 4. Don't call a French friend to ask her questions after you've already started. She probably won't understand what you're asking because it's all so obvious to her. 5. Don't try a recipe for the first time when you need to bring it for others to eat. French recipes are not straightforward, like American recipes.

Here is an example of what I am talking about:

8 gouttes d'eau de fleurs d'oranger

This sounds like eight of *some measure* of orange-flavored water, right? Not totally sure—Okay, I'll ask Dave...

"Oh, *gouttes* are spoonfuls," Dave said. *(Nope. Wrong!)*

I found *l'arôme de fleur d'oranger* at the store. That's got to be it, right? *(Wrong!)* And *sucre en poudre*—surely must be powdered sugar? *(Wrong!)* Blend the egg whites until they make a cloud (translation of *niege*). I've whipped egg whites before, but what kind of a cloud was required, a wispy one or a puffy one? I'll just call a French friend to confirm that *gouttes* are spoonfuls like Dave said.

223

"*Arrête!*" my friend shouted into the phone, which means stop! "*Gouttes* are droplets—not spoonfuls! You will poison yourselves! *L'arôme de fleur d'oranger* is not exactly right either, but it might work. How long did you blend the egg whites? You need a solid cloud. Use a blender. Start at 200 degrees and wait until they pop, eh, just until they pop, then lower it to 180," she said with her cute French accent. –*Pop?* What does that mean? I had no idea. The Madeline cookies turned out a bit heavy that first time—not enough whipping, not the right kind of sugar, and I missed the *pop*, I guess. I had no idea what that meant. (Later she invited me over to demonstrate and I found out what the *pop* was. It's when the cookies start to swell.)

February 24

I'm feeling "the end is near" panic. I made a checklist of all the things I haven't done yet, so I can get to them all. There is no chance we can stay (unless by some miracle Dave gets a job in Paris). Not having the option is actually good because I know that I have to make the most of every moment I have left. In fact, I visited three museums this week!

The Musée du Luxembourg was having a fabulous exhibit called "Miro to Warhol." Dave and I had been seeing signs for it in the Métro for a while, so we decided to go. This museum is well known by savvy travelers to Paris but I guess we needed to live in Paris awhile before we discovered it. The collection spanned Cubism, Surrealism (Miro, Dali, Ernst, Breton), Pop Art (Warhol, Klein, Soulages, Mitchell), and every great 20th-century artistic movement in between. A Portuguese collector had lent about seventy-five canvases from his private gallery to the museum. Among them were also works by Arp, de Chirico, Lichtenstein, Mondrian, Wesselmann, and Pollock. I was learning so much about art!

Then Julia and Katherine accompanied Dave and me to the Palais de Tokyo, one of the free museums of Paris. The café there is a favorite lunch spot for Julia and her friends. She had told us about the goat cheese wrapped in prosciutto many times. We tried to imitate it at home, to no avail. The Palais de Tokyo is a huge museum, set in an art-deco palace, created in 1937 for the World's Fair to house the modern art of the city of Paris. This was long before the idea for the Georges Pompidou Center, another modern art museum. It has a dramatic view of the Eiffel Tower and over eight thousand pieces of art on display. This time we all brought our drawing books and tried to draw some of the larger pieces of modern art. "It looks so easy. Anyone can do that," was a common statement from my kids when looking at some of the geometric designs. We found out it wasn't as easy as it looked.

Two museums in one week seemed like enough, but then on Sunday morning, Clare and I started chatting online. She and her kids were going to the Palais de la Découverte, part of the Grand Palais, to see—I mean smell—an exhibit there called *Nez* (which means nose). I said, "A third museum in one week? *Mais, bien sûr!''* (Of course!) We headed out walking—all of us, including Matthew this time. The Grand Palais was not far from our apartment and it was a sunny, crisp April day. The exhibit turned out to be one of the kids' all-time favorites! Designed as a large set of questions, the exhibit had ninety smells of all different types. Some of the smells elicited strong feelings, memories, and reactions. There were good smells like flowers and spices, and gross smells like garbage and dirty socks. Frequently, we knew what the smell was but we couldn't name it. What an experience! The perfume section was Julia's favorite, and she was really good at it. It's funny how she could recognize so many French perfumes.

Our family tried to squeeze in all we could, knowing that our time was limited. For example, we made lists of all our favorite things: our favorite baguette, our favorite gelato, and our favorite macarons. We ate in restaurants we hadn't tried yet, and we walked through neighborhoods we hadn't walked through before. We enjoyed sunsets and picnics on bridges and in parks, and we went on every tour we could find. We soaked all of Paris in, as much as we could. We wanted to come home with memories that would last us a lifetime.

I signed up for a class called "Writing your Learning Memoirs." It was very thought provoking, and made me realize how much I love writing. Our first assignment was to write a letter to one of our mentors. I didn't think I had any mentors, but I soon realized that my Grandma was a mentor for me. The process of writing her a letter was very enlightening! For my next assignment, I wrote a poem about my first year in Paris. I read it to my Conversation group, and Clare asked to publish in the school newsletter. Here it is:

Paris doesn't scare me any more

Pressing every sheet
Eating raw meat
Paris doesn't scare me any more

Cold and dark school days
Really hard dictées
Paris doesn't scare me any more

Tiny elevators
Rude French waiters
Paris doesn't scare me any more

Celsius and kilos
Sauces and phyllo
Paris doesn't scare me any more

Velib wheels
In high heels
Foie gras
French bras

Cigarettes
Small pets
I'll wear fur
It's cold, brrrrr
Paris doesn't scare me any more

Don't walk on the grass
No parents in the class
Paris doesn't scare me any more

Je ne comprends pas
Attention le caca
Paris doesn't scare me any more

Too many cute men
Breathe and count to ten
Paris doesn't scare me any more

New style every week
Must try to be chic
Paris doesn't scare me any more

Don't show me the butcher
With all parts of a pig
I'm going vegetarian
I'll eat sticks and twigs

I don't know what you're saying
But I don't really care
I've lived a year in Paris
I've done all that I dared

Paris doesn't scare me any more
Not any more
Not any more
Paris doesn't scare me any more

March 2009

March 3

We're driving up to Belgium and Amsterdam for our upcoming Spring Break. They're so close, how can we not take advantage of at least one vacation there before we leave? We have a lot of Starwood hotel points, and we're worried the points program (where we get free hotel rooms with our accumulated points) might disappear in the current financial crisis, so we want to use up our points. Dave rented a Peugeot—like a mini-minivan with a sunroof (no more upgrades, thank you very LITTLE) and we're heading out of Paris in the morning.

First we drove to Brussels—only about two and a half hours from Paris. Downtown Brussels was not that pretty at first sight, just a gray city in the rain. We checked into our hotel, which was in a convenient location downtown, grabbed our umbrellas, and walked out to find a place for lunch. We were on the hunt for mussels, beer, and chocolate—the things we knew Brussels was famous for. The garlic smell of a touristy restaurant enticed us. It was open to the street, so we could watch the rain. We ordered some mussels and French fries and Dave and I shared a big Belgian beer.

Then we went to find *Mannekin Pis*, the little peeing boy who is the famous mascot of Brussels in the location that he's been since the 1600's. We weren't far away. On the way there, the kids wanted to try Belgian waffles from a cart on the street—but they weren't very good. (Their grandmother in Santa Barbara makes exceptionally good waffles with homemade whipped cream and fresh berries, so my kids' "waffle palette" is quite discriminating!)

When we got to the *Mannekin Pis*, Dave said, "It should be right here." Then he pointed at a tiny little statue and said, "Ah, there it is!"

"What? Are you kidding me?" Julia said.

We were all expecting something exciting, but the statue was tiny. The little guy was less than two feet tall. The peeing boy is a fountain, we realized—the fountain being his urinating into the fountain's basin. We all got a good laugh out of that one.

March 4

Today we're going on a chocolate-tasting expedition. The Belgians and the French both think theirs is the best chocolate. We're all VERY familiar with French chocolate by now, so the taste test is on!

Later

We tasted A LOT of chocolate today. Belgian is darker than French, we found out. All of us like French better. Swiss is milk chocolate, so comparing it isn't really fair, but we tried it too, and we all still like French chocolate the best. We also tried pralines, which are nougat or cream with a chocolate shell covering. They're everywhere in Brussels, and they're divine! Basically, our entire Brussels experience has been eating so far.

March 5

We decided to try the hotel breakfast buffet this morning and had fresh, hot, crispy waffles that melted in our mouths. They were SO GOOD!! It's a Sheraton hotel, so we thought the food would be "Americanized," but it wasn't. This is THE place to get the best waffles in town. They're almost as good as Grandma's!

Later (in the car)

We left Brussels after breakfast and we're off to the medieval city of Bruges, about an hour and a half away. Bruges' nickname is "the Venice of the North" (as are a few other cities), because there are canals everywhere. I'm excited!

12:10 p.m.

We just arrived in Bruges. This town is like a picture-perfect postcard. It's SO cute!

We rented five bikes and rode through the town of Bruges to a long canal that led to another town, called Damme. It was a long ride—about four miles—but flat and straight. Dave had to push Katherine along for some of it, but she did fine. It was euphoric, riding bikes in the sunshine after so much winter weather. The canal was on one side, the bright green grass and yellow daisies on the other side, and there were even some windmills along the way. We parked our bikes at an outdoor café at the end of the canal and had snacks and coffee. On the way back, we took pictures of ourselves in the grass with the daisies behind our ears—at least the girls did!

After the snacks, we rode back to Bruges. We returned our bikes and had some gelato—always necessary to try the gelato! Everyone was tired, so we drove out of town to find the hotel, called a *gîte*. The *gîte* was a big house in the country about twenty minutes away, with a trampoline for the kids, and chickens and roosters running around. The owners came out to welcome us. *Gîtes* are what we'd call Bed and Breakfasts in America.

Later

In our room now at the gîte, or should I say: "the attic." Definitely an interesting situation here! We're all in one room, with mattresses on the floor for beds, and no bathroom in the room. The bathroom is down on the floor below—and there are no stairs. We have to climb down a ladder! You never know what you're going to find when you're traveling in Europe!

March 6

Last night we had some bathroom issues. Why here... in an attic... with a ladder? I know, s#*% happens, but why does it seem like it always happens to us?! It was NOT the easiest place to deal with that situation! I'll leave it at that. Thank goodness, we're only here for one night!

In the morning, the owners set out a nice breakfast with coffee, toast, hardboiled eggs, cheese, and pastries for all the guests. The kids jumped on the trampoline (of course there was no net around it—this is France), and we took a walk on the forest trail around the house. Then we drove to Amsterdam. (Ah, our hotel in Amsterdam... it was really, really delightful.) We were so happy we had splurged with the rest of our hotel points. We even got the kids their own adjoining room. We were in need of some modern conveniences and amenities after our *gîte* experience in the country.

This luxury hotel was on one of the most picturesque canals in the middle of the Old City. The rooms were big and modern. The kids all had their own beds with big, fluffy, down comforters, and there was a TV with shows in English. There was a pink, flowering almond tree right outside our window. It was gorgeous, but Katherine, Miss Persnickety, complained that it banged on the window all night and drove her crazy.

After checking into the hotel, we headed out to see Amsterdam. It was quaint and picturesque, with brownstone houses along the tree-lined canal. A boat went by with a group of young adults kicking back and singing, wine glasses in their hands, and looking like they were having the greatest time in the world. "Yeahhh," Julia purred. She liked Amsterdam. We walked along the cobblestone, trying not to get hit by the fast moving bikes. The bike riders were everywhere, and they did not stop for pedestrians. We realized quickly that the cyclists were the top of the food chain in Amsterdam, and it was quite dangerous. We needed to keep our kids close by.

We went to a restaurant called Pancakes and ate... yep, pancakes. I was thinking it must be a clever name for something else, but it really was a pancake restaurant. Apparently, pancakes are a traditional Dutch delicacy. The kids were thrilled. It was a happy reminder of one of their favorite breakfasts in America. (Pancakes were not something we ever ate in Paris.) Afterwards, we took a one-hour canal tour. It was fun to see the city from the water, travel under the picturesque, curved bridges, and hear about the history of the city.

After the boat tour, we wandered around town until Julia knocked a loaf of bread off the edge of a table in one of the stores, and the shopkeeper started yelling at us. I'm not sure if it was because of *la crise* (the financial crisis) or what, but he got really angry. We picked it up and put it back, but he continued yelling that we had to pay for it. Dave said, "No. That was crazy." It was perched precariously on the edge of a table, so it wasn't Julia's fault (in our opinion). (In his, it was.) Plus, it was just bread, wrapped in plastic! It was fine! We didn't understand why he was so mad. It was bizarre, and it scared the kids. It was one experience we could have lived without.

The next morning we visited the Anne Frank house. Julia had read *The Diary of Anne Frank* and couldn't believe that this was really the house where she lived, hid, and wrote in her diary. In the first room there was a film about the Holocaust. I watched it first to make sure it was kid-friendly while Dave stayed with the kids. I decided to let the kids see it. It was very sad but it was the true history of what happened. The rest of the house wasn't all that interesting. All the furniture was removed. There were photos on the wall, but we all wanted to see a real house. This was more like a museum. Still, it was worthwhile visiting it.

After that, we bought hot dogs from a street vendor and walked out to the flower market where we saw loads of colorful tulips for which Amsterdam is so famous. We some other "interesting" types of plants too, and a lot of "interesting" paraphernalia, but the kids didn't really know what they were looking at. (Thank goodness!) There were definitely some inappropriate things in the stores. At one point, I didn't realize Matthew had followed me to the back of a store—never a good idea in Amsterdam—and he was turning his head sideways, trying to figure out what he was looking at. The shopkeeper was watching the whole thing laughing, especially when he saw me realize what Matthew was looking at. (No comment!)

Dave took the kids back to the hotel while I took a quick walk through the Red Light District—because I had to see it. Dave had been there before. It was daytime, but the Red Light District was still too weird for me. I kept my eyes down because Dave said "not to meet eyes" with anyone. I walked briskly, peeking quickly at the window displays, but I didn't stop to go inside any stores. I was surprised at my lack of bravery and curiosity. I wasn't interested in all the weird stuff. I actually felt a little scared. Amsterdam prides itself on its liberal and tolerant attitude. Instead of criminalizing everything, the city invites you to experience things that are illegal everywhere else in the world. I definitely wanted to see the Red Light District once, but once was enough. *Check!* I took a few pictures of some amusing storefronts and headed back to my family. The next morning we headed back to Paris.

The next weekend we took the kids to the picturesque Île Saint-Louis—the other island in the middle of the Seine, and one of the prettiest neighborhoods in Paris. We found a store that had handcrafted puppets. The man who worked there showed the kids how to make the marionette puppets dance. Then we waited in the long line outside Berthillon for their famous ice cream, and ate it while meandering near the river. Katherine got her favorite: dark chocolate. Julia got salted caramel, and Matthew got mango. Dave and I shared a scoop of pistachio and a scoop of coffee. After that, we wandered along the narrow, cobblestone streets and into some of the gift stores on the island. We stopped to hear a jazz trio playing music on the street. The Île Saint-Louis is one of Paris' oldest neighborhoods, and it's quite different from the rest of Paris. It felt very old because it hasn't been modernized like other parts of Paris. The kids said it felt like we were in a real fairy tale.

March 15

*I went to a cooking demonstration called
"Demystifying the Meringue" today. I was not so
much mystified by the meringue as I was mystified by
Clare, who demonstrated all the recipes. Clare made
five different recipes simultaneously... in front of a
group of twenty women... in less than two hours. She
also made a professional-looking handout for everyone
with color photos and recipes, and she even made sure
to LAMINATE hers, to keep it from getting dirty.
If an "Overachievers Anonymous" group existed, she'd
be a member... No, she'd probably be the president! I
also learned a bunch of new British words today:
"squidgy" (like mud), "wizened" (wrinkled),
"mucking" and "gungy" (both meaning grungy, I
think).*

Our second Easter in Paris (*Pâques* in French) was celebrated with all the Santa Barbarans that we knew, living in Paris. The country mice invited us all out to an Easter egg hunt and brunch at their house in Moret. Harper made crêpes with asparagus, salmon, and hollandaise, an egg and sausage casserole, a leek quiche, and a carrot and curry soup. I made raspberry financiers, the little almond cakes with a raspberry in the middle from Clare's recipe. While we drank mimosas, the kids made daisy chains and played "try to flip your friend off the hammock." After coffee and dessert, we went for a hike in the Fontainebleau forest.

On March 25th I turned forty. Six girlfriends and I made a plan for dinner and maybe some dancing afterwards. Karolina picked me up in her royal blue Mini convertible with the top down. *("Yeahhh," as Julia would say.)* Dave walked me down to the car, and I could tell he was a little skeptical when he watched us drive off—music blasting and our hair blowing in the wind. But we were off, speeding down Boulevard St. Germain to Alcazar, a hip and fun restaurant. A cute, gay, French waiter gave us very attentive service. My party consisted of two French friends, Bridgit and Adrienne, my German friend Karolina, three American friends—two of whom were from Santa Barbara— Harper and Lisa, and Rhiann, Katherine's best friend's Mom. I also invited a few other friends that couldn't make it.

My French friends chipped in on a black leather Christian Dior wallet, which they said: "is as French as it gets" to remind me of Paris. The waiter came by to check it out and said, *"Oh! J'adore Dior!"* It was classic! Then we went downstairs to dance, but the dance floor was empty. It was only 11:00 p.m. and the dancing crowd didn't come out that early. We danced as enthusiastically as we could for a while, but being the only ones there, we decided to call it a night.

I went to see an exhibit called "Bonaparte and Egypt" with the school tour group at the Institut du Monde Arabe, a museum in the fifth arrondissement. We learned about Napoleon Bonaparte's campaign in Egypt in 1798. It showed many aspects of the French expedition into Egypt and the later Egyptian influence on the French. *Quelle surprise!* (What a surprise!) I didn't know there had been any history between the two countries. It was very educational for me. Also, I learned some fascinating history about the famous giraffe that Egypt gave as a gift to the King of France (Charles X) in the early 1820's. This giraffe was sent by boat to Marseilles on a thirty-two day voyage. The giraffe then walked nine hundred kilometers to Paris, which took forty-one days. She was quite the spectacle in each town she passed through. Then she lived in the menagerie at the Jardin des Plants for eighteen years. I bet that's why Sophie the Giraffe—the squeaky toy Julia received as a baby gift—is a popular toy from France.

April 2009

April 7

I'm home alone. Dave's in Santa Barbara, once again. I'm not in the mood for cleaning. I'm not in the mood for reading. It's freezing outside. I feel like doing nothing but drinking tea. Maybe I should do yoga or Pilates or plan a weekend trip. The world's economy is in shambles. Even Santa Barbara has been hit. I looked at real estate prices today, and the value of our house has gone down to half what it was worth when we left. Ugh!!! The stock market will go back up eventually. That's what everybody says. I can't let myself think so negatively. No worrying! Get busy and do something!

April 13

Dave's back now. I've noticed that we definitely have an adjustment period after each of his long trips. This time was the longest so far, almost three weeks. Then, as soon as we return to normal, he has to leave again. I know that our Paris experience could not have taken place without this unusual way of life, but it's definitely hard on a relationship.

April 18

Okay, I've planned a one-day trip to Leonardo da Vinci's house in the Loire Valley tomorrow. It will be good to get out of town for a family day, and it should also be educational! Dave and I visited the Loire

Valley before we had kids, but we didn't know that Leonardo da Vinci had lived there. (I recently found out about this from some Santa Barbara friends who were in Paris with their kids for the junior high Europe trip. Yes, parents are invited to come along, unlike in France.) Dave already picked up the rental car, so we can leave first thing in the morning.

In the morning, we woke up early and drove to Amboise, just over two hours from Paris. We parked our car across the river from the town so we could have a scenic view while we ate our picnic lunch. The Castle of Amboise was impressively perched on a hill, overlooking the town. Suddenly, disaster struck in the form of big, black ants! We had just laid out a blanket and started eating when they attacked. We literally ran back to the car, jumped inside, and finished our lunch there. Happily, none of us got any bites, but we had never seen such big ants!

After lunch, we headed across the bridge to the town. We decided to skip the tour of the castle and instead headed up, about a third of a mile, to Clos Lucé, Leonardo da Vinci's home and gardens. Clos Lucé was built in 1471 and was, for hundreds of years, a royal summer residence of the kings of France. But in 1516, Leonardo da Vinci (age sixty-four at the time) was invited to come and live in France by King François I. Leonardo lived at Clos Lucé for the last three years of his life. François I appointed him: "First painter, architect and engineer of the King," and he was free to dream and to work there. His job, basically, was to amuse the king.

Surprisingly, the tour of the house was not as impressive as the park and gardens outside. However, one thing we found very interesting was that there was a copy of the *Mona Lisa* on the wall. (The real one is in the Louvre, of course.) Apparently, Leonardo brought the *Mona Lisa* to Clos Lucé when he moved from Rome, and it was there that he finished it. In the basement of the house, there were small models, drawings, and descriptions of his many inventions. Seeing these examples of his brilliant, engineering, innovative mind was truly impressive.

Outside the house were forty full-size replicas of the miniatures we'd seen inside—model machines produced from da Vinci's original drawings, such as the first flying machine—which was the forerunner of the airplane, the first automobile, the first tank, first helicopter, first parachute, and the first swing bridge. It was shocking how many things he invented. Even more inspiring were the grounds around the house, where we saw all his sources of inspiration. We learned that he devised everything by observing nature. To emphasize the point, each model was placed in the garden next to each inspirational source.

Leonardo, the anatomist, was displayed with pictures of the human body; such as his famous *Vitruvian Man*, where he captured movement, strength, and in his view, the souls of the creatures he was representing by working from the inside out. In the garden, these drawings were purposefully placed by the muscular looking bark of the plane trees. To illustrate his treatments of shadow and light, his paintings of giant faces were placed where the light shines through the trees onto them.

Next, we saw Leonardo, the architect. The functional city he designed was yet another example of his brilliance. There was a mill, operated by Leonardo's gearing. We walked across a big oak bridge, also designed by him. He revolutionized every field in which he took an interest.

After that, we headed back to Amboise for coffee and gelato, and then off to another château in the Loire. Katherine wanted to see "Sleeping Beauty's castle"—not the one at Disneyland—but the one that inspired Walt Disney: the Château of Ussé. Unfortunately, Ussé was the farthest away, and with only a one-day trip planned, we couldn't make it that far.

Instead, we decided to go to Azay le Rideau, one of the earliest French Renaissance châteaux. We toured the inside, and then Julia and Katherine relaxed in the sunshine, making daisy-chain headbands, while Dave, Matt, and I wandered around the moat. We imagined the drawbridge coming down and what life might have been like in those times. We had a nice dinner in town before driving back to Paris. Two castles were it for one day. We would have liked to fit in one more but it was great that we could do a day trip to the Loire. We could come back again, of course. Living in Europe, so many locations are within reach. That's one of the highlights of this experience.

Everyone in our extended families knew we were leaving Paris soon, so they all came to visit us. Dave's brother, his wife, and their daughter came first. We went to see the Eiffel Tour lit up at night, toured Notre Dame, walked through the Tuileries, ate lunch at Ladurée, had the famous hot chocolate at Angelina's, walked on the rue de Rivoli, went up to the Sacré-Coeur, and more! All this, while babysitting for Rose the Turtle, Katherine's class pet, who we had at our apartment for the weekend.

April 21

We took everyone to an outdoor market, under the raised Métro on the Boulevard de Grenelle today. All the skinned animals hanging around, stinky cheese, and vendors yelling in French can be quite an ultra-sensory experience, but hey, this is France, and they wanted "authentic"!

April 22

Today we went to the Pompidou Center and saw the "Alexander Calder - Les Années Parisiennes, 1926-1933" exhibit. Alexander Calder was an American sculptor and artist who is best known for inventing the mobile. Dave and I really liked the drawings he did with one continuous line and the wire sculptures: He twists wire into 3-D designs of animals, people, and other ingenious designs... yet ANOTHER fabulous exhibition! This has inspired Dave to try his own wire art. (And he's really good!)

April 24

*Dave's Mom is here to visit now. She and the kids
and I went to see the current exhibition at the Grand
Palais yesterday. It's called "Une Image Peut en
Cacher une Autre," which means: "one image can be
hiding in another." It was a great exhibit for the kids
because it was full of optical illusions and visual
puzzles. I wonder if any other city in the world has as
many exhibits and museums as Paris!? I also found a
"trick cigarette" in Julia's bag today. Hmmm…*

The last week of April, Katherine left on a seven-night
Classe Verte (Green Trip) with her *CP* (first grade) class. They
were headed to Arcachon, by Bordeaux, to learn about oysters,
feed baby animals, climb dunes, and spend time at the beach. I
think most Americans would be pretty nervous about sending
off their first grader for a weeklong trip with only the teacher
and one helper. No parents were allowed. But, the *Class Verte* is
one of the first steps in the French effort toward autonomy.
They believe it's empowering and beneficial for a small child to
have a successful separation from their parents at a young age,
and that it leads to positive emotional development. *(Makes
sense…)* The trips also create stronger relationships between
students and teacher. *(Probably true…)* Any way, Katherine was
excited to go, because they'd been talking about it all year.

April 29

*Every night we receive a recorded phone call from
Katherine's class. It's so cute! Two or three kids talk
each time (in French, of course) about what they did
that day. Tonight it was Katherine's little voice. I
could barely understand her, but oh, how I wish I
could keep that message forever! Dave and I are getting
out a lot with Katherine gone. We went to the Musée
d'Orsay this morning. Last night we saw "Angels and
Demons" (in English) in Saint-Germain-des-Prés.*

It's nice to be able to go out, but it's weird having Katherine gone, my "velcro" girl.

May 2009

May 1

Katherine is back. She had a great time! She made a book about her trip, and we just looked at it. I find it hilarious that three pages are dedicated entirely to the menu of what they ate for breakfast, lunch and dinner—it's so important here!

Today is May Day (which we celebrate in America as Labor Day). It's also La Fête du Muguet. The tradition here is to give the ones you love a little bouquet of muguets for good luck and to celebrate the arrival of spring. Muguets are what Americans call lilies-of-the-valley. They are for sale on every corner in Paris right now.

There were a number of other school holidays in May too. It seemed like the kids were never in school. For me, it was a good history lesson. May 8th was Victory Day—the commemoration of the end of World War II. Next came May 21st—yet another vacation. It was a Christian holiday, Ascension Thursday, but kids of all religions got the day off in Paris. Then, American kids, not the French kids, have another vacation on May 31st (American Memorial Day). Many Americans visit the American cemetery in Normandy or the Picpus Cemetery in Paris, where the American flag flew on Memorial Day, even during the German occupation of France.

May 12

Today, we took the kids to another museum, which we hadn't visited yet—the Museum of Natural History at the Jardin des Plantes. There were several museums in the Jardin des Plantes but we decided on the Gallery of Comparative Anatomy and Paleontology. I have never seen so many bones in all my life. Wow! The kids said, "No! Not another museum," but they loved it! It was one of their favorite museums of our entire Paris stay.

May 20

The Upper School had a Fashion Show today. Julia was in it, as were many of her friends. All they had to do was make their own outfit. Valentina's Mom, Sofia, helped Julia and Valentina sew their outfits. It was quite an impressive show. The gymnasium was set up like a real fashion show with a runway through the middle and judges in the first row. The kids were each assigned to a continent, with about ten kids in each group: North America, Europe, South America, Asia, and Africa (Julia's group). The Terminale (Senior) student announcers spoke in perfect French and perfect English, with absolutely no accents in either language. There was a DJ who played current music. Could this school be any cooler???

June 2009

June 5

I haven't felt like writing much. I guess I'm depressed about leaving. We have one month left of our life in Paris. I feel like I have to breathe in deeply every time I go outside. I know most people would die for a month in Paris, but for me, having only a month left, is REALLY hard.

June 14

We are planning a huge, three-way, thirteenth birthday party for Julia, Valentina, and Jasmin. They've invited about seventy kids, and all seventy accepted. We're going to make each of the birthday girls a separate, homemade, birthday cake and hire a man to make crêpes at the party. The kids all have iPods, so they said we don't need to hire a DJ.

June 21

The party was a blast! —Well, except for all the crying about Julia being about to leave. We kept trying to find "happy music" to stop everyone from crying. Then, smoke started filling the rooms. I had accidentally set the timer wrong (way too long—twenty minutes instead of two, oops!) on a bag of microwave popcorn. It smelled terrible. But besides that fiasco, the kids all danced like crazy, and it was a night we'll always remember.

*Do we have to leave?? I keep asking myself
this... Yes! Dave's company wants him in Santa
Barbara. He can't keep this up—going back and
forth every month. It's not possible. (I sound so
French!) But it isn't fair to him, or to them. It's too
far. He's jet-lagged all the time, and it's definitely
putting a strain on our relationship.*

Dave and I were used to a great relationship. We had always felt lucky about that, but we were not connecting as well. It felt as though we were on different wavelengths as well as different time zones. Dave did a lot when he was around—helping with the kids' homework, dropping them off, picking them up, fixing things, etc. He also helped me cook and clean up dinner, and we ran errands together. But when he was gone, I had to do everything on my own. It was hard, but when I knew I didn't have help, I figured out how to make it work. When he came back, he wanted to help with everything, just as he always did. But that often made things more complicated. My organization was changed around, and everything had to be reconfigured.

When he was there, he was all there, and when he was gone, he was really far away. So going back and forth, literally and figuratively, every month, made us have to figure everything out, over and over again. Luckily, Dave is a very good communicator (much better than me actually), or this situation could have been a lot worse. We worked hard at making it all work but we knew things couldn't go on like that forever. The decision to return to America was the right one.

Even knowing we were making the right decision, I still couldn't believe it when we actually bought our tickets to go home. I felt like my heart dropped into my stomach when we hit the "pay now" button. I wanted to keep delaying it. I still wanted to wait for a miracle to happen. I know it was good to get it over with and buy the tickets, but I immediately got "buyer's remorse." I was so unsure of everything. In addition, I really felt bad for Julia. She did NOT want to leave. She loved her life in Paris. She was crying about everything. She loved her freedom, loved her art class, and loved her friends. Matthew and Katherine were happy in Paris, but they were excited to go back to Santa Barbara, which made it much easier for them. For Julia, leaving Paris was just about unbearable.

June 30

Am I really ready to leave? No and yes. I am completely conflicted. There are unanswered questions in my mind: What if Dave actually could get a job in Paris? He hasn't really tried. Would the kids do okay in school here for the long term? Would they get into more or less trouble in high school in Paris? They wouldn't be driving around in cars, which is one of the most dangerous parts of high school in America. Then again, I'm not sure I'd want to live in Paris forever. I feel as though I've done it now. (Of course, there's always more to do.)

July 2009

July 1

I have anxiety. Take Mom's advice: "Don't worry about things until they happen." Why can't I do that? What am I so worried about?!! Ugh!

July 6

Okay, the school year is finished, and it's time to start packing. But wait! One last trip! Amanda just called and said they're going on a vacation to Norway. We can stay in their house in Geneva for a few days if we want. How can we pass that up? Geneva is only a five-hour drive from here—that is, if you have GPS or can read a map. So for us it could be more of a seven-hour drive. (Yeah, I'm not so good at reading maps… but I have other good attributes…)

We arrived in Geneva and found the house. Then, we immediately went out to see the *Jet d'Eau*, one of the highest fountains in the world, which shoots 500 liters (132 gallons) of water per second 140 meters (459 feet) into the air. We found a curious, old, climbing tree at the beach by the lake—its trunk completely wrapped with bike tires, which the kids had a lot of fun climbing on. We took a one-hour drive to Chamonix, one of the oldest ski resorts in France. It's at the base of Mont Blanc, the highest summit in the Alps, with stunning, panoramic views, straight out of a James Bond movie. We planned on taking a hike up the mountain, but the guides told us a storm was in the forecast. That was a big deterrent there because this area is known for extreme weather conditions, and when a storm comes, it comes fast and hard, with a lot of rain. We decided to risk it (even though we did not have umbrellas or rain gear), because this was our only chance to hike in Chamonix.

We rode up in a cable car, then took a chairlift to the starting point of the hike, and headed off. The views were striking, and we saw a bunch of mountain goats—one was very close to us. Thankfully, we avoided the storm that was predicted. It never came. *Whew!* Back at the house, we swam in the pool, played ping-pong, and barbequed. On the 4th of July, in honor of American Independence Day, we sat at the picnic table and had delicious, grilled, All-American cheeseburgers.

When we got back to Paris, the goodbyes were unavoidable. We had a picnic farewell with friends on our bridge, the Pont de Solferino. We had many goodbye lunches and dinners. We had a Grand Goodbye on a boat with fireworks on France's Independence Day, the 14th of July—just two days before we left. The boat was parked in the Seine, right next to the Eiffel Tower, with the fireworks shooting off of it in all directions, very apropos for our final departure. We toasted with our champagne glasses, *"Au revoir, Paris!"*

Finally, we made ourselves start packing up to leave. We were all feeling sad and melancholy. We had to get rid of many things. I sold my rolling grocery bag that I was so attached to—I used it every day! The kids did NOT like giving their scooters away. We took apart and sold the bunk bed. We gave all our books and toys away to our friends. I sold my favorite, warm coat. It all hurt.

July 16 (driving to Charles De Gaulle Airport)

We just left our apartment. I locked the door for the last time and came downstairs to the waiting taxi van, filled with all our lives' belongings in twenty-two bags. I just looked at Julia and I feel my throat starting to hurt. I'm trying not to cry. I'm trying to write to distract myself. Matthew asked Dave for the apartment keys, because he wants to run back up to say "bye" to his home in Paris. Dave went with him

*and said that Matthew went into each room to say
"bye." (He's being very dramatic, and it isn't helping
anyone's disposition.) He's saying "bye" to all the
places we drive by: "Bye alimentation man, bye favorite
bakery, bye Métro stop, etc." It's tearing at my
heartstrings and Julia can't take it, I can tell. She just
screamed at Matthew to "STOP IT!!!" She's crying
now as we drive away... "notre beau Paris" (our
beautiful Paris).*

Once we arrived at the airport, it was so hectic we couldn't dwell anymore. Of course, our flight was delayed. A helpful porter handled our twenty-two bags and got us on a different flight. I wrote a poem just before we left Paris. It was kind of corny, but here it is:

<u>Changes</u>
Change of scenery
Change of pace
Lots to look forward to
Back to home base
Goodbye to friends
We'll keep in touch
It won't be the same though
We'll miss them so much
Beaches and mountains
Not museums and cafés
Driving all over
Not walking on quais
New Uggs and flip-flops
Packed away scarves
New schools and memories
New lives we will carve

I have to think positive
There's no looking back
It's another adventure
Something we don't lack

July 17

We're on the airplane now, moving back to Santa Barbara. Some people move many times in their lives, but I haven't. Phoenix was home for my whole childhood, and Santa Barbara was for the next twenty years. Now, Paris feels like home. Living in Paris has been enlightening. The name "The City of Light" makes sense to me. Now I understand. I see everything in a different light. It was in Paris that my eyes were opened to a new and different way of life. I was challenged intellectually every day. History, art, and philosophy interest me now. I have a diverse group of friends from all over the world that I'll have for the rest of my life. The city and the culture, so beautiful and unique, are really going to be missed. We'll go back to visit, sure, but it won't be the same. And Santa Barbara feels like home too, thankfully. It's what's keeping me going right now.

Afterward

So many people have said to me, "We'd like to do something like that with our kids someday," but maybe they think it's too complicated or not worth the effort. I'm here to say that it is worth it, because I know the true value of this experience was not evident before we did it. More and more considerable and growing evidence is emerging that living abroad for a significant amount of time, outside of one's parents' cultures, can yield substantial benefits and advantages.

Kids who have done this have been called cultural hybrids, cultural chameleons, and Third Culture Kids in a book called *Third Culture Kids: Growing up Among Worlds* by David Pollock and Ruth Van Reken. Children become Third Culture Kids for many reasons. Some have parents with international careers. Some are there for religious reasons. But a new trend is the parents who are taking their kids abroad because they want to or because they can. In Pollock and Van Reken's book they recount research showing common characteristics found among Third Culture Kids such as: adaptability, less prejudice, spontaneity, good social skills, and good linguistic skills. They also tend to be tough, responsible, and self-reliant." [8] We found evidence of the characteristics they reported in our kids, and I will describe our observations related to each of their findings.

Adaptability has innumerable benefits in our ever-changing world. One aspect of adaptability is blending in, which Third Culture Kids learn to master. "Their observational skills become highly developed. They learn to observe the nuances of a new culture—seeing how the natives behave in various situations—so that they can avoid saying or doing things that are inappropriate. This helps them gain acceptance instead of rejection. Then, once they realize they can blend in, they are

---

[8] Third Culture Kids: Growing Up Among Worlds, Pollock & Van Reken, 1999

more confident in new situations. Because of this they are sometimes called cultural chameleons." [9]

On the way to and from school, I watched and listened to the bilingual kids on the Métro. They would talk to each other in French, then switch to English—mid-conversation—then back to French. An observer would not be able to tell which was their first language. They had no audible accent in either language. Besides language, there were also cultural adaptations, which they had perfected: gestures, slang, intonations of certain words, and mannerisms, just like Pollock and Van Reken described.

"Third Culture Kids tend to be blind to color, race, and religions of other kids." [10] It's true. My kids have no prejudice when it comes to other kids. They learned that they like kids of all races, nationalities, and religions just as much or more than friends who are "the same" as them. "Due to their cross-cultural enrichment Third Culture Kids are able to see the world from multiple perspectives. They tend to become the natural mediators amongst their friends. They can understand different points of view and make others see the reasoning behind them. This will also makes them good teachers and mentors when they get older. They are sensitive to other peoples' feelings and more empathetic." [11]

When we returned from Paris, I noticed that my kids were drawn to other "new kids" even though they had old friends from before they left. The "new kids" understood what it was like to move and adapt, and they could relate to each other's feelings. They were also more perceptive to each other's struggles and shared insight from similar experiences. I don't think this would've happened if they had never been "the new kid."

---

[9] [10] [11] Third Culture Kids: Growing Up Among Worlds, Pollock & Van Reken, 1999

254

"The Importance of Now is another characteristic of Third Culture Kids, especially ones that have moved a lot. They tend to live in the moment because they know that situations can change quickly."[12] For kids who've never had to deal with change in their lives, change can be scary, but because Third Culture Kids expect things to change, they know they had better make the most of each experience while they can.

How many times do we miss an opportunity to have a great experience because we think we'll be able to do it later? Maybe we will, but maybe we won't. Spontaneity—being unconstrained and able to act on impulse—is a valuable trait. Remember how we were invited to the Champs de Mars for a last minute picnic and I almost said no? I have since learned to be more spontaneous. I think that's due, in part, to my experiences as a Third Culture Adult. As for my kids, they're very spontaneous. They will almost always drop what they're doing to join a family hike or to see a great sunset. Maybe it's because they don't want to miss anything, or because they've learned that life can change quickly like the clouds in the sky, but you have to have seen different skies to understand that.

"Third Culture Kids have an appreciation for authority."[13] This means they like to know that there are rules or a set of understandable guidelines to follow, so that once they learn them, they will fit in. This was easily observed at our kids' schools. There were a lot of rules, and if the rules weren't followed, there were consequences. Our kids knew they'd be in trouble for doing things wrong at school. But they also knew that other kids would get in trouble if they did something wrong. That made it fair and okay. Once they understood the rules, they could abide by them because they wanted to fit in. When actions lead to authoritative and predictable consequences, life makes sense.

---

[12] [13] Third Culture Kids: Growing Up Among Worlds, Pollock & Van Reken, 1999

French school really toughened my kids up. Some teachers called the kids names, and sometimes they even slapped them with a ruler. (Note: I did NOT like this behavior, but it did happen.) They even threatened to spank kids in the younger grades, but according to Katherine, thankfully, they never did it. They gave negative grades. That's right, they actually gave grades below zero for bad work. When I met with Julia's teachers (in my very efficient five-minute conferences) it was obvious that they were empowering taskmasters that gave grades out fairly. Her teachers wanted her to try harder. They knew she could do it, but they weren't going to give her any credit unless she earned it. Julia needed to hear that—from them, not us.

Kids were a lot more physical with each other in Paris. The rule "no touching each other" didn't exist there. For one thing, there wasn't enough space for that to be possible. The courtyard at Katherine's school was the size of a large American living room. It was the only outdoor area for the kids to play in, and there were at least a hundred kids playing out there at a time. The outdoor space at Julia and Matthew's school was bigger, but still very small for the number of kids at the school. These were inner city schools. There was no big, green field with unlimited space to run and play, so they had to adjust.

After school, Matthew liked to go to the churchyard to play. All the neighborhood kids went there to kick soccer balls with each other and against the church wall. (In a city with so many rules, this was somehow allowed, which was surprising.) Older ladies and men would come in and out of the church, and it never seemed to bother them. Even the priests came outside and kicked the ball around with the kids. Often, the French boys would steal Matthew's ball and run off down the street, or throw it over a fence so he couldn't get it. He and his friend Martin, who also lived in the neighborhood, would have to chase them down to get it back. But Matthew forbade me to interfere. According to him, it got pretty rough sometimes, but it didn't deter him. He still went back every day "to play."

The physicality he learned in Paris did cause him problems when he got back to Santa Barbara. In the classroom,

French school was strict, but on the playground there were no rules. The opposite was true in Santa Barbara. Matthew got sent to the Principal's office at the beginning of fifth grade for pushing a kid over on the playground. When he told me about it, he said the kid kept poking him with his index finger saying, "Matthew, Matthew, Matthew, Matthew…" until he couldn't take it anymore. He wouldn't stop when Matthew asked him to stop, so finally Matthew just pushed him away, and he fell over. That would be a fine way to deal with this situation in Paris. (But NOT in Santa Barbara.) No pushing was allowed. (I guess poking was though.) Matthew got suspended for a day.

More differences appeared: In Santa Barbara, jumping off the swings or running on the pavement was not allowed. In Paris, it was perfectly okay. My kids tried an after school cooking class when they got back to Santa Barbara, but they wouldn't them use knives. Knives were too dangerous. How do you have a cooking class without using knives? They cut everything for them! In Paris, Kate used a knife in a cooking course when she was six. Paris had the "intimidation factor" but their school in Santa Barbara had the "paranoia factor." Matthew felt like he was being treated like a baby, and that the rules were ridiculous. He preferred the physicality of boys in France and the "play at your own risk" way of life.

"What are they so worried about?" Matthew asked.

"Lawsuits," we told him.

When Julia got back to her American junior high school, she had an experience with bullying. A girl would walk by Julia's desk and knock her notebook off, onto the floor. That was until Julia saw her coming and tripped her. Clearly, Julia had developed a strong backbone living in Paris! The girl never tried it again. The same girl also tried to bully her in P.E. class, but when Julia stood up for herself, the girl gave up. In fact, she was so impressed with Julia she tried to befriend her.

Matthew was also bullied when he got to the junior high school, but it was almost a welcome respite to take off "the kid gloves" he had to wear at the elementary school. On one of his first days in seventh grade, an eighth grade boy stole his P.E.

clothes and locked them in a locker, just before class was about to start. So Matthew grabbed the kid's shoes and locked them in *his* locker. He said, "I'll give you back your shoes when you give me back my clothes." The kid gave them right back and never bullied him again. He also stood up for his friends when they were bullied at school. It was the right thing to do (and it made me proud). I have a sense of security knowing that my kids can stick up for themselves and their friends. I feel certain that was a result of their experience as Third Culture Kids.

A sense of responsibility developed from the French autonomy training ("the frame method" I wrote about earlier), but it also developed out of necessity for my kids. When Dave was gone, it was impossible for me to take both Matthew and Katherine to school in the mornings. Their schools started at the same time in two different locations. I had to take Katherine, so Matthew had to either go by himself or go with Julia, who was already going on her own. Matthew didn't want to go with Julia for a host of reasons: For one, Julia's school started thirty minutes earlier than his. Moreover, when he did accompany her, she and her friends would either ignore him or try to kiss him, which were both unattractive options to him at that age. At the beginning, when I realized Matthew had to take the Métro to school by himself, we tried to organize his meeting up with Martin and his dad. That quickly became too much trouble, so he just ended up going alone most days. Yes, my nine-year-old went to and from school alone, on the Métro, in the fourth grade. He knew what to do, and he did it all by himself—even without a cell phone!

He also became the little man of the house. Every morning when he woke up, he put on his coat, hat, and gloves, took €1.30 from the change bowl, and went out to buy a fresh baguette for the family. I couldn't go because I couldn't leave Katherine alone in the house, and it was a lot of trouble to get her all dressed first thing in the morning to go out for bread. Furthermore, Julia had no interest in going out. She would rather sleep longer. So Matthew did it for me. At first he wanted to have the exact change for the baguette. But later, he recognized the French coins well enough to count them out with ease.

I remember the first day I sent him out alone. I was so nervous. We lived two blocks from Boulevard St. Germain, a busy four-lane street, which he needed to cross to get to the bakery. There was a Métro stop on both sides of the street, so it was possible for him to go under the street instead, which was safer. When he got more comfortable, he started crossing the street up above. He was very mature and responsible about it. We talked about the buses—how they came right up to the curb—and he said he was always careful not to stand too close. So I let him do it. (Brave Mommy, huh?)

This bravery, independence, and confidence, along with all the other characteristics I've just described, developed from living in a different and new environment, one that was not as easy as the life our kids had in United States. People sometimes made fun of us when we say that we wanted to make things more challenging for our kids by moving abroad. Friends have teased, "So you moved to Paris? Oh please!" But life there was more difficult in many ways: We didn't have a car. The kids had to walk everywhere, and they had to get themselves around alone a lot of the time. We didn't speak a word of French when we arrived, and we all had to learn it to communicate. We didn't have a lot of money to spend, like many of the friends we made. We had to budget, cook, and clean our own apartment. Our kids went to a French school, where they had to learn how to behave in a highly restrictive classroom environment—completely different from the ones they had left. They had to make new friends. They had to eat new and different foods. They had to learn to adapt and fit into a whole new culture.

One morning on the way to Katherine's school, I had an "Aha!" moment. I was talking to the mother of one of Katherine's friends. I knew she worked full-time, but she wasn't dressed for work that day. She told me she had been laid off with two weeks notice. She worked for an American company, and the economic downslide had really started to hit. They were closing down the company. She was upset but not worried. "Oh,

259

I'll get another job. I mean, I'm completely bilingual. Actually, I can speak a lot of languages. I might have to do something different, but I won't have a problem getting a job," she told me. *Wow*, I thought. *How fortuitous it is to speak other languages. It really opens doors.*

But it's not just bilingualism that's important. Bilingualism also gives social skills and perspective. It's a "cultural education." As Norma M. McCaig, the Founder of Global Nomads International, is quoted as saying, "The benefits of a cross-cultural upbringing need to be underscored: In an era when global vision is an imperative, when skills in intercultural communication, linguistic ability, mediation, diplomacy, and the management of diversity are critical, global nomads are better equipped in these areas by the age of eighteen than are many adults. These intercultural and linguistic skills are the markings of the cultural chameleon—the young participant-observer— who takes note of verbal and nonverbal cues, and readjusts accordingly, taking on enough of the coloration of the social surroundings to gain acceptance, while maintaining some vestige of identity as a different animal, an 'other'. Our world is changing, and global visionaries are in high demand. We can no longer rest on our laurels here in the U.S. We need to understand and value the bigger world around us."[14]

"Because of these reasons, a lot of Third Culture Kids go into international careers. They have skills that others don't have, gained from immersion in a foreign culture."[15] The founder of the school my kids attended is quoted as saying, "Learning a foreign language is, by itself, important; it is also a means to better understand others, to be able to think like them—it provides access to the world. The education is more than learning how to translate and say the right words. When you learn the idioms and perceive the nuances, then you begin to think (and even dream) in another language. Ultimately, you

---

[14] Norma McCaig, Founder of Global Nomads International

[15] Third Culture Kids: Growing Up Among Worlds, Pollock & Van Reken, 1999

begin to see how a French/German/Spanish, etc. person thinks, and how all the nuances fit in, and it is then that you start to understand the culture. In our multicultural and global world, this can help in social and business situations, and can certainly help Third Culture Kids in their careers, and in life."[16]

---

[16] Jeannine Manuel, founder of École Jeannine Manuel (originally École Active Bilingue Jeannine Manuel)

Where is home?

Yes, your adventure ends when you return home, but that is absolutely not the end of the story. You will have to readjust to your old culture in the same way you had to adjust to the new culture. Your old culture will be new again, and you will have changed. As my friend Brad, an American tour guide who has lived in Paris for over twenty years told me, "I feel as if both places are home, and both are foreign. I exist somewhere in between the two. It's not a bad place to be. I'm never completely at home in either place, but I get to experience the excitement in both places that being in a foreign place brings."

For some, reintegrating into your old life may be the hardest part. It was definitely that way for me. I don't say this to discourage anyone, but it's good to know what to expect. For a long time after we got back, I couldn't figure out what to talk about with my friends in Santa Barbara. Because all my experiences for the past two years were in Paris, it was hard not to talk about them. But I could hear how it sounded; it seemed like I was always comparing everything in Santa Barbara to Paris. Once, one of my best friends actually said, "If you miss it so much, why don't you just go back?" I wasn't trying to say it was better. It was just different. My kids thought it sounded like they were bragging if they talked about Paris, so they didn't talk about it at all.

We felt lucky to come back to Santa Barbara. We reunited with friends, and there was comfort in old friendships. Santa Barbara is a beautiful place—one of the most scenic in the world—so that part was easy to appreciate. Since it's a small town, we ran into friends everywhere we went. People asked how we liked Paris, but the scope of the experience was too deep to relay in a couple sentences. A short conversation didn't do it justice. The first question people asked was almost always, "Can you speak French now?" That was definitely one of our main reasons for going, but there was so much more to the experience beyond learning French. There just wasn't a way to explain it. (Thus this book!)

When school started for the kids, I thought I'd have time to "find my groove," but that was when things got even tougher for me. It was back to the "car culture." I certainly didn't need to get dressed up in the morning to go out. I could drive the kids to school in my pajamas if I wanted to. (And I DID many days!) I missed the brisk walk and the conversations with other moms at drop off. I missed the Métro ride with the *20 Minutes*—the free, daily, French newspaper that challenged me every morning. One of my favorite activities was trying to figure out what my French horoscope meant. I missed the warm, fresh baguette from the bakery and the butter with the crunchy sea salt crystals that we had for breakfast every morning.

One of my first days back, I wore a linen skirt, a white blouse, and sandals to the tennis club. This would've been an everyday, casual outfit to wear on any warm day in Paris. But in Santa Barbara, every person I saw asked me why I was dressed up. Was I going out to lunch or something? It reminded me of the time when I wanted to wear my exercise clothes around Paris. It didn't work there, and getting "dressed up" didn't work in Santa Barbara. I succumbed. I went out and bought some new tee shirts and shorts.

Two years was a long time to live somewhere, and we all felt different. It was definitely the hardest for Julia. She went to a new school where she only knew a few kids from before. Socially, she didn't know where she fit in. She told me she was a "group hopper" because she didn't fit into any group. Academically, there were—and still are—definite holes. Sixth and seventh grades were significant years to miss in the U.S. For instance, she had taken math in French for two years, so she didn't know any of the math terms in English. She couldn't even describe how to do math in English, only in French. Interestingly though, her ability to reflect on words from the French language helped her writing. She was more analytical. Her writing was different from her peers, who only knew how to communicate in one language. There was, and is still, a flexibility and creativity in her writing that I assume is a result of the knowledge of another set of words.

Matthew had some difficulties coming back too, as I already talked about. He also was going to a new school, and he got into trouble a lot. The independence and toughness he learned in Paris were not the way things worked in Santa Barbara. He felt overprotected. But, academically, he got lucky. He had learned a lot of French and European history in the two years in Paris, but he hadn't learned any American history. He could name all the French kings in perfect order, all the countries in the EU, and when they joined, but he didn't know that Ohio was one of the fifty states. He had never heard of Ohio. In fifth grade in Santa Barbara, American history was the focus. They even had a class trip to Washington D.C. that year.

On Katherine and Matthew's second day of school, I drove into the drive-thru parking lot where a school monitor or guard would usually take them in. On that day, the principal of the school was standing there, ready to take them from me, smiling her huge smile, and in a loud voice she said, "Hi there! ARE WE GOING TO HAVE ANOTHER GREAT DAY TODAY?" Matthew and Katherine looked stunned.

"Is she a clown?" Katherine asked.

"No, that's the principal," I said.

Side note to explain why she thought that: There were clowns at every birthday party Katherine attended in Paris. (That's just what they did for all the young kids' parties there.) But Katherine was always scared of clowns. French Directrices and teachers didn't smile such huge smiles or act so excited to see them.

"Why is she talking like that?" Matthew asked.

"That's how she talks," I told them. "She's really nice."

Matthew held Katherine's hand and they "bravely" went in. Katherine couldn't get over how friendly everybody was at school. But she too had some obstacles to overcome. She didn't know how to read or write in English, but fortunately, the school gave her a (free) private tutor to help her get up to speed, and it only took her two weeks to catch up to the same reading level as her class in English. She also had to learn how to print her letters. (In Paris she had only learned to write in cursive.) Lunchtime was very different too. Katherine was used to an hour and a half to eat, while being constantly reprimanded to sit up straight, push in her chair, and have her manners corrected incessantly. In Santa Barbara it was much more relaxed, but she only had fifteen minutes to eat. She wasn't used to or able to eat that fast. The guards didn't care how they ate though. Their manners weren't constantly corrected, which surprised her, but after fifteen minutes, they were shoed out, whether they were finished or not. But, they were then free to run and play in the HUGE field of green grass. It was incredible after having only a tiny courtyard to play in at her school in Paris. And there were THREE recesses! Snack time was also a new thing. There was no snack time in Paris. That helped a little, since she wasn't able to eat much of her lunch in fifteen minutes.

After the first couple of weeks, school was pretty easy for my kids. For one thing, it was all in English, but also the expectations put on them had been much higher in Paris. Their penmanship had to be perfect. They had to do daily French dictations, read novels in French, and memorize French poetry. I'm not talking about a haiku or a short poem in English either. These were long French poems, usually ten lines at a minimum, and they got longer and more difficult as the kids got older. French teachers were never sympathetic or flattering of their work. But in Santa Barbara, all their teachers were warm and nice to them. At first they were skeptical and suspicious, but once they realized it was not an act, they were appreciative of the praise and positive atmosphere.

Another benefit that materialized was that our kids were reinvigorated for their sports and music lessons. They could hardly wait to start piano lessons again. While they all were more than happy to take a break when we left, it was something they were excited about when we returned. This was because in Paris, a lot of their friends played the piano. But our kids found that they had forgotten everything when they stopped practicing.

Julia, especially, never wanted to practice before we left. When we returned, however, she practiced more than willingly, and she's still sticking with it. Of course, there are times when she wants to quit, but she remembers quitting once before, and she knows she will regret it if she does. *(Thank you, Paris!)*

It was the same with tennis for Matthew; after two years off, he was excited to start it up again. The break reenergized him, and we saw it in the effort he put forth. With Katherine, it was ballet; she wanted to take ballet in Paris, but I didn't let her. We were avoiding after school activities, but also because life in Paris was already very strict. Her teacher was strict, the behavioral expectations were strict, and ballet is a strict discipline. When we returned, I let her start ballet, and she's been totally dedicated to it ever since. Maybe it's because she had to wait, or maybe because the strictness of ballet (and the French terms) remind her of Paris. Whatever the reason… my plan worked! *("Bahahaha," as Matthew would say.)* The feelings of entitlement that I wrote about in the beginning of the book were gone. They all were grateful and appreciative to do their music and sports again, and that made me happy.

What about me? Well, I'm a dweller! I try to appreciate both Santa Barbara and Paris for the beneficial qualities each brings (and brought) to my life. I notice that I am acutely aware of the differences though. I notice behaviors that were appropriate in Paris, but are not appropriate in Santa Barbara, and vice-versa. For example: when Dave and I went to a hotel for our anniversary recently, we went to get a drink in the bar. It was a small hotel, and the owner was also the bartender. As every person came up to the bar, the owner/bartender would ask, "So what do you do?" In France, that would be an extremely private question to ask someone. In fact, most personal questions are inappropriate there. But in the U.S., it's perfectly normal. Kissing in public is considered inappropriate in the U.S. In France it's normal. French people don't give you their names. They'll have a long conversation with you, even at a dinner party, and never ask your name, or tell you theirs. With Americans, it's uncomfortable when you haven't been properly introduced. Typically, the first thing we Americans do, when we're with someone we don't know, is offer our name and expect the other person to offer theirs. Different cultural norms and ideas of privacy get blurred when you've lived in another culture.

When we got back to Santa Barbara, we found we had new perspectives on many things that we wanted to share, but trying to make others see them only worked in certain situations, and quite a few times we found ourselves pushing the limits too far. In Paris, our conversations were often about arguing our differing opinions. I was even told that French people don't trust you if you're too nice or don't state your opinion on things. This was great for Dave and me, since we're both very opinionated, and both come from families of arguers. But in America (at least in Santa Barbara) it's generally inappropriate to argue in public. This is especially true with couples. Of course, American couples have differing opinions, but they usually keep quiet about them when in public. In France, they think there is something wrong with a couple that doesn't contradict one another.

I'm also more judgmental of my children's manners than I used to be. In Paris, children were required to come to the door to welcome guests and to go to the door to say goodbye when guests left. In the Santa Barbara, nobody does this. My kids think it's crazy to demand things like that, because it's not necessary. It's much more relaxed and casual here, so I've had to alter my demands and expectations.

It was hard getting used to the late dinner hour in Paris, and then it was hard getting readapted to the early dinner hour in Santa Barbara. Dinner parties in Paris began around 9:00 p.m. with dinner being served around 10:30 p.m. We usually left around 1:00 a.m. (because that was when people without cars had to catch the last Métro). It was rude to leave earlier. When we moved back to Santa Barbara, everyone was eating dinner at 5:30 p.m. or earlier. That was the hour of *le goûter* in Paris. The difference was extreme.

"Why so early?" I asked my friend when our first invitation for dinner arrived. "Can we do it a little later?" (Dave usually wasn't even finished with work by then, and he wanted to work out.)

"Well, is 6:00 okay then? We had a late dinner last night," my friend said. *(Ah, geez, okay!)*

Other things were hard to adjust to as well—especially the "freedom factor." Our kids were used to a lot of freedom, which also gave me a lot of freedom. By the second year, both Julia and Matthew were getting themselves around Paris alone on the Métro. Julia also had the bus routes figured out. Unfortunately, the public transportation in Santa Barbara is terrible, and it's impossible for my kids to get around by themselves, so I have to drive them. Daily, I find myself in my car for four hours when they get out of school, with a packed cooler in the back to keep everyone nourished and hydrated, bags of clothes and uniforms for quick changes, music books for lessons, and files of paperwork and agendas. My brain is overloaded with organization. I now realize how significantly good, public transportation benefited my quality of life. Lastly, not overscheduling my kids was a big difference in my lifestyle in Paris, and unfortunately, I fell right back into my old ways when we moved back to Santa Barbara.

People ask me all the time, "Do I miss Paris?" Of course! I miss small things: such as the light on the apartment building across the street from us, with its gray and white striped awnings, the three mini Cypress trees on each windowsill, and the dormer window up on top. I miss Côte d'Or dark chocolate with caramelized pistachios or hazelnuts. I miss the smell of the chestnut trees after rainstorms, and the smell of hot bread wafting out of the bakeries. I even miss the smelly cheese stores! I miss that everything in Paris was treated like a work of art, such as the way they packaged up flowers at the flower stores; they always seemed to take such pleasure in wrapping my purchase for *un cadeau* (a gift), even if I only bought an inexpensive plant. I loved how the shopkeepers always placed their fruit and vegetables out on display. Once, I remember watching the man who worked in our neighborhood fruit stand place one cherry at a time, in row after row, outside his shop. I miss my daily shopping trip, not in my car, but walking with my rolling bag to the open-air market or to the Franprix, where I'd have discussions with the in-store butcher. He'd always ask me how I was going to cook the meat I bought, and I'd play along: *"Je ne sais pas,"* (I don't know. How would you cook it?") Then he'd tell me the temperature I should use and hand me a spice rub, or explain more about how I should cook it. He always wanted to make sure I cooked the meat properly!

I miss big things like the Paris sky, the Eiffel Tower, and the Seine. I miss the good friends I made. I miss the ease of travel in Europe and having all those school holidays. That really spoiled us. After enjoying the fabulous Parent Group for two years, I miss the constant camaraderie of group outings and international potlucks. I loved meeting new people from different countries, hearing about different cultures, and trying different ethnic foods. I miss learning about art and history by living it. Every time I went on a neighborhood tour or museum exhibition, I blogged about it, but in order to write about it I had to do research to understand the history. In those experiences and research I learned a great deal.

I miss the rituals that are such a big part of life in France—like the yearly celebration of the new Beaujolais wines every November. Parisians welcome the arrival of each new vintage with uncharacteristic enthusiasm. I miss October's *Nuit Blanche*, when everyone stays up until the early morning hours, walking around and enjoying fire and light displays that light up the streets and parks. And I miss the yearly *Fête de la Musique* every June, where musicians performed all around the city.

I miss dressing up. (I can't believe I just said that!) But I did feel good about myself when I got dressed up. I'm too lazy to do it here, since I don't have to, and most everyone wears workout clothes all day. But every time I walked out the door in Paris, I had to dress up. Having three kids who also needed to be dressed up at all times was expensive, but once we purchased the dressy coats, fancy shoes, blouses, and dresses, it was fun to see them looking sharp all the time.

There's something in Paris I'd call "the look." This is hard to explain, but it's something to which one becomes accustomed. There's more eye contact when people walk by each other. They don't smile. They just see each other. When I returned to Santa Barbara, it felt like no one looked at me. I wondered, "Did I look ugly?" It's true that I wasn't getting dressed up the way I did in Paris, but I still tried to look attractive! I don't know if you'd call it flirting, but to the French and other Europeans, it's just normal to acknowledge each other with a look. I guess it makes all the effort required worth it!

I also miss the French language. I was just getting it when we left. I remember one of my last Conversation Group meetings when the French flowed out of my mouth—without thinking. I didn't have to translate what I wanted to say first in my head. I just started speaking. "Wait, was that right? Did I say that right?" I couldn't believe it when they said yes. I was SO excited! I also miss using all the French expressions I learned and had become accustomed to using. Sometimes a French word or saying just fits a situation!

Another thing: we had worked so hard to get our kids to learn French, we didn't want them to lose it, but it seemed almost inevitable. Julia was too advanced to take French in junior high. It was French 1-2. Matthew and Katherine didn't have an option to take French at their school. So, when we returned to America our attempt to keep the kids speaking French was to hire Daphne, a charming, half-French, 19-year-old babysitter, once per week, who would speak only French with them. Also, I'd buy the ingredients for a French themed meal: crêpes, croque monsieurs, quiche, soups or salads. Daphne and the kids would cook the French dinner and eat together. Then they'd either play games or memorize a skit (all in French). Dave and I would go out to dinner while Daphne was there, enjoying a date night together, and when we returned home we'd enjoy a funny skit they'd all perform for us. That worked for a year, until Daphne left for college. We tried a few more French sitters, but after a while, we gave up.

I miss all the time I had with Dave. When Dave was in Paris, he worked in the evenings, so he was around in the daytime. We had lunch together almost every day. We'd make big, fresh salads, which we'd usually enjoy with a glass of wine, and we'd talk and relax. We'd go on walks and tours and outings. We'd even run errands together. Here, we're mostly like ships passing in the night.

But don't get me wrong; the Santa Barbara lifestyle is great. I love being able to drive to the beach for a walk after I drop the kids off at school. The ocean was the thing I missed the most while in Paris. When we first returned, I went to the beach almost every day, even if it was just to look out at the water and breathe in the salt air. That was my refuge. I love the small town feel of Santa Barbara, and knowing if I go to the beach or the tennis club, I will almost always run into friends. I love fresh Mexican food, and I love being tan year-round. The weather is great. It's almost always sunny, which helps my disposition. I also like that Americans are so friendly. We can't help but strike up conversations with the person next to us when we're waiting in line, standing in elevators, or sitting next to someone. I love how easy it is to return things, and how the customer is always right instead of always wrong! I totally appreciate that there are bathrooms everywhere, toilets that flush—with toilet seats, toilet seat covers, hot water, and paper towels. I love that my dryer actually dries our clothes, and that I don't have to iron everything (or anything, actually) and no one notices! I love that my kids can run and play on the grass. I love wearing running shoes all day long. I even love Cheetos, Ranch Doritos, Fruit by the Foot, and a few other preservative-laden foods, which I couldn't get in Paris.

And there are many things I don't miss, such as the perfectionism of Paris. I don't miss Katherine being sick all the time. My car, while I complain that I am in it too much, is definitely a convenience, especially in winter, when I can walk into my warm garage and not take a step outside, or into a full Métro car, inevitably containing sick people who'd cough or sneeze on me. I don't miss all the random Métro strikes, which

271

made my life very difficult. Public urination, smelly underarms, and cigarette smoke are happily left behind. I don't miss my pallid skin. I don't miss the squeaky, wood floor in our apartment, and I don't miss French haircuts. Oh, how happy I am to have my favorite hairdresser back—who speaks English! My kids' teeth are all looking good, thanks to our favorite American orthodontist and dentist. We love having barbecues and pool parties. Thankfully, I have found my "happy place" in Santa Barbara once again, and my kids are happy, as is Dave, who is back to surfing and rollerblading at lunch.

The deep impact of our experience is acknowledged every day by us and by people around us. I believe it was the biggest gift we could ever give our kids and ourselves. They appreciate it more and more as time passes. Different aspects of their experiences have been the subjects of countless school assignments, and I bet it will be a part, if not the topic of their college essays. As their parents, we see benefits in so many areas, but I think the thing I notice most is that our kids seek out challenging situations. Interestingly, the word challenge means "an invitation to take part in something." Challenges are a choice, and challenges are opportunities to grow. I'm happy that our kids don't shy away from them. New things are not scary to my children any more. New foods and strong spices intrigue them. They appreciate other people's unique styles of dress. They're open-minded listeners. They've learned that there are reasons behind other people's perspectives, and that Americans are also different to people of other cultures.

Timing was definitely an important factor, but there isn't one perfect age for this kind of experience. The brother of one of Julia's best friends was a sophomore in high school during his year abroad, and had a fabulous time, but I think in most cases, it's more difficult for a kid to move when they're in high school. They're usually more serious about school, might have serious relationships, and they know that college depends on how well they do in high school. There is also the issue of the "window of opportunity" when it's easier for kids to learn a foreign language. As the study I referenced earlier reported, that window closes at around twelve to thirteen years of age. But kids benefit differently at different ages. And while bilingualism is beneficial in so many ways, "semilingualism" is a challenge one must be ready to face. When a kid learns two languages, they may be challenged by a lack of proficiency in both. Of course, there are many factors related to this, such as time spent and age at the time of learning, but a smaller vocabulary, poor grammar, and trouble expressing complex thoughts are difficulties children may experience.

And living in another culture is not for everyone. The difficulties lie both in the small things and the big things, and they should all be considered. Language is a big thing. If the language spoken in the foreign culture is not English, learning a foreign language is, for sure, the biggest challenge. Do you want to learn a foreign language? Does your spouse? How about your kids? Then there's the financial issue: Can you work from afar, or can you take a sabbatical? If you are part of a couple, is this both of your decisions or only one of yours? Does your personality type fit? Do you enjoy the process of learning new things? Do you like change? Are you open-minded? Do you think your way is the only way, or are you adaptable? Do you have a sense of humor? How do you handle ambiguity and frustration? How well are you and your family members able to tolerate failure?

Additionally, there are many small things that one must be able to adjust to, accept, and live with. Do you mind dogs in restaurants? In Paris they are welcome almost everywhere! Do you need ice in your glass when you order a soft drink? In Paris, you will only get one cube, no matter how many times you ask. Patience is necessary, and satisfaction is not a given. Other cultures may be more or less formal than you're used to, and cultural differences can take awhile to get used to. You have to be truly open-minded to accept these differences and grow from them. Americans tend to take for granted how easy life is, but other cultures may not have the same ease or comforts. Are you okay with that? For some people, these are minor inconveniences they are glad to live with in order to reap the benefits. But for others, all of these things may add up and tip the scales to make the experience too difficult to appreciate. Some adults adjust easily. Some don't. Some kids adjust easily. Some don't. Many factors affect each kid's adjustment: such as the parents' attitude and support, each kid's confidence level, the relationships they make, and their academic and social capabilities.

When you immerse your kids in an international environment, they see the world with "new eyes." Because my kids made so many friends from all over the world they learned how BIG the world is, and where they fit into it. They're American. They're Californian. They're Santa Barbaran. It makes them who they are. In Paris, it was how other people came to know them. Before they moved away, they didn't realize that where they came from was an important part of who they are. As Clare, my dear friend, related the famous quote in her speech at the beginning of the school year, "Two of the greatest gifts you can give your children are roots and wings."[17] The roots are the knowledge of who they are and where they come from, and the wings are the confidence to go out on their own.

Before we left Santa Barbara, our kids were fighting like cats and dogs. But when they got to Paris, they were BEST friends. This was because they were each other's ONLY friends. They needed each other. Home was our safe haven... haven from the French language, haven from the cold, haven from the unknown, and haven from all the complications inherent in these new experiences. Home was a comforting place. When it was freezing cold outside, we felt like we were hibernating in our cozy, warm apartment, closing all the curtains, getting in our "comfy clothes," and hanging out together. In the depth of winter, I loved seeing my kids cuddled up next to each other, under a blanket—usually watching French cartoons! We were all just happy to be inside, warm, safe, and together. When we got back to Santa Barbara, that bond—strengthened due to circumstances, memories, and experiences—has provided

---

[17] W. Hodding Carter

constant comfort for our family. As Dumbledore said in *Harry Potter and the Goblet of Fire*: "We are only as strong as we are united, as weak as we are divided."[18] This experience will unite you.

There are so many lessons we learned from our two-year stint abroad. We have friends from all over the planet now—friends that are different from us in culture, language, and behavior. We learned that different makes life more interesting. These friendships have been easy to maintain with Skype and the Internet. We have already begun to travel and visit each other, and look forward to more reconnecting in the future. The memories of good and bad times and "mis-adventures" will last forever, and they will pepper our family's conversations for the rest of our lives.

Travel broadens your horizons, but living abroad changes you. I know that for us, what started as a crazy dream, turned into the best decision we ever made. It has shaped all of us into open-minded, confident, world travelers who know we can survive anything. As Helen Keller said: "Life is either an adventure or it is nothing." An experience like this is mind opening, full of surprises, challenges, and fulfillment. It is for the curious-minded and the brave. It's not necessarily what you're looking for, but what you'll come across along the way… and it's in those discoveries that life becomes an adventure. If this sounds good to you, and there is a way… ANY WAY to make it happen… I say, "All Abroad!"

---

[18] *Harry Potter and the Goblet of Fire* by J.K. Rowling, July 2000

Made in the USA
San Bernardino, CA
09 May 2018